Communication
and
Litigation
Case Studies of Famous Trials

Janice Schuetz and Kathryn Holmes Snedaker

With a Foreword by Peter E. Kane

Southern Illinois University Press
Carbondale and Edwardsville

Copyright © 1988 by the Board of Trustees, Southern Illinois
     University
All rights reserved
Printed in the United States of America
Designed by Jody Dyer Jasinski
Production supervised by Natalia Nadraga
91 90 89 88   4 3 2 1

Library of Congress Cataloging-in-Publication Data
     Schuetz, Janice E.
          Communication and litigation

          Bibliography: p.
          Includes index.
          1. Trials—United States. 2. Trial practice—
United States. 3. Forensic orations. I. Snedaker,
Kathryn Holmes, 1958–. II. Title.
KF220.S38 1988 347.73'7 87-35654
ISBN 0-8093-1456-8 347.3077

The paper used in this publication meets the minimum requirements of
American National Standard for Information Sciences Permanence of
Paper for Printed Library Materials, ANSI Z39.48-1984. ∞

Contents

Contents

Foreword

The study of communication in the field of law is one that has recently received a great deal of attention from both lawyers and communication scholars. One of the newer interest groups in the Speech Communication Association is the Commission on Communication and Law. New organizations have sprung up to provide academic consultants to the legal profession and to promote the interchange of ideas among those consultants. Some law schools have even included courses in communciation in their curricula. Communication in the law is a hot field.

However, for those like Janice Schuetz and Kathryn Holmes Snedaker who are familiar with the classical tradition in rhetorical theory, communication in the law is certainly not a new field. The origin of the study of rhetoric in Western culture is generally credited to Corax, a Sicilian theorist and instructor who flourished during the first half of the fifth century B.C.—over twenty-five hundred years ago. Corax focused his attention on legal disputes and instructed citizens, who at that time served as their own lawyers, in how best to prepare and present their cases. His ideas were based upon his observations and analyses of actual trial practices. Corax was thus observing and analyzing real trials, drawing theoretical conclusions based on that observation and analysis, and then instructing others in the use of these insights.

This volume by Schuetz and Snedaker is in the best tradition of the study of rhetoric as Corax first presented it. Like Corax, they have looked at actual trial practices and have analyzed those practices to arrive at theoretical understandings communicated to us through this volume that uniquely provides the reader with the entire intellectual process. Trial materials from celebrated court cases are presented. These fascinating narratives provide the foundation for the analysis and theoretical observations that follow. Finally, the reader is offered insightful commentary on Schuetz and Snedaker's work by communication scholars, legal practitioners, and in one case a participant in the events that Schuetz and Snedaker describe.

In this study the trial process is broken into five phases from opening statement to appeal of the trial court decision. For each of these five phases Schuetz and Snedaker have selected and developed a narrative from an appropriate historically important criminal case.

vii

The cases—those of the defendants in the Haymarket riot trial, Bruno Richard Hauptmann, Sacco-Vanzetti, the Rosenbergs, Sam Sheppard—are familiar to most of us. These cases are part of our popular culture as well as, in one way or another, landmarks in the history of law in the United States. The nature of the rhetorical (persuasive) discourse in each of these five phases of the trial process is analyzed. Conclusions are then drawn, based on this narrative and analysis, regarding the expectations for the discourse at each of these phases and what the practitioners in each case actually did.

Two additional chapters at the beginning and end of the volume focus on more global issues that transcend particular phases in the trial process. The first of these looks at a compelling case with massive pretrial publicity—the case arising from John Hinckley's attempt to kill the president of the United States. While the topic of pretrial publicity has received much attention, no treatment is more clear and succinct than that provided here. The second, dealing with the Chicago Eight, develops the theme of trial as a form of theater, an important concept that is often overlooked even though trials have been a frequent subject for drama (*Merchant of Venice, The Crucible, The Caine Mutiny,* and many others). Daniel Berrigan even turned the transcript of one of his own trials into a successful play *(The Trial of the Catonsville Nine).*

What Schuetz and Snedaker have produced is that most difficult and most rewarding type of intellectual activity—a synthesis. Drawing on concepts from classical to contemporary, they have synthesized a communication theory that illuminates the actual trial activities presented. This theory is then joined to legal theory regarding appropriate trial practice at the various phases of trial that Schuetz and Snedaker consider. The resulting final synthesis brings together in a unified whole the best insights from the fields of both law and communication.

In traditional rhetorical theory the ends or goals of discourse are often identified as "to inform," "to persuade," and "to entertain." Janice Schuetz and Kathryn Holmes Snedaker have produced an additional level of synthesis by achieving all three of these ends simultaneously in a discourse that offers meaningful levels for response for both novices and experts in communication and law.

Peter E. Kane

State University of New York at Brockport

Preface

The relationship between communication and law dates back to the early theories of Aristotle and Isocrates in the fourth century B.C. Students attending Aristotle's school of rhetoric learned how to prepare and deliver forensic (legal), deliberative (political), and epideictic (special occasion) speeches. The Roman teachers Cicero and Quintilian elaborated the Greek ideas about forensic and deliberative speaking in several formal treatises on rhetoric, which then served as the textbooks for the training of young men for careers in law and politics. During the Middle Ages, many of Cicero's principles of courtroom logic and evidence continued to be central ideas of the curriculum.

During the Renaissance, the curriculum for students of law used Ciceronian concepts but focused the content more on philosophy than rhetoric. Despite this shift, when the first law school in the United States opened at Harvard in 1756, the curriculum featured the study of Aristotle's *Rhetoric* and Cicero's *De Oratore*. Many famous legal practitioners, including Daniel Webster, Rufus Choate, and William Ewarts, studied rhetoric as a preparation for their distinguished legal careers (Oliver, 1965). As schools of law became more specialized, however, rhetoric gradually disappeared from the curriculum.

In this century, the study of communication in the courtroom is found in two broad categories of periodicals: social science journals and legal journals. The literature found in the social science journals consists almost entirely of experimental research examining, for example, the impact of defendant variables and witness characteristics on juror perceptions. In contrast, the material published in the legal journals typically includes hypotheses by advocates explaining their personal uses of trial techniques, rather than developing strategies based upon a systematic analysis. In recent years, however, there has been an increased interest in identifying strategies of successful courtroom communication.

This resurgence of interest in the relationship between rhetorical theory and the study of law is evident in the research of scholars in both disciplines (Mauet, 1980; Bennett & Feldman, 1981; Dicks, 1981; Rieke, 1982, 1986; Tanford, 1983). Trial lawyers also have shown new interest in communication. As former Supreme Court Justice Tom Clark noted: "Most trial attorneys are knowledgeable

of the law. Many, however, don't communicate well in the courtroom. They don't know how to construct persuasive oral arguments
and don't know what kinds of techniques influence a judge or jury"
(Frontes & Bunden, 1980, p. 251). Moreover, the late Irving Younger,
well-known criminal lawyer and trial consultant, recommended that
lawyers could learn a great deal about the strategies of successful
courtroom communication by reading about historical trials. The
responses by legal scholars and practitioners, following each of the
chapters in this volume, point to the importance of communication
to successful litigation. This volume contributes to this academic
debate by directly applying communication theories in a legal context. Our goal is to illuminate how the critical analyses of celebrated
trials can enhance understanding of both the traditional and contemporary connections between communication and law.

Goals and Content

The present volume explicates the relationship of communication to litigation through the analysis of trial discourse. The trial
process functions as a sequence of persuasive arguments. This sequence begins with the media coverage of the trial; enters into the
courtroom persuasion by way of opening statement, direct examination, cross-examination, and closing argument; and often culminates in appellate arguments. The entire trial operates as a
persuasive unit, and yet each segment functions as a distinctive and
identifiable part of the case.

We analyze one process of litigation in each of the seven historical cases—Hinckley, Chicago Anarchists (Haymarket), Hauptmann, Sacco-Vanzetti, Rosenberg, Sheppard, and the Chicago Eight.
Each chapter uses a critical approach that integrates theories of
communication with principles of advocacy.

The case study of the press coverage in the Hinckley trial (chapter 1) demonstrates how media coverage of trials may result in overt
persuasive content in the form of slanted depictions, agenda setting,
and social scapegoating. Understanding how the "opening statement" of the press persuades the public about the accused, attorneys,
judges, witnesses, and evidence will aid litigators in jury selection,
selection of theme, and presentation of the case.

Our rhetorical analysis of opening statement (chapter 2) demonstrates how effective opening speeches should preview the un-

derlying story structure of the case, which in turn establishes the perceptual framework for all subsequent persuasion in the trial. Specifically, the chapter on opening statement systematically reveals the preferred form, content, and style of effective opening statements.

The chapter on direct examination (chapter 3) distinguishes between narratives that are likely to persuade during this segment of the trial and those that are not. The chapter further contributes by delineating how the prosecution and defense should construct the stories, how direct questioning should be conducted, and why some stories are more persuasive for jurors than the competing narrative.

In contrast to the direct examiner who seeks to create a narrative, the strategies available to the cross-examiner are investigated in chapter 4. The chapter details the recommended approaches to cross-examination, and demonstrates how cross-examinations can be more persuasive by adoption of specific communication strategies and tactics.

Our analysis reveals participatory persuasion as the basis for effective closing argument (chapter 5). This analysis demonstrates how advocates can enhance the persuasive content of their closing speeches, communicating in ways that stimulate thought, mental activity, and sensory involvement.

The chapter on appellate brief writing (chapter 6) identifies the persuasive strategies underlying effective brief writing. Our approach reveals the components of effective arguments and demonstrates how these components can be manipulated in the effective advocate's brief.

The Chicago Eight chapter (chapter 7) considers the communicative universe of the courtroom, the complete courtroom drama—characters, plot, denouement, action, setting, as well as narrative. Understanding the trial drama makes sense of the trial interaction as a whole and demonstrates the importance of the assumptions that underlie the justice system.

This analysis results in a trade-off between depth and breadth. On the one hand, by analyzing only one part of each trial, we risk overlooking the whole process of that trial. On the other hand, by examining seven trials, using a unique theoretical perspective for each, we gain the advantage of a broader and more comprehensive investigation of the role of communication in the litigation process than otherwise possible.

Trial Selection

Each of the trials analyzed in this volume was selected according to several criteria. First, each of the trials qualifies as a sensational case because of the nature of the crime, the social and political affiliations of the defendants, or the questionable legal practices of the litigants, judge, jury, or media. Second, the cases represent different decades and hence different historical, social, and legal influences on the trial. Third, each of the trials marks an historical milestone in the legal process, showing the potential of the courts and the media for abridging the rights of the defendants to an impartial and public trial, due process, and freedom from prejudicial press coverage. Fourth, each of the cases demonstrates the important role that communication plays in the enactment of legal drama. Finally, our analysis shows that public opinion often influences the persuasion inside of the courtroom. Among the many trials in the last century that qualify as "sensational," the seven cases selected stand out as a representative sample in that they show diverse contexts, feature different decades, reveal unique persuasive strategies, and point to the impact of political climate upon the process of litigation.

Although the focus of our study is not on legal change per se, we recognize that the last century has witnessed a number of legal changes. Some of these changes are noteworthy. For example, at the time of the Haymarket and Sacco-Vanzetti trials, women were not allowed to serve on juries. In the trials prior to 1960, opening and closing arguments often consumed as much time as the advocates wanted, whereas contemporary judges often impose strict time limits upon advocates' speeches. Before current laws required that jurors be summoned from voter registration rolls, judges could constitute juries from meetings at a local lodge, as was done in the Sacco-Vanzetti case. Prior to the Miranda laws, Sacco and Vanzetti and the Rosenbergs could be interrogated and forced to disclose self-incriminating evidence without their attorneys present. The police's ransacking of the Hauptmanns' home and the prosecution's withholding of evidence from the defense in the Lindbergh case would not have occurred under present laws. Prior to the restraints on media, mandated by the Supreme Court in the Sheppard decision in 1966, the press covered trials with very little concern for the defendants. In contemporary cases, defendants would not be brought into the courtroom in cages as Sacco and Vanzetti were in 1921. Under current Codes of the American Bar Association, litigants and judges would not talk to the press prior to and during the trial, as they did in Haymarket, Sacco-Vanzetti, Hauptmann, Rosenberg, and the Chicago Eight cases. From the time of the Haymarket case until the Hinckley trial, the law has evolved to give greater protection to the rights of the accused.

Because statutes and legal practices evolve over time, the actions or procedures in historical cases might seem to contemporary readers to be obvious infractions of the rights of defendants. In fact, however, these actions were routine practices at the time of the trial. Our analysis necessarily incorporates contemporary legal assumptions and communication practices. However, when pertinent, we have noted the legal norms and practices that existed at the time the trial took place.

Rhetorical Criticism of Narrative

Rhetorical criticism is our method of analysis. This method seeks to understand how the symbols used within the trial or in discourse about the case persuade audiences. The focus of this method of criticism is on rhetoric, persuasive discourse. In its broadest sense, Wallace (1971) defines rhetoric as the "art of discourse" (p. 3). Nichols (1963) clarifies the definition, noting that "rhetoric is the practice of the verbal mode of presenting judgment and choice, knowledge and feeling" (p. 7). The "Report of the Committee on the Scope of Rhetoric" (1971) broadens the definition further claiming: "Rhetorical studies are properly concerned with the processes by which symbols have influence on beliefs, values, attitudes, and actions" (p. 208).

We use the word "rhetoric" as synonymous with persuasive communication. Rhetoric includes verbal and nonverbal symbols that influence beliefs and attitudes, judgment and choice, and knowledge and feeling. More specifically, this analysis of litigation processes looks at rhetoric as it occurs in the narrative arguments found in the press' reconstruction of the arrest, indictment, and trial; the prepared speeches of advocates; the questions and answers between advocates and witnesses; the appellate briefs of advocates and legal opinions of appellate judges; and the complex dramatic interaction within the trial as a whole. It is not surprising that legal philosopher Chaim Perelman (1963, 1967, 1980) recommends the law be interpreted in terms of rhetorical choices that incorporate the values and understandings of the audiences addressed by litigators.

Each chapter investigates in three phases the elements of persuasion with the litigation process. First, the chapter describes the trial and the circumstances in which it occurred. The background information is followed by an explanation of a theoretical framework accounting for the choices made by advocates in that particular unit of the trial. Second, each chapter analyzes one segment of each trial by comparing the theoretical framework to the communication prior to or during the trial. Finally, each chapter evaluates one part of the case, judging its merits and suggesting how the conclusions might assist contemporary legal or communication practitioners in understanding the trial persuasion.

In particular, the focus on persuasion identifies the situational factors that produce the form, style, and content of the discourse. This approach is distinctive in several ways. First, it differs from typical works on celebrated trials in that it is not just a description of the trial nor a systematic history of the trial given in an attempt to justify or debate the verdict. Our purpose is not to discern the guilt or innocence of the parties involved. Instead, we seek to understand how the public opinion of the era enters into the trial and to identify how the communicative practices work. Quite simply, our goal is to understand how each part of the trial functions as persuasion and, in doing so, give a glimpse of the difference between the ideal of what should occur and the reality of what actually takes place.

Second, our analysis attempts to illuminate how theories of persuasion contribute to an understanding of all aspects of the practices associated with litigation. Most legal scholars develop theories of trial advocacy simply from the standpoint of the practitioner. Tanford (1983), an exception to the usual practice, recognizes the contribution of the other disciplines to advocacy, but his work does not apply these theories to legal discourse.

Finally, the method used here is analytical rather than merely descriptive and seeks to answer the question: How does trial discourse work as persuasion? The volume investigates the adequate and deficient aspects of the choices, constructions, and uses of the discourse prior to or during the trial. By noting the factors that make the persuasion strong or weak in each case, we make recommendations in each chapter about what contemporary practitioners can learn from the successes and failures of the litigators.

The communication prior to and during the trial takes the form of narrative persuasion or storytelling. Fisher (1984) defines narrative in general as "the words and/or deeds—that have sequence and meaning" for others (p. 2). If we apply Fisher's definition to the courtroom, the words and deeds have order and meaning for the press, attorneys, witnesses, accused, jurors, and judge. The litigation stories feature several storytellers, stories, and story listeners. In the pretrial phase, the press tells the story through their medium to the public. Inside the courtroom, the advocates and witnesses tell their story through the opening statement, direct and cross-examination, and closing argument. The judge, jurors, and public listen to the stories given inside the trial. As storytellers, the goal of the press, advocates, and witnesses is to develop narrative accounts that are corroborated, relevant, consistent, and probable. In particular, the story is the message jurors use to decide the guilt or innocence of the accused.

Story has several defining traits. According to Chatman (1978) the first trait is content, that is, the chain of events or actions. The events, actions, and happenings of litigation stories pertain to the facts of the case and point to the charges of the indictment. The second trait, according to Chatman (1978), consists of existents, the characters and setting of the story. In stories relating to the trial, the existents include the people and places associated with the alleged criminal actions and all of the actors holding information relevant to the indictments. In particular, both the press and the advocates seek information about the times, places, people, and relationships that pertain to each case. The final trait is the discourse (Chatman, 1978), the linguistic means by which the content and the existents are presented by those who tell the story to those who listen and evaluate the accounts. The discourse includes descriptions of people, places, and things; claims of fact and the inferences and evidence presented in support of the arguments; refutation and rebuttal of others' stories; instructions about courtroom rules and issues of law; and the enactment of the crime story in the external and internal dramas within the trial.

Our critical analysis focuses on story as rhetoric as it investigates the role of narrative in litigation processes. Although each chapter is independent of the others, the theory we develop for each segment of one trial is generalizable and can be applied to the parallel segment of the other trials in the volume. However, because of the unique circumstances and indictments of each case, the application of the theory will differ slightly with each individual case.

Organization

The following chapters are organized according to the chronology of the trial process: pretrial press coverage in the Hinckley trial (1982), opening statement in the Chicago Anarchists (Haymarket) case (1886), direct examination in the Hauptmann case (1935), cross-examination in the Sacco-Vanzetti case (1921), closing argument in the Rosenberg case (1951), appellate argument in the Sheppard case (1954–66), and trials as drama in the Chicago Eight case (1969). The chronology emphasizes the story and how that story is disjointedly presented in the media, prefaced in opening statement, elaborated in direct examination, refuted and reshaped in cross-examination, reemphasized in closing argument, validated or invalidated by appellate arguments, and carried out in the dramatic theme of the trial as a whole.

Since the book stresses the communicative perspective, we asked well-known scholars and legal practitioners to comment on the chapters from their perspectives. Their responses point to experiences and perceptions that are not likely to emerge from an analysis of the transcripts, such as the historical changes in the law, the adverse conditions under which defense attorneys must present a case, the personalities of the litigants, the importance of preparation that occurs prior to the trial, and the poetic perceptions of a litigator about the case in which he served as one of the defense attorneys. These insights add more depth to our conclusions and provide an additional interpretive point of view for our readers.

Acknowledgments

We acknowledge the helpful comments of our colleagues at the University of New Mexico. We are especially indebted to Michele S. G. Hermann, Professor of Law, for her encouragement in the early stages of the project and for her critical comments on the manuscript. Andrew S. Burgess, Associate Professor of Philosophy, read and commented on each of the chapters. Robert Schwartz, Associate Professor of Law, and Joyce Rogers, Associate Professor of University Studies, provided encouragement at each stage of the project.

We are also indebted to Vincent Fuller, defense attorney for John Hinckley, who read and commented on chapter 1. The Honorable Judith M. Billings, Utah Court of Appeals, gave helpful advice on chapter 6. Each of the respondents added insight about each of the chapters through comments and clarifications in their responses. We also appreciate the ongoing personal and moral support given by Andy and Lee.

Communication
and
Litigation

1
The Press Coverage
of the Hinckley Case:
A Case Study
of a Crime News Serial

The case of John W. Hinckley, Jr., exemplifies how the press presents its story to the public prior to the opening of the trial. This chapter explains how the press historically has covered sensational trials, including all of the cases analyzed in this volume. The chapter then surveys the codes and standards of both the legal and journalistic professions, examines how reporters reconstruct crimes into news stories, and explains the social effects of the news coverage of trials. This analysis of the pretrial press coverage of the Hinckley case is developed through a content analysis of 120 articles in the *Washington Post* during a thirteen-month period, extending from the day of the shooting until the opening of the trial.

In the Hinckley case, the *Washington Post* presented the story of the attempted assassination of President Ronald Reagan to the public as the details of the crime emerged. This narrative took the form of serial news containing distinct frames and several episodes within each frame. Our analysis uncovers overt persuasive content in the form of slanted depictions, efforts to set the agenda, and social scapegoating. Even though both the press and the trial participants adhered to the legal restraints and abided by the journalistic codes, the pretrial publicity still presented a persuasive point of view. Our analysis calls the story of the press "the opening statement before the opening statement." This kind of media persuasion chooses witnesses as its sources, presents evidence, and judges the accused or the prosecution before the trial has begun.

The Trial

At 2:25 P.M. on March 30, 1981, John W. Hinckley, Jr., shot President Ronald Reagan, press aide James Brady, a Secret Service agent, and a Washington, D.C., policeman. Just as in some other assassination attempts, the press was covering Reagan at the time of the crime. Thus the press observed the crime firsthand and created these vivid reconstructions of the event in the *Washington Post*. For example, Cannon (31 March 1981) gave this account:

> Reagan had delivered his basic speech appealing for support of his economic program and exploring the increase in violent crime. . . . Outside the hotel room more than 100 persons had gathered. Reagan, as he usually does, paused and waved to the crowd. . . . Abruptly, the scene changed. Shots rang out, six of them in quick succession. . . . The shots appeared to come from the roped off press area (p. A1).

That same day, Broder (31 March 1981) assured readers that "five hours after the shooting, the president was out of surgery and in stable condition . . . clear of head and should be able to make decisions tomorrow" (p. A1). In the same edition, Shaffer and Henry gave a detailed profile of the assailant, claiming his arrest "followed several years of aimless drifting—years during which the 25 year old son of a wealthy oil man dropped in and out of college in Texas and traveled in Colorado and California in search of a job" (p. A9).

The case opened on April 27, 1982. Hinckley was tried on the plea, "not guilty by reason of insanity," in the United States District Court in Washington, D.C. Vincent J. Fuller conducted the defense for Hinckley, assisted by Gregory P. Craig, Judith A. Miller, and Lon S. Babby. Roger M. Adelman directed the prosecution and was assisted by Robert R. Chapman and Marc B. Tucker. Given the nature of the plea, the prosecution had the obligation to prove that Hinckley was sane at the time of the shooting. After forty-two days of trial, the jury returned the verdict that Hinckley was "not guilty by reason of insanity." In posttrial hearings, Judge Barrington Parker remanded Hinckley to the care of St. Elizabeth's Psychiatric Hospital in Washington, D.C., and he remains in that hospital today.

Many investigators have analyzed the press coverage during a trial and the decisions given in appellate courts that have followed a trial. A great deal of this literature centers on the issue of free press as it relates to the fair trial of the defendants (Stephenson, 1979; Lieberman, 1980; Marcus, 1982). Other sources have focused

2

on the verdicts in which the press has prejudiced the trial outcome (Lofton, 1966; Friendly & Goldfarb, 1967; Dreschel, 1983). Researchers studying press coverage have acknowledged its impact only when the case has been appealed on First Amendment grounds, as it was in the Sheppard trial.

This chapter seeks to answer the question: How does the press cover a sensational case prior to the trial? To accomplish this goal, the chapter (1) summarizes the history of press coverage of trials in general and reviews the coverage of other trials analyzed in this volume; (2) explains how the press reports news about trials; (3) examines how the *Washington Post* covered the Hinckley case prior to the opening of the trial; and (4) draws implications from the press coverage of other sensational cases.

History of Press Coverage of Trials

The newspapers and their stories about crime and violence share a long history. As early as 1807, in the Aaron Burr case, the press got involved in news coverage of sensational cases. The newspapers reported the Burr trial by taking sides long before the trial started. Both the Federalist papers, the *Virginia Gazette* and the *Daily Advertiser*, supported the position of the defense and spoke out vehemently for the accused; whereas the *National Intelligencer* in Washington supported the prosecution and tried to use their paper to establish Burr's guilt (Lofton, 1966).

By the 1830s, the "penny press" named for its one-cent dailies, was designed to reach the uneducated public who had a thirst for crime and violence, so it dealt exclusively with police reports about drunkenness, wife beating, prostitution, and vagabonds (Mott, 1952). This press flourished through the Civil War period, covering cases such as the Webster-Parkman case in 1850 (the trial of Webster for the murder of Parkman, to whom Webster owed money), the case of the conspirators aiding John Wilkes Booth in the assassination of Abraham Lincoln, and the impeachment of President Andrew Johnson (Mott, 1952).

In the 1880s, Joseph Pulitzer revamped the *New York World* by encouraging his reporters to cover crime and scandal and to use headlines enticing readers to buy the paper. The success of the *World* encouraged other papers to emphasize the reporting of sensational crimes. As a result, the *New York Herald*, the *New York Sun*, the *Cincinnati Enquirer*, the *Chicago Times*, and the *San Francisco Examiner* followed the lead of Pulitzer, who featured the coverage of sensational crimes as the primary content of his newspapers (Mott, 1952).

At the time of the Haymarket riots in Chicago in 1886, the *Chicago Tribune* took an active advocacy role, urging the public to respond violently toward the labor strikers at Haymarket Square, a factor that helped inspire the riots. As part of the rioting at this labor gathering, dynamite exploded killing seven Chicago policemen and injuring six citizens. Subsequent to the explosion and the rioting at Haymarket Square, newspapers, including the *Chicago Tribune*, advocated the conviction of the accused labor leaders. After the trial, the local press cheered the guilty verdict and applauded the impending execution of some of the Haymarket defendants (Lum, 1969; Avrick, 1984).

In the late 1800s, William Randolph Hearst labeled his press' emphasis on crime and violence the "new journalism." His stress on crime, scandal, and disaster also transformed the *San Francisco Examiner* into a financially successful paper and led to Hearst's purchase of the *New York Morning Journal.* Together with Pulitzer's *New York World*, Hearst developed what scholars call "yellow journalism," a type of news reporting that featured crime and scandal, using scare headlines in large black type and graphic pictures to attract attention to this kind of news (Mott, 1952).

The advent of the twentieth century saw continued newspaper preoccupation with crime. The most sensational national cases between 1900 and 1920 concerned labor leaders who were charged with conspiracy, rioting, and other felony crimes, such as the cases of Thomas J. Mooney and Warren Billings, Eugene Debs, and the Wobblies. In all of these cases, the press supported the state and overtly called for the conviction, stiff sentencing, and even the execution of the defendants (Hays, 1933).

By the time of the Sacco-Vanzetti case in 1921, the press engaged in the active reporting of cases from the pretrial stage through the appellate process. Prior to and during the Sacco-Vanzetti case, the *New York Times, Boston Transcript*, the *Boston Herald*, and other Massachusetts papers condemned the defendants as anarchists, communists, and disloyal men who deserved to be convicted of murder. Only after the international press got involved in the case, as the result of the guilty verdict and death sentence, did some American papers actually speak out against the injustice of the trial and in favor of the defendants. Among the papers that alleged unfairness in the trial were the *St. Louis Post Dispatch* and the *New York World*. During 1926, shortly before the execution of Sacco and Vanzetti, the *Boston Herald* reversed its earlier guilty proclamations and called for a new trial (Joughin & Morgan, 1948).

Because aviator Charles A. Lindbergh and his wife Anne were national celebrities, the press covered the kidnapping and death of their child in 1932 as a serial crime story. Thus, no one was surprised when the arrest of Bruno Richard Hauptmann in September 1934 received unprecedented media attention. Prior to the trial of Hauptmann, a news columnist for the *Daily Mirror*, Walter Winchell, claimed that Hauptmann was guilty and even called for his execution. Additionally though, two hundred newspapers covered the trial and over eleven million words were written about the case (Waller, 1961; Kennedy, 1985). Adding to this overwhelming publicity, the Hearst newspaper chain paid for the defense of Hauptmann in exchange for exclusive rights to the filming of the trial. By current standards, the press jeopardized Hauptmann's fair trial, yet the legal restraints of the time did not preclude such coverage.

The 1951 trial of Julius and Ethel Rosenberg also received extensive coverage throughout each stage of the case. This publicity directly implicated the Rosenbergs and their codefendant, Morton Sobell, in communist activities; took the side of the prosecution in calling for a guilty verdict and the death penalty; and endorsed the stiff sentences and long pre-execution incarceration of the defendants. Just as in the Sacco-Vanzetti case, the American press changed its position only after the international press lashed out at the injustice in the case. For the most part, the major newspapers throughout the country supported the position of the state against the Rosenbergs (Radosh & Milton, 1983).

Although the Sheppard trial took place in 1954, the legal ramifications of the case did not begin to affect the court system until twelve years later. In 1966 the Supreme Court granted Sheppard a new trial, and warned the courts they must adopt strict measures to guard against trial by press and ensure the fairness of the proceeding for the accused. As explained in chapter 6, the *Cleveland Press'* coverage of the Sheppard murder case was sensational, prejudicial, and extensive. Additionally, many of the leading newspapers in the country covered the trial. According to the majority Court opinion, the publicity about the Sheppard trial was "massive, pervasive, and prejudicial" (*Sheppard v. Maxwell*, 384 U.S. 333 [1966]). The Court faulted the media coverage of the trial for the amount of pretrial publicity, the printing of names of veniremen, the prejudicial photography, the debate and commentary about the trial in the press, and the disruption of the courtroom decorum by reporters.

As a result of the Sheppard case, the Court ordered judges in future cases to take steps to preclude the prejudicial atmosphere created by the media. These steps significantly changed the way the press was permitted to cover trials. These precautionary steps applied to judges and included: issuing a motion of continuance, that is, delaying the date of the trial to wait for the publicity to fade; requiring a change of venue so that the trial would not be held in the same location in which the crime occurred; conducting a rigorous *voir dire* to eliminate jurors who had been strongly influenced by the media; sequestering the jury so that they would not be subject to press coverage during the trial; having the judge give deliberate instructions to warn jurors about press influence; issuing gag orders to restrict the media legally from releasing information about the trial; and issuing silence orders to prohibit trial participants from talking to the press prior to and during the trial.

The Sheppard ruling did result in judges taking preventive measures in future trials. Even though these restraints resulted in some protection of the jury from prejudicial testimony, in 1968 the participants of the Chicago Eight trial circumvented these orders and created media events outside of the trial with specific intent to influence the press. The political nature of the trial aroused the *Chicago Tribune* to take an advocacy position condemning the defendants. During the course of the trial, the *Tribune* called the lawyers "hooligans" and the defendants "the Riot 7" (referring to the defendants after Seale left the trial), praised Judge Hoffman, published polls favoring the conviction of defendants, and generally tried to encourage a guilty verdict for the defendants (Dee, 1985).

By the time the Hinckley case took its place on the front pages of newspapers in 1981, the overt prejudicial reporting, characteristic of trials prior to 1966, was not evident. Whereas the assassins of Lincoln, Garfield, McKinley, and Kennedy had been the victims of the press, the newspapers reacted to the Hinckley assassination attempt with greater restraint and decorum than in other similar historical cases. Judge Parker issued silence orders on the trial attorneys, and the trial attorneys voluntarily silenced their expert witnesses. However, the trial was not moved out of Washington, and the jury was not sequestered because of the time lapse between the crime and the trial because the accused admitted the crime in his plea.

Even though the prejudicial treatment of Hinckley was not overt, the pretrial news coverage of this trial provides an illuminating case study of some of the covert practices of news reporters that do contribute to slanted and persuasive coverage of sensational trials.

News Coverage and Criminal Trials

News coverage of sensational criminal trials can be examined from two points of view: the legal standards and the reporters' methods of reconstructing the event. Although each point of view is separated for the purpose of our discussion, in reality the legal standards affected the reporters' reconstruction and the reconstruction affected the implementation of the standards.

Legal Standards

The Constitution, through the Due Process Clause and the Sixth Amendment, guarantees the accused a verdict determined by an impartial judge and/or jury in a fair proceeding. In particular, Justice Holmes argued that "conclusions to be reached in a case will be induced only by evidence and argument in open courts and not by outside influence, whether private talk or public print" (*Patterson v. Colorado*, 205 U.S. 454, 462 [1907]). At the same time, the First Amendment guarantees the press the freedom to publish information about the crime, indictment, trial, and appellate processes. This guarantee results from the fact that "a trial is a public event. What transpires in the courtroom is public property" (*Craig v. Harney*, 331 U.S. 368, 374 [1947]). In the Hinckley case, the public certainly had a right to know about the circumstances and the suspect who tried to kill their president.

When do the rights for a free press conflict with those for a fair trial? In *Sherbert v. Verner*, 374 U.S. 398 (1963), the Supreme Court concluded that the rights of the press can be limited only when the judge decides that "no alternate form of regulation would combat such abuses" as the media might create for a fair trial. The right of the press to cover trials is affirmed later in *Nebr. Press Assoc. v. Stuart*, 427 U.S. 539, 587 (1976), when Justice Brennan writes: "Commentary and reporting of the criminal justice system is at the core of the First Amendment values, for the operation and integrity of that system is of crucial import to citizens concerned with the administration of government." The American system of reporting differs significantly from that in England, where the press refrains from publishing any information about a case that goes to court. However under the American system of government, the press

7

is a watchdog of the police, courts, prosecutors, and thus has a responsibility to monitor the activities of the public representatives.

In the Hinckley case, the press monitored the legal system in its reporting by questioning the adequacy of the Secret Service protection of the president, commenting on the failure of Tennessee legal authorities to report the arrest of Hinckley for trying to board a plane with concealed weapons, noting the limitations and abuses of the "not guilty by reason of insanity" plea, describing the seizure by the prison guards of Hinckley's private writings, and questioning the reputation of Judge Parker by inquiring into his previous decisions and his failure to sequester the jury.

During the 1960s and subsequently, the press and the bar associations jointly developed codes that have lessened the prejudicial reporting of trials. For example in 1962, the State Bar Association of Oregon, the Newspaper Publishers Association, and the Association of Broadcasters adopted the following code concerning the news coverage of criminal cases:

> (1) The news media have the right and the responsibility to broadcast the truth. (2) The public has a right to be informed. The accused has a right to be judged in an atmosphere free from undue prejudice. (3) Morbid and sensational details of criminal behavior should not be exploited. (4) The editor or news director . . . should consider that—an accused person is presumed innocent until proven guilty, readers are potential jurors, and no person's reputation should be injured needlessly.

Codes, such as this one, gave additional direction to the editors and reporters who covered criminal cases.

In l983, the American Bar Association Model Rules of Professional Conduct, Rule 3.6(a) applied additional ethical standards to attorneys, restricting the kind of information they give to the press. The rule states: "A lawyer shall not make any extra-judicial statements that a reasonable person would expect to be disseminated by means of public communication if the lawyer knows it will have a substantial likelihood of materially prejudicing an adjudicative proceeding" (Harper, 1984). In the Hinckley case, the attorneys were ordered by the judge to refrain from speaking with the press. This order was followed; the *Post* included no references to information from attorneys on either side of the case prior to or during the trial.

Both the laws and codes about free press and fair trial seek open access of the press to the trial, and yet they try to protect the defendants so the accused can have a trial free from harmful press information. These restrictions do not entirely eliminate prejudicial information because the press must create interesting stories that attract and sustain the attention of its audiences.

Reporter Reconstruction Strategies

The press' goal of creating interesting stories is sometimes incompatible with the legal mandates for a fair trial with an impartial jury. Since the newspaper is usually the "first agent of the community to enter a case," the press can formulate public impressions about the crime and the accused (Lofton, 1966, p. 139). In the Hinckley case, the reporters for the *Post* observed the crime and were therefore able to give an eyewitness account of what they perceived. In most cases, however, reporters rely solely on external sources for reconstructing the event.

Denniston (1980) advises trial reporters against becoming involved with legal issues and developments and suggests instead that they concentrate on the dramatic elements of the trial. He recognizes that reporters tell better stories about crimes and trials when the "legalities and technicalities are woven around the story of the persons involved" (p. 110). Denniston counsels reporters to create interesting stories that will attract the public attention.

Gans (1979) outlines several strategies for reconstructing interesting and involving news stories. First, the story must have substantive content and newsworthiness. The substance derives from developing the importance of the people involved in the event and from the national impact of the actions. Gans specifies that the most important news stems from "known" individuals who play "a key role in national events" (p. 8). The Hinckley case obviously fits this first characteristic. The case involved the attempted assassination of President Reagan and the injury of James Brady, a Secret Service agent, and a policeman. John Hinckley, an unknown, was arrested shortly after the crime and the police found letters and poems written by the accused to actress Jodie Foster, a movie celebrity. The crime was committed against the leader of the country, and the motive seemed to be that Hinckley tried to kill Reagan to win the favor of Jodie Foster, a well-known actress.

A second feature of an involving news story is that it must have a high degree of activity. Gans (1979) views activity as conflict, disagreement, decision, protest, violence, or scandal (p. 16). The

Hinckley case maintained front page coverage for a long period of time because the story had a great deal of violent and bizarre twists to it. This activity began with the shooting incidents but was followed by accounts of the psychological struggles of the accused, the legal struggles of the Hinckley attorneys in protecting the client, the suicide attempts of the defendant, the survival struggle of James Brady, the search for motives of the accused, the ploys of the defendant to get additional attention by writing letters to leading news magazines and newspapers, and the struggles of Hinckley's family to help him.

Finally, Gans notes that sensational stories focus upon the issues of moral disorder in society, that is, the disruptions of the traditional values prized by most members of society. The Hinckley case raised a plethora of social and moral questions. Because Hinckley had purchased a half dozen guns and exploder bullets legally, the event raised questions about the sale of guns and ammunition. Because Hinckley grew up in an upper-class family that gave him money that enabled him to complete the crime, the case raised questions about discipline and the breakdown of family values. Because Hinckley committed the crime and admitted his act and yet pleaded "not guilty by reason of insanity," the case raised concern about the legitimacy of the insanity plea. Because Hinckley's own writings suggested a motive for the crime that paralleled the motive of Travis Bickle in the movie *Taxi Driver*, the case raised public concern about the influence of film on criminal behavior. Taken together these factors suggested causes of moral disorder in society.

In order to write an involving story for readers, reporters feature well-known characters, imbue the story with conflict, and raise social and moral questions. For the most part, the stories written about the Hinckley case met the legal standards for both a free press and fair trial. However, at times the stories seemed to violate some journalistic codes, such as reporting intimate and sordid details about the accused and abridging the rights to privacy of the Hinckley family. The subsequent analysis delineates some of the violations and emphasizes how the press covertly persuades the public.

Analysis of the Hinckley Trial Press Coverage

The Hinckley trial received extensive coverage in all the mass media particularly television, news magazines, and newspapers. This coverage commenced on the day of the shooting and continued for the year prior to the case, and during the six weeks of the trial.

Since this time, the press has continued to cover developments in the status of Hinckley while he has been incarcerated at St. Elizabeth's Hospital. Our analysis considers the way the pretrial coverage in the *Post* serves as a kind of opening statement to the public prior to the opening statement in the courtroom.

Post Coverage

The following analysis focuses on the media coverage of the Hinckley case from the day of the shooting, March 30, 1981, until the date of the trial opening over a year later, April 27, 1982. Several reasons govern the choice of the *Washington Post* for the analysis. First, the *Post* is the major newspaper in Washington, D.C., the location of the crime and the residence of the victims as well as the place where the trial was held.

Second, the *Post* is a national newspaper and its stories are frequently reprinted by other newspapers; excerpts are used for radio broadcasts, and information from the paper reappears in television news on the national networks. The *Post* is likely to give a representative sample of media coverage because stories are the product of "pack journalism," that is, the television networks, newspapers, radio, and magazines jointly report stories with the same dramatic slant (Bennett, 1983, pp. 14–16). Moreover, Epstein (1973) notes that most of the news comes from the same wire services causing television stations and magazines to print or broadcast the same information as the newspapers.

A final reason for selecting the *Post* is that their coverage of the news is presented in more detail and with greater thoroughness than the other media. The coverage occurred on a regular basis and in a large quantity throughout the thirteen months between the crime and the trial. Moreover, the *Post* was likely to cover the attempted assassination and its aftermath because of its Washington location and its national focus, factors central to the Hinckley case.

Harper (1984) explains that pretrial media coverage illustrates how the press works with the courts to ensure an outcome in line with the free press and fair trial principles. The media covering the trial are the average person's only source of information about the case. Moreover, members of the public use the sensational trial as the model for formulating their opinions about the efficiency and fairness of the trial process. Denniston (1980) notes that the average citizen "reads no court opinions, watches few proceedings in court, studies no law review articles, has no regular contact with legal

11

personnel" (p. xx). For this reason, what the press says is happening is what members of the public perceive to be reality; the media coverage is the public's only perceptual view for understanding how the legal system and its personnel work to combat crime.

Press Coverage as Opening Statement

As famous criminal attorney Melvin Belli notes: "Media coverage prior to the trial is the opening statement before the opening statement" (Harper, 1984, p. 79). Media opening statements resemble the in-trial opening statements in several ways. First, the media purport to be objective and claim to present only factual information about the people and happenings related to the case. Just as in the actual opening statements during the trial, the media statements persuade the audience without appearing to do so. Second, media coverage outlines the theories of the case for the public just as the attorneys use opening statements in the trial to outline their theory of the case for the judge and jury. The media, however, outline the theories of both sides of the case, often in a single news story. Moreover, the theories outlined by the media are speculations and inferences rather than summaries of the pertinent legal facts of the case. Third, the press anticipates the evidence that will be presented and predicts the order, quantity, and quality of witnesses who are likely to appear.

Several differences also show how the press' opening statements contrast with those delivered by attorneys in the trial. The purpose differs. The press seeks to interest the audience and sell newspapers by the conflict, novelty, and drama developed in their stories (Tuchman, 1978; Gans, 1979; Bennett, 1983). In contrast, attorneys outline the story of their respective cases to preview the order, the content, and the motives of the trial. The audience for the press is the public, whereas the judge and jurors are the main target audience of attorneys. The press' opening statements are often thousands of column inches in length and published over many months of time. This contrasts with the in-trial opening statements, which are often restricted to thirty minutes. Finally, each attorney in the trial focuses on one side of the case in order to place the pivotal characters, actions, and motives into a narrative, previewing their side's story of the case. The press' statements, on the other hand, weigh the competing theories of both sides and speculate about the social, political, and legal implications arising from the outcomes of the trial.

Understanding how the opening statements of the press persuade the public about the accused, the attorneys, the judge, the legal process, and the law necessitates a breakdown of the coverage into its structure, the content of frames, and its persuasive strategies and effects.

The Structure of Pretrial Coverage

Pretrial coverage of sensational cases is both intensive and extensive. The coverage is intensive because it exploits each conflict and personal struggle so as to involve the readers with the victims, the defendant, the trial process, and the legal system. At the same time, reporting about the case is extensive, covering various angles of the case with multiple stories in one issue or diffusing the coverage over a long period of time. Evidence of the extensiveness of the coverage of the Hinckley case is found in the multiple articles on the trial in many editions. For example, the *Post* had over 120 different articles about the case over the thirteen month period from the day of the crime to the opening of the trial. In one edition of the *Post* following the crime, there were five long, multiple column, front page articles related to the case.

The structural divisions account for both the intensive and the extensive characteristics of the coverage. Structure refers to organizational units, that is, the principles of arrangement that separate the news coverage of the Hinckley trial according to issue, setting, and characters. The general structure is serial news; the serials are separated into episodes, and the episodes are subdivided into frames.

News Serial

Coverage of sensational trials such as the Hinckley case qualifies as "serial news." Bennett (1983) explains that serial news develops from "long playing events" that "capture the attention and shape the emotion of the public." News serials are "real life dramas that unfold on the world stage" (p. 5). Examples of news serials are the coverage of the protests against the Vietnam War, the hostage drama in Iran, the hostages in Lebanon, and numerous sensational trials, such as the Haymarket, Hauptmann, Sacco-Vanzetti, Rosenberg, Sheppard, and Chicago Eight cases.

Serial news resembles other serials on television or in books in that the historical derivation of the event, the major characters, and the dominant themes remain constant even while the main narrative develops significantly throughout a long period of time. Just as in other serials, the coverage of the contexts of the trials, the minor characters, and the themes change as the narrative develops.

In the Hinckley coverage, the historical event remained the same even though the serial evolved. The key elements were the shooting and the victims, the type of gun used to commit the crime, the lack of security surrounding the president, the assailant's willingness to be caught, and Hinckley's confession immediately after the crime without a lawyer present.

In the initial coverage, the main characters of the story were the victims: President Reagan, Press Secretary James Brady, Secret Service agent Timothy McCarthy, and Washington policeman Thomas Delahanty. In later coverage, the president and Brady became the main character-victims. After the first two weeks, the news reported comparatively little information about the victims.

As the story progressed, however, the main character in the news serial became John Hinckley, the defendant. Broder (31 March 1981) characterized Hinckley on the day after the shooting in these terms: "The 25-year-old son of a wealthy Evergreen, Colo., businessman" (p. A1). The wealth of the defendant became an important descriptive term in the ongoing character development of the defendant, appearing over twenty times in the news coverage. Shaffer and Henry's portrait included other elaborations about Hinckley's character referring to him as a gun collector, a psychiatric patient, and a friendless drifter. All of these depictions were repeated many times in the news about the case.

The main themes of the narrative began as laments about "when will this needless violence end," placing the attempt on Reagan's life in the same category with the assassination that year of Anwar Sadat and the assassination attempt on Pope John Paul II. In each episode of the serial, similar character profiles and actions were the issues. An episode evolves into another episode when the themes and context of the story change.

Episodes

Whereas the serial is the overall structure and content of the coverage of the trial, the episodes are the subdivisions of the serial into separate sequences according to time, character relationships, theme development, and changing causal forces. The analysis that follows identifies the four major episodes of the trial coverage of the Hinckley case.

Episode One. The first episode reported the crime in a fragmented way. The episode occurred during the five days following the crime through twenty different stories, most appearing on the front page and running several columns in length. The main character in each narrative was John Hinckley. The *Post* featured victims of the crime, primarily President Reagan and James Brady. At this stage in the coverage, the press mentioned Jodie Foster as a possible leading character.

In this episode, the *Post* concentrated on the details of the crime story. The news coverage was both fragmented and diffuse, featuring many unsupported claims, speculations, and side issues about the motive for the crime. The *Post* bombarded the public with a large amount of loosely connected information to satisfy public curiosity about this sensational crime. Even though each individual story gave a coherent account of an issue, the articles encouraged controversy about issues not directly linked to this crime, such as the question of assassination in general, mental illness, and family responsibility. Because the public desired information about the crime, the *Post* tried to cater to their appetite even though reporters had limited information available. As a result, the news consisted of everything remotely related to the crime. The coverage was not narrated with any overall coherent plot or story line; instead a configuration of ideas surfaced, and the only link among them was that each had some connection to Hinckley or to his assassination attempt. In these early reports, the news reporters drew from a large variety of sources.

Episode Two. The second episode reconstructed the crime and its background by providing a chronological history of the day of the crime and a life history of the assailant. This part of the news serial occurred between April 5 and April 25, a period featuring nine stories and other related items appearing in the editorial section. The *Post* focused on the life and possible motives of John Hinckley. At this time, the news linked Hinckley directly to Jodie Foster through letters and tapes found in his motel room on the day of the crime.

The reconstruction episode developed a central theme—that Hinckley committed the crime to win the favor of the real Jodie Foster just as Travis Bickle tried to win the favor of Betsy (played by Foster) in the movie *Taxi Driver*. The story moved from fragmented narrative speculating about the crime to a clearly developed theory of the case constructed by the *Post*. The theory emerged in this story line:

(1) Hinckley was a disturbed young man, a drifter searching for some purpose in his life.

(2) Hinckley became obsessed with the plot of the film *Taxi Driver* and found some purpose in his life by identifying his goals with those of the character Travis Bickle.

(3) Just as Bickle won the affection and loyalty of Betsy (Jodie) by assassinating a president, Hinckley believed he could perform a similar feat for the real Jodie Foster by assassinating Ronald Reagan.

(4) To accomplish his goal, Hinckley stalked President Carter in several cities in 1980, but he did not get a good opportunity to shoot him.

(5) However, on March 30, 1981, because of the lack of security at the location of Reagan's exit from the Hilton Hotel, Hinckley found the opportunity to gun down President Reagan.

The *Post*'s theory of the case closely paralleled the theory by the defense. By the time of the second episode, reporters had narrowed the scope of their narrative and, as a result, they limited the number of types of information they included in their stories.

Episode Three. The third phase of the coverage occurred at the time of Hinckley's incarceration and during the period when he was evaluated psychologically by teams of defense and prosecution doctors. This episode resulted in limited coverage because very little action and hence little information was available to the press. The period extended from April 25 to August 24, 1981, and the coverage appeared in ten different articles.

Hinckley remained the major character in the news about the case. During this time, the *Post* emphasized Hinckley's first suicide attempt and speculated about the approach of his defense lawyers to the case. This part of the serial repeated previously reported information, foreshadowed the plea Hinckley was likely to make of "not guilty by reason of insanity," and suggested names of those likely to appear on the list of defense witnesses, drawing on the public information about the names of psychological experts examining the defendant. By this time, the public interest in the case had waned, and therefore most of the stories of the case appeared on the back pages of the newspaper.

Instead of many writers covering the crime, as occurred in the first two episodes, the news assignments for the case seemed at this point to be given almost exclusively to Laura A. Kiernan. The fact that one writer created most of the stories here and also in the final episode added more continuity and coherence to the news coverage than previously and also reduced the amount of redundancy that typified the first two phases of reporting. Many of the sources of news dried up, although a minimal amount of information came from the prison officials, who reported about Hinckley's ongoing mental tests.

Episode Four. In the fourth phase of the coverage, the news centered on the legal maneuvers prior to the opening of the trial. This episode extended over seven months, from August 25, 1981 to April 27, 1982. The period featured fifty articles, occurring in segments that chronologically followed the sequence of the legal actions.

Although Hinckley retained his celebrity status in the news, he shared the spotlight with several legal participants, including the prosecutors, chief defense counsel Vincent Fuller, and Judge Barrington Parker. Since the judge and attorneys were the agents of legal action, they became the main characters of this news episode. However, Hinckley upstaged them in two instances: he attempted suicide and almost succeeded, and he offered to provide information to the press by writing letters from his prison cell to leading newspapers and magazines, who then featured his responses in their stories.

The legal maneuvers themselves were each presented in a brief and unexplained form in the news. During this last episode, the following actions were covered: Hinckley's plea of not guilty by reason of insanity, a defense motion to exclude from trial evidence diaries and personal papers seized by prison guards, a defense motion to prohibit video presentations of the crime to the jury, a defense motion to exclude blown-up photos of Hinckley taken at a Colorado shooting range, and a judicial decision not to sequester the jury. The public legal records of the action were the sources of the press' information. Just prior to the opening of the trial, some feature articles in the *Post* chronicled the biographies of the judge and the attorneys.

Many of the news reports during the episode of legal maneuvering lacked information about the reasons for these motions. The press failed to explain how the legal maneuvers worked to protect the defendant's rights or the impartial climate of the litigation process. Additionally, this news episode seemed to suggest that the motions had created unnecessary delays in the trial. Despite the fact that the press was the only source of information most people had

17

about the legal procedures, the media failed to give definitions or explanations sufficient to inform the public about the legal process.

The *Post*'s reporting of the plea and the pretrial motions confirms Denniston's conclusion that the public's perceptions of legal procedures are often in error because of the "inattention or ineptness of the press as a chronicler of the legal process" (p. xix). Perhaps the press slighted its coverage of the legal process because the information received in press releases lacked inherent dramatic elements of conflict, human interest, or novelty; that is, legal motions are boring. Or perhaps the news reporters lacked sufficient background and knowledge to inform the public about the meaning of the legal procedures.

The pretrial episodes concluded with the opening of the trial on April 27. But prior to the trial, the *Post* featured many articles about the crime itself, the motive for the crime, the defense's theory of the case, the plea and its consequences, the list of key witnesses, the legal background of the litigators, and the record of the legal procedures prior to the trial. For regular readers, the press' opening statement about the trial offered a comprehensive portrait of what was going to transpire in the trial. Although extensive press coverage in highly celebrated trials tends to prejudice the jury against the defendants, the *Post*'s coverage of this case seemed to help the defense, because the news episodes told Hinckley's story, implying the defendant was psychologically unstable, erratic in his behavior, and unclear about his reasons for acting. Our investigation uncovered few articles that supported the prosecution's theory of the case, that Hinckley was sane at the time he committed the crime.

Content of Frames

The crime is a news serial that is divided into episodes. Each episode is then subdivided into frames, individual story units within the episode. Tuchman (1978) notes, frames organize "strips of the everyday world." "Strips" mean the "slices or cuts" of information that reporters make from the stream of available information (pp. 1–14). After writers select information, they transform the bits and pieces into a single story that embodies the content of the episode. The frames of news stories usually include sufficient documentation to make the stories appear to be hard news. Each frame typically gathers information that is both pertinent to the legal case and important to the public's right to know.

Frames and Hard News

Frames can include either "hard" or "soft" news. Tuchman (1978) defines hard news as factual occurrences and soft news as interesting details about the lives of human beings (p. 48). Hard news focuses primarily on news events, whereas soft news focuses on people and their problems. In hard news, the goals of reporters are to be objective, refrain from pursuing personal goals, and disregard the consequences of the story (Gans, 1979). Reporters of hard news want to create the impression that their stories are objective. To do this, they heavily *quote sources* so that others do the talking; make references to *locators* (precise times, places, and relationships); use concrete *descriptors* that give the impression that the reporter was an eyewitness to the event; and employ persuasive appeals to relate the story to accepted American *attitudes and values*.

In the coverage of the Hinckley case, some frames were a mixture of hard news and soft news. On the day following the shooting, Broder (31 March 1981) exemplified the ideal of objectivity in this excerpt from his hard news article about the assassination:

At 7:25 P.M. [locator], five hours after the shooting the president was out of surgery in stable condition. Dr. Dennis Leary [source] told reporters the "70 year old chief executive's prognosis is excellent" adding that at no time was he in danger. . . . The president's good spirits survived the traumatic day [values]. At 8:50 P.M. [locator], according to White House aide Lyn Nofziger, [source] with drainage tubes still in his throat [descriptors], Reagan wrote a note to his doctors saying: "All in all I'd rather be in Philadelphia," the line uttered by W. C. Fields when facing a lynching in *My Little Chickadee* [values].

In the same frame, however, Broder presented inferences that violated the norms of hard news, such as unsubstantiated claims of facts, controversy, judgments about the significance of events, and exclusions of quoted statements.

The following segment of news illustrates these violations:

Forty minutes later, with the president in surgery, Haig himself came to the White House briefing room [unsubstantiated claim]. "As of now," he said, "I am in control here at the White House . . ." [exclusion of information]. The comment was an ironic footnote to last week's publicized dispute [controversy], when Haig protested Reagan's decision to name Bush as crisis manager in a foreign or domestic

19

emergency [controversy]. But there was some confusion over Haig's exact role [judgment]. He said that during the afternoon appearance that "constitutionally" you have "the president, the vice president, and the secretary of state in that order . . ." [exclusion of information]. But in fact the order of succession to the president is speaker of the House and president pro-tempore of the Senate before secretary of State [controversy].

Although the article as a whole followed the norms of hard news, the writer deviated from this standard by raising controversy and by bringing the words and actions of a controversial political character into a story that otherwise focused on the crime.

The *Post* contained numerous other articles that do not qualify as hard news. These articles appeared to focus on people and problems but, instead of documenting the claims that were made, the articles revealed a tone and content usually associated with editorials. On the front page of the *Post* (1 April 1981), five articles developed the following themes: Reagan's recovery and good spirits, an explanation of how government runs without Reagan, Brady's slow recovery, Hinckley's love letter to Jodie Foster, and a report on Hinckley's travels before the crime. Some articles were predominantly hard news and others were not.

The frame about Hinckley's letter to Jodie Foster exemplified how reporters abridged the standards for hard news. The frame avoided content that would associate it with norms of objective reporting. An excerpt of the article from Knight and Henry (1 April 1981) follows:

> The young loner [judgment] charged with shooting President Reagan had a fixation [unsubstantiated claim] for teenage movie star, Jodie Foster, and attempted to assassinate the president in a grotesque attempt to get her attention [judgment] according to a letter found in his Washington hotel room. John W. Hinckley, an aimless unemployed, mentally troubled drifter [judgment, unsubstantiated claim] who in his 25 years made few friends [judgment, unsubstantiated claim] had sent several affectionate letters to the actress he had never met.

Some of the conclusions labeled "unsubstantiated claims" may have been documented in other frames of this episode, but these reporters drew conclusions that appeared to be factual when they more closely resembled editorializing than news.

Reporters of the Hinckley events expected audiences to accept the claims in this article based on evidence presented in other frames of this news story. In doing so, they took for granted that audiences had read those frames and understood the evidence from one frame must be transferred to another in order to make it factual. Knight and Henry did the talking rather than letting others talk for them. In the same article, these reporters concluded that Hinckley was "a man of few aims or cause"; he struggled with "loneliness, desperation, and disillusionment"; he was "bitter and nihilistic about American life and politics"; he had "an apparent fascination with guns"; and he exhibited "bizarre" behavior. This frame of news generalized far beyond the evidence in the article or evidence in this entire edition of the paper. Although the characterization was interesting, it violated the principles of news objectivity and the use of sources. Instead the frame catalogued a list of prejudicial information against the defendant. Nonetheless, this piece was placed as a news story on the front page of the *Post*.

Frames and Evidence

Besides lacking objectivity, the news about trials often presents stories that are subjective, one-sided, not corroborated, and not challenged. Although the public likely believes the information presented in the newspaper to be factual and accurate, the process of handling the evidence differs significantly from that of the courts. In news serials, each frame attempts to report news in an objective way letting the participants tell the story for the reporter. Additionally, each frame gathers and presents evidence about the case. Reporters present their "facts" of the case to public adjudicators, but in a fragmented way through many different frames. They expect the public to piece together the fragments into a meaningful interpretive framework. In contrast, the court requires that attorneys present facts in a clear and direct manner through a witness, who is then subjected to cross-examination in an attempt to verify the evidence. Whereas the public adjudicators (the readers of the news) judge the guilt or innocence, morality or immorality, or the fairness or unfairness of the legal case from fragmented and unverified evidence in the news, the jury decides only the guilt or innocence according to the disputed facts presented in the courtroom.

A second difference is in the way evidence is presented. Each frame is part of the entire news serial, just as the testimony of one witness creates one frame within the trial. The reporter's method of presenting evidence differs significantly from that of the in-court

21

testimony. First, the reporters present a one-sided point of view, whereas the testimony of a witness offers a two-sided argument that includes the questions of opposing counsel. Although the norms of news objectivity imply that the reporters present both sides, most news reports of a trial promote one controversial theme, adopt one point of view, and exclude evidence not supporting their position (Tuchman, 1978; Paletz & Entman, 1981; Bennett, 1983).

Third, news reporters do not present their own beliefs or recollections as witnesses are supposed to do. Instead, the press summarizes, paraphrases, and selects from the statements of others. For example, the *Post*'s coverage of the Hinckley case incorporated, in very abbreviated form, the testimony of others and then mixed together the testimony of several witnesses to create the evidence for a single frame. This evidence then supported the theme of the writer. Shaffer and Henry (2 April 1981) reconstructed the character of John Hinckley from a half dozen sources ranging from a bartender to a taxi driver. The reporter gave no credentials for the witnesses except their names and occupations. Cannon (5 April 1981) borrowed bits and pieces of testimony from over twenty sources and used all of this testimony to support his claims in the article. The problem with this reporter's selection was that he decided what parts of the testimony to use and gave no indication to the reader what interviews, documents, or letters had been excluded from these news reports.

Finally, the testimony of newspaper witnesses is not subject to any evidentiary rules. No evidence is overruled because it is the result of conjecture, opinion, or leading questions. No evidence is excluded because it is prejudicial or conclusionary. The reporters have almost absolute freedom in their selection of evidence, but the evidence allowed in courts is limited, restricted, and contested. Quite clearly, then, the reporters' evidence is of an entirely different quality from the evidence allowed in court, yet the public accepts the newspaper evidence as factual, makes judgments about the legal process, assumes the merits of the news reporter and the quality of the newspaper, and defines what constitutes justice for the accused without knowing about the credibility of the witnesses or the accuracy of the evidence. Obviously, in Hinckley and other trials, the newspaper tries to do its job well just as the courts attempt to do their job effectively. A problem arises when the public assumes that the "facts" given in the newspaper are of the same caliber as evidence presented in the court; this assumption is incorrect.

Persuasive Strategies of News

In addition to the episodic structure of the news serial and the content of the frames of news, the news embodies inherently persuasive elements. Three different elements appeared in the reporting of the Hinckley assassination through slanted depictions, agenda-setting, and scapegoating.

Slanted Depictions

Depictions can be both verbal and graphic representations of the crime, the accused, the victims, the weapons, and/or the context. Depictions in news articles take the form of dramatic narratives with villains, victims, conflict, and violence (Bennett, 1983). Several factors contribute to the persuasiveness of the depictions, including visual depictions and verbal headlines, connections between the story and other emotional issues, and accumulations of evidence supporting one side of the case.

In the Hinckley case, the headlines offered "factual" conclusions about the crime and the motive. These headlines accentuated the symbolic evidence of the pictures, and the graphics confirmed the conclusions in the headlines. In the first episode, five frames showed the slanted depictions of the crime (Table 1).

The early episodes contained many more visual depictions than

Table 1. Slanted Depictions

Headline	Visual
Presidential shooting suspect "Aimless Drifter"	Hinckley looking out of a police car window
"Aimless Wandering of Sick Boy"	Graphics of map of travels marked with logos and a swastika
"Letter Portrays Historical Deed"	Hinckley identified in a Nazi uniform (picture was retracted later as it was not a picture of Hinckley)
"Love Letter Offers Clue to Motive"	Picture of smiling Jodie Foster
"Sanity Test for Hinckley"	Courtroom sketch of Hinckley appearing in court after his arrest

the later ones. In episode four, the only pictures that appeared were one of Judge Barrington Parker, two of Hinckley's parents, one of the guards at the court house, and one of Hinckley after his suicide attempt. The frames in this final episode relied on headlines to report the legal procedures of the case. Among the headlines were the following: "Hinckley Pleads Not Guilty to Assassination Attempt," "Hinckley's Lawyers Act on Searches," "Jodie Foster Confirms That She and Hinckley Talked by Phone," "Psychologists, Psychiatrists End Examination of Hinckley," "No Nonsense Judge Plans an Active Role in Hinckley Trial," "Defense Headed by Bulldog," "Top Prosecutor, Intense Veteran," "Judge Won't Let Networks Tape Video-Taped Testimony," and "Hinckley Team May Widen Insanity Defense." These headlines established the theme, and the subsequent stories suggested that the legal activity was routine, cumbersome, and not very interesting.

Within each episode, the depictions of the crime were connected to other emotional issues by frames that elaborated and related the stories of the crime to larger social or political issues. In episode one, the crime was linked to other assassinations, the security of the president, gun control, social violence, and family breakdowns. In episode two, the crime was linked to the role of film in societal violence, celebrity creation, mental illness, right wing radicalism, and criminal conspiracies. In episode three, Hinckley's incarceration was described in connection with suicide and drugs, prison security, accuracy of diagnosis of mental illness, and "copycat" assassination plots. In the fourth episode, the paper connected the crime to the propriety of the insanity defense, suicide and depression, prisoner rights, and repeated delays of the trial because of legal motions. Finally, as the trial opened, the case was presented as a public drama in which the public wanted revenge on Hinckley for his crime.

The depictions also developed the character of Hinckley in the various news reports. At first glance, these depictions seemed to gather evidence pointing to Hinckley's criminal behavior and thus favored the prosecution. The *Post*'s depictions of criminality included repeated statements of his arrest record, his purchase of guns, his theft of money from his parents, his deceptive letters to his family, his lies about his travels, and his "stalking" of President Carter. In the same editions, the *Post* accumulated evidence of Hinckley's insanity; noting that he lacked the ability to show feeling, had been under psychiatric care, attended school erratically, seemed obsessed with Jodie Foster, and had exhibited bizarre habits. On balance, the evidence suggested Hinckley's insanity and thereby

24

favored the story of the case presented by the defense. This slant was countered by editorials and features that suggested the insanity plea was legal manipulation, speculated that Hinckley would be out on the street because the insanity plea let criminals get off, and questioned the ability of psychiatrists accurately to diagnose mental illness.

Slanted headlines and visuals sometimes betray the lack of objective reporting. Just as often, however, the slanting goes unnoticed and the depictions convey to audiences that the reporter's point of view is factual and accurate and is thus the "truth" of the criminal case. In addition to slanted depictions, newspapers set the agenda for what the public and the rest of the press should consider important.

Agenda Setting

Agenda setting is a second effect of the press coverage of news. By clustering and focusing the news reports on certain issues and excluding other issues, the press can "set the agenda," that is, delineate what is important for their readers to think and talk about regarding a crime. McCombs and Shaw (1972) explain agenda setting as the ability of the media to establish the important issues by giving them prominent media attention. Because readers take their cues about what is important from the media, the press succeeds in establishing priorities about the significance of the news they cover. Although previous research has centered upon political news, we believe that agenda setting also occurs with legal news.

Unlike the political news, which tends to be disseminated in a two-step flow, the public reads and interprets legal news directly. Friendly and Goldfarb (1967) note that the best-read items in any newspaper are those about crime, and the public's "fascination with the news of crime is insatiable" (p. 3). Because the public responds directly to such news, and because it has very little information about the criminal process, it accepts without question the agenda about what is important in the crime and trial.

Not only does the press set the agenda about legal priorities, but the national newspapers, such as the *Washington Post*, set an agenda for what other newspapers, magazines, radio, and television are likely to accept as the key issues about the crime and the legal process. For example, during the early stages of the case, television, radio, and magazines borrowed sources from the press and offered approximately the same theory of the case as the *Post* used. In the later episodes of the coverage, the news magazines and the broadcast media seemed to use the same press releases as the *Post*, a pattern of pack journalism (Epstein, 1973; Paletz & Entman, 1981; Ranney, 1983). The importance of pack journalism for crime reporting is that journalists collaborate in their decisions about what is important and what is not. In turn, their collaboration is a joint effort on the part of the media to decide what they want the public to see and hear about the case.

Agenda setting seems to follow a dialectic of threats and reassurance; in one frame the news threatens and in later frames of the same episode it reassures the public about how its fears are being dealt with by legal and political authorities (Paletz & Entman, 1981). The threat/reassurance pattern characterized the agenda of the *Post*'s coverage of the Hinckley case (Table 2).

Table 2. Patterns of Threat and Reassurance

Threat	Reassurance
Death/disability of victims.	Reagan is recovering nicely.
Lack of political leadership during Reagan's absence.	Haig and Bush are running government and in contact with Reagan.
Copycat assassination plots and conspiracies.	Political plans to stiffen penalities against assassins.
Guns are available to everyone.	Congress has hearings on gun control.
Hinckley may succeed in killing himself and deprive the public of a trial.	Hinckley recovers, new measures taken to prevent accused from committing suicide.
Hinckley's crime parallels those of other assassins.	Hinckley receives mental tests.
Hinckley may be free soon because of insanity plea.	Government hearing as attempt to limit use of insanity plea.
Hinckley nearly kills self a second time.	Hinckley recovers.
Hinckley may get off.	Injured Secret Service agent and Washington policeman suing Hinckley for a total of $14 million.
Defense is limiting the prosecution's evidence.	Court rules against some defense motions.

In each of the episodes, the initial frame threatened the public with harmful action, and the subsequent frames reassured the public that the political, legal, and psychiatric professionals were able to solve the problems raised in the media news. The threat/reassurance dialectic promoted conflict and interest and thereby involved the readers in this serial press drama.

The press is not always in control of the agenda, although it ultimately makes the choices about what is news and what is not. In the Hinckley case, the defendant himself affected the news agenda by his two suicide attempts, writing letters to the press and volunteering his participation in their reporting, and composing notes for his diary in his prison cell. The defense, prosecution, and judge entered into the news by their motions and legal actions. Potential witnesses, such as Jodie Foster and the psychological experts, helped the press focus and establish those issues as the public agenda.

Scapegoating

By slanted depictions and agenda setting, the press points to public scapegoats. Burke (1950, 1964, 1966) explains that scapegoats arise from the disruption of the social order. In a social order, there exists a hierarchy of different classes of people with various modes of living and patterns of action. This hierarchy makes division and conflict inevitable. When conflict occurs or the society is disrupted in some way, the social order experiences guilt and tries to relieve itself of guilt by victimage or mortification. Foss, Foss, and Trapp (1985) note that victimage is the process of transferring guilt to a person or event so that the person or event acts as a scapegoat to suffer for the evils present in society. Mortification differs from victimage because it is a process of "self-inflicted punishment, self-sacrifice, or self-imposed denials or restrictions" (p. 181).

Wilkie (1981) explains that contemporary societies do not transfer their guilt to effigies or animals as they did in ancient times. Instead the public selects its scapegoats through the press coverage of public crimes. Wilkie explains that journalists transform defendants into "symbolically fitting victims whose character and transgressions represent the ills present in society" (p. 102). Thus, the public participated through the media in a consensus about the guilt of the Haymarket defendants, Sacco and Vanzetti, Hauptmann, the Rosenbergs, and Sheppard. The media tried to restore the social order through making these accused persons into its victims.

To achieve this purgation, the press in the Hinckley case used

27

scapegoating as an underlying motif for its coverage in these four phases: the discussion of the pollution of the social hierarchy, description of the presence of guilt, characterization of the scapegoat as a symbolic victim, and the search for redemption.

The crime was an example of *pollution of the social order* both in the way it occurred and the way it was reported. The President of the United States, the designated symbolic leader, was gunned down by an "aimless drifter" who shot Reagan so he could be a celebrity and win the favor of Jodie Foster. Denton (1982) notes that an effective symbolic national leader must act as the nation's personal and moral leader by symbolizing the past and future greatness of America and radiating inspirational confidence. At the time of the shooting, Reagan was a symbolic leader with high national approval ratings. Moreover, he increased the inspirational quality of his leadership after the assassination attempt by his humor after the surgery, his resilient recovery, and his attitude of compassion for the accused.

The pollution of the social order was evident when the press reported that Hinckley represented the antithesis of his victims. He was a member of the American Nazi party; lacked the approval of his family and peers; and had no understanding of the moral consequences of his acts. Whereas Reagan represented the top of the hierarchy as its admirable leader, Hinckley personified the bottom of the hierarchy, a person who had made no contribution to society. By shooting the president, Hinckley reversed the hierarchy so that the social attention would be on him rather than on the president. He switched roles with Reagan making himself into the celebrity and Reagan, the president, into the social victim.

The later coverage of the shooting portrayed society in the second stage, *guilt.* As the news stories developed about the attempted assassination of Reagan, they revealed deep sources of instability in the society, such as other assassination attempts, the societal preoccupation with violence, the availability of weapons, the inability of affluent families to give their children what they needed, the inadequacy of the mental health system, the ineffectiveness of presidential security, and the accidental but negative effects of film on the minds of people. As these social evils surfaced in the news of the case, the *Post* blamed everyone for these problems, including Hinckley's parents, the Secret Service, psychiatrists, and pawn shop owners. The press also faulted gun sellers and ammunition manufacturers, the legal system, and even the prison system. Goodman (2 April 1981) noted that society is in such bad shape that "even assassination attempts have become a cliché. . . . The swell of violence has taken its toll on each and everyone of us. Our feelings are worn around the edges by exposure to the irrational and the random, the evil. We now believe what was once unbelievable" (p. A23). Goodman concluded that violence had become routine, and we all had to bear the guilt for such a sad state in our society.

The American public had reason to want the death penalty or life imprisonment of Hinckley, because he epitomized many of the evils of society. The legal tradition of the trial and the ritual of execution (or the comfort of life imprisonment) would help relieve society of its guilt. But the *scapegoat*, John Hinckley, lacked the qualities to be that perfect *victim*, because according to the press' own portrait he was erratic, obsessed, driven by unreal motives, depressed, and unable to show feeling. In an uncharacteristic statement by a scapegoat, Hinckley declared that President Reagan was the greatest leader the country had ever had. And Reagan, in an uncharacteristic statement for a victim, said about Hinckley: "I hope indeed I pray that he can find an answer to his problem" (Szasz, 6 May 1981, p. A1).

As the coverage of the case evolved through the suicide attempts and the psychiatric tests, it became more clear that Hinckley should not be sacrificed to achieve *public redemption*. By the time he pleaded "not guilty by reason of insanity," the press had shifted its scapegoat from the assailant to the law and to those who misused it. Instead of doing away with Hinckley, the press advocated doing away with the laws that allowed him to plead not guilty and yet admit the crime. In fact, the press recommended the plea be "guilty but insane" and that the punishment combine mental treatment with imprisonment.

By the time the case came to trial, the press' stories about the accused made it difficult for the prosecution to prove that Hinckley was sane. In doing so, the social order had not been purged by the hospitalization of Hinckley, the plea had not changed, the sentencing was not altered, and the pain and suffering of Hinckley's paralyzed victim James Brady had not been lessened. In one sense, the news coverage of the case did not succeed in renewing the social order by the victimage of one of its guilty parties. But the press did create a new scapegoat, the law itself. In fact, the need for changes in the law was the theme of over twenty articles appearing in the *Post* during the week following the verdict. These news articles were reinforced by cartoons and letters to the editor that expressed the same idea, that is, the "not guilty by reason of insanity" law should be changed. In a limited sense, purgation eventually did occur because the law took some of the blame for the evils of society.

Implications of the Press and Trial Relationship

This analysis of the press coverage of the Hinckley case shows historical changes, selective coverage, serial and episodic structures, slanted content, and persuasive reconstructions of the crime and the trial. A point-by-point summary indicates how the conclusions of this study might relate to the coverage of other sensational trials.

First, this investigation shows that legal personnel, particularly judges, are mandated by law to take precautions to prevent trials from becoming circuslike events. Because of the Supreme Court decisions in Sheppard and other cases, the courts are now required to take precautions to ensure that the rights of the accused are not abridged overtly by press coverage. Additionally, the press and bar association codes give guidance to the media and the courtroom practitioners, stressing that they should refrain from prejudicial reporting and from out-of-court statements that might be detrimental to the accused. Some of the excessive prejudicial coverage of the press that occurred prior to and during the Haymarket, Sacco-Vanzetti, Hauptmann, and Sheppard trials is unlikely to happen in future cases because of current restrictions on the media.

Second, the reporting of crime news always is likely to contain a subjective element because reporters tell stories that highlight the dramatic through conflict, protest, and disagreement. Some cases will become sensational news, because the crimes involve known individuals who play a key role in national events, possess a degree of controversy, and focus upon moral disorder in society.

Third, press coverage of trials is a type of opening statement before the actual beginning of the trial itself, because the news reports evidence from witnesses, presents theories of the case from both the point of view of the prosecution and the defense, and subtly recommends a particular verdict for the accused. The opening statement made by the press presents evidence as if it were factual, even though the press lacks corroborated evidence, two-sided interrogation, and accredited witnesses.

Fourth, media coverage of sensational trials takes place in a serial drama in which the plot of the story evolves through many news articles over long periods of time about the characters and actions associated with the crime. The structure of these serials develops in episodes. The number of episodic divisions is likely to vary depending on the complexity of the case and the passage of time between the crime, the arrest, the trial, the verdict, and the appeals. Most sensational trials will include several episodes that change as the point of view and the themes of reporters vary.

Fifth, the content of the frames often abandons standards for objective news reporting by failing to quote sources, provide locators, use descriptors, and employ value appeals. Instead, some news frames make judgments, offer unsubstantiated claims, promote controversy, and give only partial testimony from sources. This lack of objectivity characterized the reporting of most of the cases included in this volume. And we predict this lack of objectivity will be the norm rather than the exception in the news reporting of sensational trials in the future.

Sixth, crime news embodies slanted depictions in the headlines and visuals that connect crime news to emotional social issues. Additionally, such news establishes an agenda for the people about the accused and the trial, and it also sacrifices defendants as scapegoats for social problems. We predict that this purging of the social order with accused criminals will continue to occur as it did in the Haymarket, Sacco-Vanzetti, Hauptmann, and Rosenberg cases. The press will seek people, objects, or actions as its scapegoats to promote purgation of the social order.

Seventh, our analysis demonstrates how the press establishes the agenda for what the people should perceive as social, moral, and political issues. By linking the larger public issues to the causes of the crime, reasons for criminal behavior, inadequacies of the law enforcement systems, unfairness of pleas and verdicts, negative social consequences of the crime, and political responses to the crime, the press will continue to decide for its readers why the case is important.

Finally, sane and insane criminals will continue to use the media to gain their own glory and to place themselves in the public spotlight. Because the press can make a criminal into a celebrity by the massive attention it bestows, criminals will continue to seek this attention as they have done throughout history.

Our investigation of the pretrial news coverage of the Hinckley case has some limitations. By definition, it is a partial press portrait and does not complete the story, thus some news episodes are left out. However, analysis of the pretrial press does explain why and how publicity prior to a case (even under the most restrained conditions) can and does have an impact upon potential jurors and

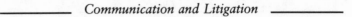

indirectly on prosecutors and judges. The public is largely unaware of the way pretrial press coverage occurs; this case study illuminates the persuasiveness present in news stories about sensational crimes such as the Hinckley case.

A Political Scientist's Reaction

W. Lance Bennett

Shooting the president, for whatever reason, qualifies the assailant as crazy on commonsense grounds. Even a political zealot exceeds the bounds of popular reason by risking life and liberty in pursuit of political justice through assassination. When an assassin acts for reasons beyond the political pale, the social preoccupation with insanity is engaged in the extreme. John Hinckley's personal adaptation of a movie plot inspired by his fantasies about the actress is the stuff of which the tabloids were made.

In comparison to the sensationalist press in the days of Hearst and Pulitzer, the coverage of the Hinckley trial was relatively tasteful. One cannot imagine the *Washington Post* offering to pay for Hinckley's defense in exchange for the movie rights, as happened when the Hearst chain paid Bruno Richard Hauptmann's legal fees in exchange for exclusive newsreel rights in the Lindbergh kidnapping trial of 1935. However, media preoccupations with Hinckley's sordid motives may have been nonetheless prejudicial to the grounds for his defense. In this case, the prejudice was favorable to a defense based on claims of insanity, but prejudice is prejudice no matter which side it benefits. If civilization continues to advance at the same pace it has since the Lindbergh case, critics may look back fifty years hence and judge the contemporary media guilty of no less rabble-rousing than before. If there has been some improvement, it may be that the rabble, not the media, have raised their standards.

The question of media-induced prejudice is important for the conduct of legal proceedings, and the conduct of legal proceedings, in turn, is important for the quality of civilization. Kangaroo courts may, for all we know, produce a high level of justice as far as the

W. Lance Bennett teaches political science at the University of Washington. He received his Ph.D. degree from Yale University in 1977. His writings on criminal trials and the news media include: *Reconstruction Reality in the Courtroom* (with Martha J. Feldman), and *News: The Politics of Illusion*. Mr. Bennet has also published several articles on criminal trials.

verdicts go, but they are sadly inadequate in terms of the reasonableness of those verdicts.

If we adopt a narrow legalistic focus on the outcomes of the Hinckley trial, it is hard to argue whether justice would have been served better by electrocution, life in prison, or a good long sting in the asylum. These matters would seem better suited to divine judgment than to academic deliberation. However, in terms of the way in which media coverage may have prejudiced broader social understanding of the issues in the case, there is something we can say. It is in terms of prejudicing social reasoning about legal issues that the press continues to join with the weakest link in the chain of human imagination. Rather than addressing the larger social question raised by the case, the media followed the course of least social resistance. The result was a sort of low key yellow journalism for yuppie tastes.

What were the larger issues lost to popular consciousness as a result of prejudicing the news plot in terms of Hinckley's palpable insanity? Well, with a little less insanity, this might have been an occasion to introduce gun control into the headlines rather than give the issue brief mention, once again, in the back pages. Perhaps this was also an occasion to draw popular attention to the sex and violence in the American culture—a culture that celebrates movies like *Taxi Driver* from which Hinckley drew his inspiration. Instead, the news sustained popular fascination with sex and violence through an unreflective portrayal of a real life episode laden with the stuff. Rather than raising the tired question of whether insanity should be allowed as an excuse for crimes like this, the media might have explored the reasons for so much violent insanity in this society to begin with. And, as long as the psychoanalysts on the news desk were comfortable explaining Hinckley's displacement of sexual frustration onto the President, perhaps they could have considered the possibility that the assassin sensed and responded intuitively to the rage felt by the millions of people socially marginalized by the president's less than altruistic social policies. Instead of addressing any of these, or other social themes, the media settled for a story line that trivialized the crime as one man's insanity, while casting the victim in larger than life heroic terms as he walked bravely into the hospital with a bullet lodged in his chest.

It is easy to explain why media coverage of the Reagan assassination attempt was prejudiced along story lines of the lone lunatic and the heroic survivor. The media in the United States operate under oligopolistic market conditions in which imitation passes for competition. As long as some chord of audience response is struck, an audience is secured, no matter how low that chord may be on the scale of human responses. The media, in turn, can justify pandering to the masses on grounds that they have dutifully responded to what the masses want. As for the critic who calls for more than lowest common denominator news, media executives respond with the "law" of the market: any attempt to play to higher levels of popular taste and reason would result in lost audience shares and consequent market death.

In light of the media market imperative, it is no wonder that the strides in quality of coverage have not been great since Booth shot Lincoln. It is also not surprising that any evident progress against prejudice is attributable more to legal restraint than to any self-induced elevation of professional standards on the part of the media. True, we cannot imagine the *Washington Post* paying legal fees in exchange for movie rights, but what is less clear is whether the *Post*'s journalistic imagination was constrained more by law or by some higher sense of journalistic purpose. While it is clearly against the law to intervene in a trial today the way Hearst did in the Lindbergh case, it isn't clear what higher journalistic principle could be cited for this act of restraint.

If the press is to transcend social prejudice in coverage of legal issues, it must not wait for the law to be its guide. Rather, the media must assess their social responsibility and aspire to be critics rather than collaborators in the base morality of the times. Even if market motives cannot be ignored, the media could engage in professional dialogue aimed at standardizing their oligopolistic product at a higher level of taste, thereby drawing their captive audience along with them. In other words, the media might embark on a quest for profitability not at odds with social sensibility. This sort of enlightened oligopoly would seem preferable to the current one in which profits are taken at the expense of a downward spiral of social taste and prejudice.

What would be entailed for the media to cover trials with less prejudice and more social insight? For one thing, journalists could stand to develop greater insight into the process through which they construct socially acceptable news. At present, the process of writing news resembles less a describable method than a spiritual medium in which the successful reporter is able to "find" or "be at one with" the popular wavelength. I recall with wonder the remarkably insightful comment of a national political reporter for a large newspaper chain who was called away from a conference we attended to go on special assignment to Cuba. He said, and I must paraphrase here: The reason they send me on assignments like this is that they know that no matter what I encounter down there, I will find a way to describe it that won't disturb the average reader.

It is this sense of stories developing somehow on their own, out of some implicit understanding between the journalist and the popular subsconscious, that must be changed if resulting prejudice in news coverage is to be replaced by some higher sort of reason. BIG STORIES, as another journalist once said, arise as if from Ur and take on a life of their own. Stories like the Hinckley case just seem to write themselves. It is hard to imagine a more "natural" course for the Hinckley story than the one that emerged: crazed son of wealthy family sees movie, falls in love with heroine, decides that re-creating plot would be way to win her heart in real life. Indeed, this is deep cultural feedback in action. Yet, the news does not serve the culture well if all it does is keep us in touch with our second nature. The news might serve us better as an agent of change rather than as a purveyor of prejudice.

When BIG STORIES like the Hinckley case virtually write themselves, we are in trouble as a society. The verdict of quilty-by-reason-of-insanity was a foregone conclusion in the Hinckley story as told by the press. When the jury delivered the verdict, it seemed that reality, if not justice, had been done. Another chapter in our stream-of-consciousness social saga ended cleanly, plausibly, and with the dramatic flourish of real life.

2
Storytelling in Opening Statements: The Chicago Anarchists' (Haymarket) Trial

The actual opening statement of the trial follows the stories presented in the media. This chapter investigates how an opening statement previews the underlying story structure of the case, and thereby establishes the perceptual framework into which all subsequent trial persuasion will fit. The chapter delineates how the elements of form, content, style, purpose, context, and audience contribute to the development of a persuasive opening statement in this historical case and thereby suggests to contemporary advocates how to develop their opening statements.

In an atmosphere of hysterical concern over public safety, the trial of eight men charged with murder, conspiracy, riot, and unlawful assembly began in the city of Chicago. The trial itself reflected Chicago's—and the nation's—mood of alarm and vengefulness, due in part to the influx of immigrant labor into the country. All the defendants were known anarchists, noted for their strong discontent with the government of the United States; all were associated with one of Chicago's several anarchist newspapers; all were found guilty of conspiracy to murder. For these reasons, studying the opening statement of the Chicago Anarchists' trial offers insight into how the opening statement in this case, and by inference in other cases, functions to address the broader questions of the nature of society and the social order, thus entwining forensic (legal) and deliberative (political) issues. The opening statements delivered at the trial of the Chicago Anarchists thus serve as the vehicle for focusing on this important phase of the litigation process.

37

The Trial

For the United States the decades between the end of Reconstruction and the beginning of World War I were a period of rapid industrial development and also an era of increasing conflict between capital and labor. During these years struggles for power and economic advantage pitting businessmen against workers were the principal source of American political trials. Tensions between labor and capital lay behind the 1886 Haymarket trial of eight Chicago anarchists, against whom prejudice was strong and the evidence weak.

In order to set the Haymarket affair in its proper perspective, the general social conditions of the overall labor force in Chicago at the time must be considered. The early 1880s were marked by a labor force that was growing in unrest and discontent. A number of factors were responsible for this labor unrest including the intense rate of postwar industrialization, the rapid development of industrial urban centers, the increase in the flow of immigrant labor into the country, and the economic and social position of the American working class (David, 1936, p. 49). In addition, the depression of 1883–86 created severe distress, filling the industrial centers with throngs of idle and destitute persons. In Chicago alone, it is estimated that thirty-four thousand were out of work (Avrick, 1984, p. 79).

Thus, it was a time of misery and suffering for many; moreover, immigration remained heavy, compounding the problem of unemployment. It is hardly surprising that such circumstances inspired a wave of social unrest; indeed, a vigorous revolutionary movement was taking shape. Open struggles between labor and capital, in the form of strikes, demonstrations, and boycotts became more and more frequent. Strike after strike witnessed police brutality and the use of militia, scabs, and private detectives, not to mention blacklists and lockouts.

It was this social fabric that made the times favorable for the rapid growth of the International Working People's Association, a revolutionary anarchist organization. In addition to having a crowded immigrant population and having a long history of labor unrest, Chicago was the seat of an active anarchist press and capable anarchist leaders; thus, the city of Chicago was fertile soil for anarchist propaganda and organization. Between the years 1883 and 1886, the anarchist movement picked up considerable momentum, with groups of the IWPA multiplying from year to year, and their membership increasing steadily (Avrick, 1984, p. 82). The goal of the IWPA was not only to end capitalism and government but also to promote a total revolution in human relations, cultural as well as political and economic. One of the focuses of anarchist propaganda during this period was the growing subdivision of labor, with its corrosive effects on the human spirit (Avrick, 1984, p. 89). A climax was reached during the early months of 1886 with a nationwide crusade for the eight-hour day, one of the most intense labor struggles in American history.

On May 4, 1886, a meeting of working people was called in the Haymarket district in downtown Chicago, for the purpose of discussing the worsening conditions of labor in the city. As the meeting approached a close, a cadre of policemen charged into the crowd and ordered the meeting to disperse. As they entered, a dynamite bomb was thrown into the midst of policemen. Within less than five minutes the Haymarket "riot" was over. Seven police officers died as a result of injuries sustained at the Haymarket meeting and sixty more were seriously wounded.

The Haymarket explosion brought on the first major "Red Scare" in American history (David, 1936, p. 528). News of the incident provoked a demand for justice that soon became universal; the feeling was that radicalism must be suppressed and all radicals punished. The panic ran deepest in Chicago. Within a week the police had arrested almost every prominent anarchist in the city, while the condemnation of radicalism reached a feverish pitch.

The eight men who were finally indicted and brought to trial, charged with murder, conspiracy, riot, and unlawful assembly, were August Spies, Michael Schwab, Samuel Fielden, Albert Parsons, Adolph Fischer, George Engel, Louis Lingg, and Oscar Neebe. The defendants were interrelated in several ways. All were known anarchists, noted for their strong discontent with the labor conditions of the day. All had vigorously expressed their views publicly; the authorities considered these men to be the leaders of the anarchist cause of Chicago. Also, almost all of the men were associated with one of Chicago's several anarchist newspapers.

The trial began in June, 1886, in an atmosphere of hysterical concern over the public safety. Presiding was the Honorable Joseph E. Gary, with William Perkins Black, a prominent corporation lawyer, representing the defendants and Julius S. Grinnell representing the state. On August 20, almost two months after the opening of the trial, the jury returned their verdict, finding Spies, Schwab, Fielden, Parsons, Fischer, Engel and Lingg guilty of conspiracy to murder, fixing the penalty at death, and Neebe guilty of conspiracy to murder, but fixing the penalty at imprisonment for fifteen years. The Supreme Court of Illinois affirmed the verdict; the Supreme Court of the United States denied the defense's application for *writ of error*. Lingg then committed suicide; Spies, Parsons, Fischer and Engel were executed; the sentences of Schwab and Fielden were commuted to imprisonment for life and they, together with Neebe, were pardoned after serving seven years, by John P. Altgeld, then Governor of Illinois.

The Chicago Anarchists' trial was unsurpassed in dramatic intensity in the city's legal history and remained so, perhaps, until the Chicago Eight case in 1969. The trial reflected the popular mood of alarm and vengefulness; in such circumstances it would have been difficult to secure a fair trial for the defendants. What took place has been called a "farce and an abomination" and has been characterized as "the grossest travesty of justice ever perpetrated in an American court" (Avrick, 1984, p. 262). Not only were the impaneled jurors admittedly biased in favor of the state (Avrick, 1984, pp. 266–67), but the presiding judge was openly prejudiced and, moreover, the prosecuting attorney subsequently was accused of deliberately offering perjured testimony in connection with the case (Avrick, 1984, p. 270).

Despite the defense attorney's evidencing airtight alibis that the defendants either were not present when the explosion occurred, were never at the Haymarket at all that night, or were on the speakers' wagon in full view of the audience when the bomb was thrown (Avrick, 1984, pp. 270–71), all eight men were found guilty of conspiracy to murder. On the whole, it seems, the defendants were ably represented; the verdict does not appear to have resulted from any inadequacies on the part of the defense. Indeed, it is difficult to imagine what might have been changed to alter the outcome. What, then, can explain this result?

The purpose of this chapter is to investigate how the opening statement of a trial serves as an important phase of the litigation process. The essay posits that a persuasive opening statement is significant in producing a successful outcome of the trial. This investigation seeks to understand how the elements of a persuasive opening statement can serve to preview the underlying story structure of the case, and thereby establish the perceptual framework into which all subsequent trial persuasion will fit. Further, the essay considers how the opening statement in political trials functions to address the broader questions of the nature of society and the social order, thus entwining forensic and deliberative issues.

To achieve this end, the essay (1) examines the importance of the opening statement in the trial process; (2) identifies the story form as the communication strategy underlying successful opening statements; (3) considers how the elements of form, content, style, purpose, context, and audience contribute to the development of a persuasive opening statement; (4) analyzes the opening statements of the prosecution and defense in the Haymarket trial according to each of these elements; and (5) suggests the implications of the investigation for trial practice.

Framing the Argumentation of the Trial: Opening Statement

Legal Procedure and Norms

Opening statements in judicial proceedings are unique as speech situations. As a type of argumentation, the opening statement presents a very special case. Opening statements cannot, according to trial procedure, be argumentative. The United States Supreme Court has limited opening statements to informing "the jurors concerning the nature of the action and the issues involved and to give them an outline of the case so that they can better understand the testimony" (Starr, 1983, p. 426). However, while the opening statement is technically nonargumentative, it is the anticipation and promise of what is to come; thus, it is also the quintessence of argument, for this segment of the trial must persuade without appearing to do so (Wessel, 1976, p. 189). For these reasons, it is easy to understand why the subtle persuasion of opening statement is so highly valued by the trial attorney.

Several authorities on trial advocacy suggest the opening statement is one of the most important phases of the persuasion process and, therefore, also the most significant aspect of any trial. Effective advocates suggest that an opening statement can win the trial of any lawsuit (Julien, 1980, p. 1); in fact, there is no single tool that has more potential for persuasion than the opening statement (Sumpter, 1978, p. 34). Spangenberg (1977) emphasizes that the opening statement is the most important statement a lawyer will ever make in a case (p. 13) and further suggests that if faced with

41

the necessity of choosing just one time to speak—to argue a case to the jury—he would certainly make it the opening statement (1982, pp. 3–11). Morrill (1972) claims the opening statement is the most valuable tool in courtroom persuasion in that it enables a lawyer to "paint a picture in the mind's eye" through the use of words (p. 22).

The opening statement is the first opportunity for the attorney to persuade, and persuasion is the goal of the courtroom advocate. Moreover, it focuses the attention of jurors on lines of reasoning the advocates hope the panel will adopt for the entire trial proceeding. Thus, identifying why one opening statement is more effective and persuasive than another is critically important; the analysis contains a theoretical framework that can point the way to effective practices for lawyers.

Communicative Features of Opening Statement

In their analysis, Bennett and Feldman (1981) conclude that effective advocates achieve favorable verdicts by telling believable stories to jurors (p. 2). By binding together large volumes of complicated and disjunctive argumentation, attorneys can provide a persuasive connective thread for the entire proceeding. Stories told in trials fit with Fisher's (1984) conception of narrative argument; he believes narrative works are a justification for beliefs and values since they supply description that "offers an account, an understanding, of any instance of human choice and action" (p. 15). Thus, stories influence verdicts in criminal trials when jurors use the experiences of their lives as a basis for evaluating the stories told in opening statements.

Whereas storytelling is the form underlying the narrative argument of the opening discourse, the genre of opening statement itself is more complex. An analysis of genre must specify the type of argumentation as a distinctive kind of discourse in the trial proceeding, examine the internal workings of the discourse, and specify the contexts, motives, and effects of this segment of the trial.

Harrell and Linkugel (1980) explain the genre theory of rhetoric as a method of classifying discourse according to its type or kind. This method of categorizing discourse identifies the norms and central tendencies of a representative sample, catalogs "linguistic and organizational" features of the discourse, and maps the course to be followed by future speakers who may wish to develop this kind of discourse. Delineating genre is possible because one group of discourse shares some important characteristics that distinguish it from other discourse (Harrell & Linkugel, 1980, pp. 405–6). Since there are a limited number of ways to respond rhetorically to any given situation type, and since situations recur historically, they spawn similar responses by speakers in common situations (Campbell & Jamieson, 1976, p. 14). Thus, opening statements constitute a genre of discourse because there are a limited number of ways for attorneys to achieve a rhetorical purpose when legal contexts and restraints are similar.

The opening statement is a narrative argument or story that enables a cast of courtroom characters to follow the development of a case and reason about the issues in it. Although Bennett and Feldman (1981) view all processes of the trial as contributing to a common story, it is the opening statement that outlines the plot, describes the characters, depicts the setting, attributes the motives, and portrays the action of the story.

In the opening statement, the advocates develop the crucial parts of their theory of the case by presenting a kernel of a story. Chatman (1978) explains that these kernels are "nodes or hinges" in the narratives (p. 53); that is, they are major claims that underlie the advocate's theory of the case. The nodes in an opening statement supply the incidents that explain why a crime does or does not fit the allegations of the criminal indictment. Even though the story of opening statement must be brief, it weaves a core narrative that becomes the central interpretive framework for the entire trial. Whereas the kernel is the skeletal story, satellite narratives fill out, elaborate, and extend the narrative through the information gathered during the examination of witnesses (Chatman, 1978, p. 54).

The effectiveness of the argument in a criminal trial depends on the ability of attorneys to persuade the jury by reflecting the social understanding common in society and incorporating changes in these understandings over time (Bennett & Feldman, 1981, p. 21). The story works as a "frame" for interpretation; that is, it imposes structure on diverse information, forces images to coalesce within the story, and establishes consistency among characters, setting, motive, and action (Bennett & Feldman, 1981, p. 9). Moreover, this type of narrative argument permits jurors, who are often unsophisticated and from diverse backgrounds, to find common interpretations, to compare competing stories from the prosecution and defense, and to make sense out of large quantities of isolated and diverse bits of information presented during the course of the trial.

Elements of Storytelling

Stories, then, are vehicles for assisting jurors to consolidate and interpret courtroom evidence and to understand an advocate's theory of a case. By understanding the power of narrative, an advocate gains insight into how the trial discourse enters into the judgments of jurors and produces a verdict. The specific story of opening statement is important to the trial outcome because it previews, outlines, and directs the more developed story that emerges during the trial. Not only are stories a systematic way of reordering, contrasting, and interpreting information, but they generally illuminate the methods and strategies of case construction and predict the form, content, and style of this genre.

Form

Form is the connective structure that gives a pattern and shape to the discourse (Burke, 1941, rpt. 1973, pp. 110–11). Bennett, in his framework for the systematic analysis of trials, states that the storytelling strategy is the underlying form of trial discourse (Bennett, 1978, p. 1). Bennett and Dicks show that stories in criminal trials are fit together by definition, connecting evidence, and credibility (Bennett, 1978, p. 1; 1979, pp. 311–23; Bennett & Feldman, 1981, pp. 4–6; Dicks, 1981, p. 190). They explain that advocates create this form as they convey their theory of the case.

More specifically, definition locates the central action of the story, focuses on the key elements of the narrative, and graphically depicts the accused and the witnesses. Then, by way of inference or linking, advocates relate evidence in such a way that certain persons are directly connected to specific key events and actions. In doing so, advocates lay the foundation for refutation of opposing witnesses and develop strategies of vilification that will degrade the opponents and their witnesses. In this way, the story of the opening statement is the key for connecting all participants and actions depicted in the trial and establishing a perceptual framework into which all subsequent discourse should fit.

Content

Whereas form supplies the links between ideas, content presents the ideas themselves. Content includes the justifications offered to the jurors to persuade them to vote for acquittal or conviction. The content of opening statement seeks to meet several purposes of this phase of the trial process: to promote the theory of the case, to introduce what the evidence will reveal, to educate the jury with regard to legal standards with which they may be unfamiliar, and to appeal to the jury in an effort to gain a favorable decision (Mauet, 1980, ch. 3). The content of the story reflects traditional factors studied by communication scholars such as issues, strategy of presentation, and tactics to induce resistance to persuasion.

Qualities of the content deserve further explanation. Issues include major claims and their accompanying evidence. For example, the issues in a criminal trial stem from the criminal indictment and concern such actions as whether persons committed murder in the first, second, or third degree; persons conspired to overthrow the government; or persons committed rape or criminal assault against another person. The issues are bound closely to the pleadings and the indictments.

Strategy of presentation refers to the one- or two-sided communication and order of presentation. A communication is one-sided when it addresses one view of an event; in contrast, a two-sided communication sets forth a particular interpretation and also refutes the counterposition. Research on persuasion suggests that a two-sided appeal is preferable when you are addressing an unfamiliar audience, one that is unaware of the issues, and a one-sided appeal should be used when addressing a familiar audience (Dipboye, 1977, p. 125). Additional research reveals that if the audience is aware that there are two plausible sides to an issue, a two-sided communication is preferable (Jones & Brehm, 1970, p. 47). Research in this area has important implications for courtroom communications; the jury is aware that there are two plausible sides to the case but, at the same time, is necessarily unfamiliar and impartial regarding the issues.

Tactics are those appeals by the advocate that seek to identify with the interests, needs, and values of the jury. For example, an advocate for the defense might characterize the accused as a family man, an active member of the community, and a churchgoing person. The content is, therefore, the personal and legal substance of the story presented in the opening statement.

Style

Whereas the form is the connecting structure of the discourse and the content consists of the ideas, the style is the linguistic embellishment of the discourse. Just as in any act of storytelling, the story of the opening statement must be told in ways that engage the audience through the use of powerful verbs, carefully chosen adjectives, and the use of the active voice. Additionally, though, the marks of an engaging story are its use of repetition, imagery, and metaphor.

Repetition consists of repeating key phrases that reflect the point of the story; that is, reasons why the accused is either legally guilty or innocent. For example, advocates might develop the chronology of the story of the characters and actions that resulted in the indictment of an accused, but the narrative must also appeal to the attitudes of the jurors. Language using imagery and metaphors is the vehicle for that appeal. Imagery consists of word pictures that call up a vivid mental representation of persons and circumstances in the minds of the jurors. Advocates choose images laden with emotion and vividness that enhance the ability of the story to involve listeners. Whereas a prosecutor might picture the accused as a vicious animal stalking victims in the night, the defense might picture that same person as a victimized and mentally ill veteran of Vietnam who has no control over his actions. In ways similar to imagery, metaphors add vividness to the story, denoting one kind of idea or object in place of another and suggesting an analogy or likeness between them (Ehninger, Monroe, & Gronbeck, 1978, ch. 13). Metaphors in criminal trials often compare the accused to demons and traitors and their acts to destructive accidents, storms, or devastation. In this way, language draws the jurors into the reality of the story of the opening statement.

Thus, storytelling strategy is the form underlying persuasive opening statements. Effective stories in opening statement develop factors such as issues, strategy of presentation, and tactics to induce resistance to persuasion. Moreover, persuasive stories seek to engage the audience through carefully selected language, repetition, imagery, and metaphor.

Analysis of Opening Statements in the Chicago Anarchists' Trial

In an effort to delineate clearly the qualities of genre—form, content, and style—and their impact on shaping effective stories in opening statement, the prosecution's story and the defense's interpretation of the same events will each be examined in turn.

The Prosecution's Story in Opening Statement

The prosecution's interpretation of the events that transpired included portraying the defendants as conspiring maliciously to destroy property and person and endeavoring to make anarchy rule. The prosecution stated further that while none of the defendants may have personally thrown the bomb, they each abetted, encouraged, and advised the throwing of it and, therefore, were guilty of conspiring to commit the "most fearful massacre ever witnessed or heard of in this country" (Transcript of Record, p. 25).

Opening Statement for the Prosecution. [Transcript of Record, pp. 24–46]

(Introduction)
The prosecution focuses the jurors' attention on the prosecution theme—anarchy.

Gentlemen: For the first time in the history of our country are people on trial for their lives for endeavoring to make Anarchy the rule, and in that attempt for ruthlessly and awfully destroying life. I hope that while the youngest of us lives this in memory it will be the last and only time in our country when such a trial shall take place. It will or will not take place as this case is determined.

(Content)
Prosecution seeks to meet two purposes here: to educate the jury with regard to legal standards with which they may be unfamiliar and to appeal to the jurors' reasoning in an effort to get a favorable decision.

The State now and at no time hereafter will say aught to arouse your prejudices or your indignation, having confidence in the case that we present; and I hope I shall not at any time during this trial say anything to you which will in any way or manner excite your passions. I want your reason. I want your careful analysis. I want your careful attention. We—my associates and myself—ask the conviction of no man from malice, from prejudice, from anything

(Form)
Prosecution utilizes definition strategy in the following manner: locating the central action of the story at the Haymarket on the 4th of May; focusing on the key element of the story of anarchists plotting a massacre; defining the jurors' duties in relation to the charge against the defendants; indicating what subsequent testimony will reveal.

(Content)
Tactics to induce resistance to persuasion are illustrated in this excerpt—the prosecution is seeking to identify with the interests, needs, and values of the jury. Recall the context of the trial as one of hysterical concern over the anarchists' influence in Chicago and the nation; accordingly, the prosecution utlizes this known alarm by appealing to the jurors' sense of patriotism, nationalism, and democracy and

except the facts and the law. I am here, gentlemen, to maintain the law, not to break it; and, however you may believe that any of these men have broken the law through their notions of Anarchy, try them on the facts. We believe, gentlemen, that we have a case that shall command your respect, and demonstrate to you the truthfulness of all the declarations in it, and, further, that by careful attention and close analysis you can determine who are guilty and the nature of the crime.

On the 4th of May, 1886, a few short weeks ago, there occurred, at what is called Haymarket Square, the most fearful massacre ever witnessed or heard of in this country. The crime culminates there—you are to find the perpetrators. The charge against the defendants is that they are responsible for that act. The testimony that shall be presented to you will be the testimony which will show their innocence or their guilty complicity in that crime.

We have been in this city inclined to believe, as we have all through the country, that, however extravagantly men may talk about our laws and our country, however severely they may criticise [sic] our Constitution and our institutions; that as we are all in favor of full liberty, of free speech, the great good sense of our people would never permit acts based upon sentiments which meant the overthrow of law. We have believed it for *need to restore society to a state uninfluenced by the evils of anarchy.*

(Style)

Throughout this appeal, the prosecution utilizes powerful language embellished with imagery and continually repeats the nationalistic theme.

(Form)

Prosecution connects the evidence with the defendant Spies, inferring that this current attack on humanity is in keeping with known past behavior. Prosecution is also laying the foundation

years, we were taught it at our schools in our infancy, we were taught it in our maturer years in school, and all our walks in life thereafter have taught us that our institutions, founded on our Constitution, the Declaration of Independence, and our universal freedom, were above and beyond all Anarchy. The 4th of May demonstrated that we were wrong, that we had too much confidence, that a certain class of individuals, some of them recently come here, as the testimony will show, believe that here in this country our Constitution is a lie. Insults are offered to the Declaration of Independence, the name of Washington is reviled and traduced, and we are taught by these men, as the testimony will show, that freedom in this country means lawlessness and absolute license to do as we please, no matter whether it hurts others or not. In the light of the 4th of May we now know that the preachings of Anarchy, the suggestions of these defendants hourly and daily for years, have been sapping our institutions, and that where they have cried murder, bloodshed, Anarchy and dynamite, they have meant what they said, and proposed to do what they threatened.

We will prove, gentlemen, in this case, that Spies no longer ago than last February said that they were armed in this city for bloodshed and riot. We will prove that he said then that they were ready in the city of Chicago

49

for attacking this defendant's credibility.

(Style)
Prosecution has selected powerful verbs and carefully chosen adjectives to tell their story. Additionally, the prosecution uses the strategy of repetition to emphasize the "anarchist" and "conspiracy" theme. Prosecutor Grinnell also has chosen language laden with imagery—word pictures that call up strong mental images of a patriotic, democratic America. Thus, the prosecution emphasizes the central claims of their story, the key reasons why the jurors should find the defendants "guilty as charged."

(Form)
Prosecutor Grinnell specifically connects the charge with defendant Parsons and in so doing is laying a foundation for attacking the defendant's credibility.

for Anarchy, and when told, by a gentleman to whom he made the declaration, that they "would be hung like snakes," said—and there was the insult to the Father of our Country—then he said George Washington was no better than a rebel, as if there was any possible comparison between those declarations, between that sentiment of Washington's and his noble deeds, and the Anarchy of this man. He has said in public meetings—and the details of them I will not now worry you with—he has said in public meetings for the last year and a half, to go back no further—he and Neebe and Schwab and Parsons and Fielden have said in public meetings here in the city of Chicago that the only way to adjust the wrongs of any man was by bloodshed, by dynamite, by the pistol, by the Winchester rifle. They have advised, as will appear in proof here, that dynamite was cheap, and "you had better forego some luxuries, buy dynamite, kill capitalists, down with the police, murder them, dispose of the militia and then demand your rights." That is Anarchy.

* * *

I will prove to you that Parsons—be it said to the shame of our country, because I understand that he was born on our soil—that Parsons, in an infamous paper published by him, called the *Alarm*, has defined the use of dynamite, told how it should be used, how capitalists could be destroyed by it, how policemen could be absolutely wiped from the face of the earth by one bomb; and further has published a plan in his paper of street-warfare by dynamite against militia and the authorities.

(Form)
Prosecution vilifies and degrades the defendants as persons, thereby affecting their credibility.
(Style)
Prosecutor Grinnell has chosen powerful verbs and adjectives to degrade the defendants.

Gentlemen, leaders of any great cause are either heroes or cowards. The testimony in this case will show that August Spies, Parsons, Schwab and Neebe are the biggest cowards that I have ever seen in the course of my life. They have advised the use of dynamite and have advised the destruction of property for months and years in the city of Chicago, and now pitifully smile at our institutions, as they have through their lives—and, like cowards contemplating crime, they sought to establish an alibi for the 4th of May, of which I will speak directly.

* * *

(Content)
Prosecution emphasizes the importance of the audience serving as jurors in the case and their contribution to the nation if they return a favorable verdict.
(Style)
The language selected is highly embellished, dramatic, and overstated.

I want to suggest to you now, gentlemen, this is a vastly more important case than perhaps any of you have a conception of. Perhaps I have been with it so long, have investigated it so much, come in contact with such fearful and terrible things so often, that my notions may be somewhat exaggerated; but I think not. I think they are worse even than my conception has pictured. The firing upon Fort Sumter was a terrible thing to our country, but it was open warfare. I think it was nothing compared with this insidious, infamous plot to ruin our laws and our country secretly and in this

51

cowardly way; the strength of
our institutions may depend
upon this case, because there is
only one step beyond republicanism—that is Anarchy. See that
we never take that step, and let
us stand today as we have stood
for years, firmly planted on the
laws of our country.

* * *

(Content)
Prosecutor Grinnell educates the
jury with regard to the technical
legal standards with which they
may be unfamiliar and explains
how the prosecution's theory of
the case fits within the legal stan-
dards described.

This indictment is for murder, a serious charge. Under our
statute the jury fixes the penalty.
If murder, the penalty is not less
than fourteen years; it may be
for life; it may be the death penalty. For manslaughter, the lower
degree under murder, under our
statute, which is somewhat different from statutes in other
states, the penalty is any number
of years imprisonment and may
be for life. The indictment in this
case is for murder. There are a
great many counts here, but the
chief thing is the count against
these men for murder. Now, it is
not necessary in a case of this
kind, nor in any case of murder,
or any other kind, that the individual who commits the exact
and particular offense—for instance, the man who threw the
bomb—should be in court at all.
He need not even be indicted.
The question for you to determine is, having ascertained that a
murder was committed, not only
who did it, but who is responsible for it, who abetted it, assisted
it, or encouraged it? There is no
question of law in the case.

(Content)
Prosecutor Grinnell makes a fi-
nal statement indicating what the

We will show you, I
think to your entire satisfaction,
that, although perhaps none of

evidence will reveal and how that evidence relates to the legal standards just described and the prosecution's theory of the case.

(Content)
Prosecutor Grinnell ends by complimenting the jury, leaving the jury with a sense of the importance of their decision and their contribution as a jury—all as an appeal to the jury in an effort to gain a favorable decision.

these men personally threw the bomb, they each and all abetted, encouraged and advised the throwing of it, and therefore are as guilty as the individual who in fact threw it. They are accessories.

I have talked to you, gentlemen, longer than I expected to, and chiefly so that you would know something about this case, know something about the facts. I have given you not, perhaps, all the details, but I have given you, as a whole, the facts. I want you to patiently listen to the evidence in this case from both sides, and be careful in your analysis. You have, most of you, been here some time, and you have been admirably patient. Only continue that way, and be patient in the matter, and make up your minds when the testimony is all presented, and not before. It may take some days to get at the proof and to place it before you, so that you can clearly understand it. A great deal of the proof has to come from the mouths of witnesses whose language will have to be interpreted to you. That will take more time. But the whole case will finally be presented to you substantially, I think, as I have stated it. I will now leave the matter with you.

The Defense's Story of Opening Statement

The lawyers for the defense promoted a story that the defendants were not at or near the Haymarket when the crime was committed, that the meeting had been orderly, that none of the defendants had resisted the police, and that the defendants had assembled peaceably to exercise their First Amendment rights.

(Introduction)
The defense elected to present their opening statement following the prosecution's case-in-chief. Consequently, from the very beginning it is a two-sided presentation that refutes the issues and evidence of the prosecution.

(Form)
In contrast to the prosecution's defining the central action of the story as one of anarchists conspiring maliciously to destroy life, the defense's opening statement defines the story of the case as involving issues of individual rights. The defense attempts here to emphasize the defendants are not charged with anarchy and should not be convicted on the basis of their political beliefs.

The Opening Statement for the Defense. [Transcript of Record, pp. 125–30]

Mr. Salomon said the defendants had steadily refused to believe that any man on the jury would be willing to convict any of the defendants because of being an Anarchist or a Socialist. Mr. Grinnell failed to state to you that he had a person by whom he could prove who threw the bomb, and he never expected to make this proof until he found that without this proof he was unable to maintain this prosecution against these defendants; and it was as this case neared the prosecution end of it that the State suddenly changed front and produced a professional tramp and a professional liar, as we will show you, to prove that one of these defendants was connected with the throwing of it. They then recognized, as we claimed and now claim, that that is the only way they can maintain their case here.

They are not charged with Anarchy; they are not charged with Socialism; they are not charged with the fact that Anarchy and Socialism is dangerous or beneficial to the community; but, according to the law under which we are now acting, a charge specific in its nature must be made against them, and that alone must be sustained, and it is the duty of the jury to weigh the evidence as it bears upon that charge; and upon no other point can they pay attention to it.

(Content)
The defense seeks to educate the jury with regard to the technical distinctions between the law of conspiracy and that of murder/ accessory to murder, so that the jurors may understand how the defense's version of the story fits within their interpretion of the governing law.

Now, gentlemen, the charge here is shown by this indictment. This is the accusation. This is what the case involves, and upon this the defendants and the prosecution must either stand or fall. This indictment is for the murder of Mathias J. Degan. It is charged that each one of these defendants committed the crime, each defendant individually; and it is charged in a number of different ways. Now, I desire to call your attention to the law governing this indictment and to read it to you; and I am presenting the law to you now, gentlemen, so that you can understand how we view this case and how the evidence is affected by what the law is.

The law says, no matter whether these defendants advised generally the use of dynamite in the purpose which they claimed to carry out, and sought to carry out, yet if none of these defendants advised the throwing of that bomb at the Haymarket, they cannot be held responsible for the action of others at other times and other places.

* * *

(Form)
Defense attorney Black first refutes the prosecution's portrayal of the defendants and then refocuses the jurors on the defense's story of the case. The defense uses definition strategy by locating the central action of the story not at the Haymarket on the 4th of May, but the months preceding when the defendants were struggling to help their fellow-

That view of the law, that they must be proven to be accessories to the crime, is the one point only upon which the prosecution can sustain their case, and is the only one upon which this case must proceed, according to our view. Now, these defendants are not criminals; they are not robbers; they are not burglars; they are not common thieves; they descend to no small

man. *The defense focuses the ju-*
rors on key elements of their
version of the story—of laboring
men struggling to help others.

(Form)
The defense goes on to explain
the behavior of the defendants in
a manner consistent with the de-
fense narrative regarding individ-
ual rights.

(Style)
The defense uses imagery of
"suffering servants" to enhance
the story of the defense and in-
volve the audience of jurors.

criminal act. On the contrary, this evidence shows conclusively that they are men of broad feelings of humanity, that their only desire has been, and their lives have been consecrated to, the betterment of their fellow-men. They have not sought to take the life of any man, of any individual, to maliciously kill or destroy any person, nor have they sought to deprive any man of his property for their own benefit. They have not sought to get McCormick's property for themselves; they have not sought to get Marshall Field's property for themselves, and to deprive Marshall Field of it feloniously, but they have endeavored and labored to establish a different social system. It is true they have adopted means, or wanted to adopt means that were not approved of by all mankind. It is true that their methods were dangerous, perhaps; but then they should have been stopped at their inception. We shall expect to prove to you, gentlemen, that these men have stood by the man who has the least friends; that they have endeavored to better the condition of the laboring man. The laboring men have few friends enough. They have no means, without the combination and assistance of their fellow-men, to better their condition, and it was to further that purpose and to raise them above constant labor and constant toil and constant worry and constant fret, and to have their fellow-men act and be as human beings and not as animals, that these defendants have consecrated their lives and energies.

* * *

It is neither the place nor the time for counsel in this case, nor of the gentlemen of the jury, to either excuse the acts of these defendants or to encourage them. With that we have here nothing to do. Our object is simply to show that these defendants are not guilty of the murder with which they are charged in this indictment. But the issue is forced upon us to say whether it was right or wrong, and whether they had the right to advocate the bettering of their fellow-men. As Mr. Grinnell said, he wanted to hang Socialism and Anarchy; but twelve men nor twelve hundred nor twelve thousand can stamp out Anarchy nor root out Socialism, no more than they can Democracy or Republicanism, that lie within the heart and within the head. Under our forms of government every man has the right to believe and the right to express his thoughts, whether they be inimical to the present institutions or whether they favor them; but if that man, no matter what he advocates or who he be, whether Democrat, Republican, Socialist or Anarchist, kill and destroy human life deliberately and feloniously, that man, whether high or low, is amenable to criminal justice, and must be punished for his crime, and for no other.

(Form)
After first refuting the prosecution's narrative regarding anarchy, defense attorney Black focuses on the key element of the defense—the issue of individual rights—and links this issue with the fact that in this country every man has the individual right to believe and express his thoughts.

(Content)
The defense tries to anchor the defendants' story to juror values by appealing to the basic rights of persons to speak and assemble freely.

(Style)
By constantly repeating that the defendants were merely exercising their rights, the defense emphasizes their key claim that every person has fundamental individual rights that should be upheld and respected.

(Form)
The defense again emphasizes the theme of individual rights and graphically depicts the accused as suffering servants striving only to help their fellowman.

(Content)
Whereas the prosecutor frames his story into a logical series of claims about the defendants, the defense tells two stories; each with different issues and a different logic. Here the defense answers charges about the motives and character of the defendants; thus, their issues are not an independent and probable story but instead a refutation of the issues and evidence of the prosecution. In effect, the defense narrative re-presents the narrative of the prosecution for interpreting the issues. At the same time, the defense adds a scenario of its own by claiming that the defendants had come to the Haymarket and assembled there peaceably to exercise their individual rights.

* * *

We shall show you that these men, in carrying out their plan for the bettering of the condition of the workingmen, inaugurated the eight-hour movement. They inaugurated the early-closing movement. They inaugurated every movement that tended to alleviate the condition of the workingman and allow him greater time to his family, for mutual benefit. That is what these defendants set up for a defense. That is what they claim was their right to do, and that is what they claim they did do, and they did nothing more.

* * *

We expect to show you, further, that these defendants never conspired, nor any one of them, to take the life of any single individual at any time or place; that they never conspired or plotted to take, at this time or at any other time, the life of Mathias Degan or any number of policemen, except in self-defense while carrying out their original purpose. We expect, further, to show you that on the night of the 4th of May these defendants had assembled peaceably, that the purpose of the meeting was peaceable, that its objects were peaceable, that they delivered the same harangue as before, that the crowd listened, and that not a single act transpired there, previous to the coming of the policemen, by which any man in the audience could be held amenable to law. They assembled there, gentlemen, under the provision of our Constitution, to exercise the right of free speech, to discuss the situation of the workingmen, to discuss the eight-hour question. They assembled there to incidentally discuss what they deemed outrages at McCormick's. No man expected that a bomb would be thrown; no man expected that anyone would be injured at that meeting; but while some of these defendants were there and while this meeting was peaceably in progress, the police, with devilish design, as we expect to prove, came down upon that body with their revolvers in their hands and pockets, ready for immediate use, intending to destroy the life of every man that stood upon that market square.

(Form)

The defense also uses the strategy of vilification—accusing the police of disrupting the peaceful meeting—thereby degrading their opponents and their opponents' witnesses.

* * *

We expect to show you further, gentlemen, that the witness Gilmer, who testified to having seen Spies light the match which caused the destruction coming from the bomb, is a professional and constitutional liar; that no man in the city of Chicago who knows him will believe him under oath, and, indeed, I might almost say that it would scarcely need even a witness to show the falsity of his testimony, because it seems to me that it must fall of its own weight.

(Style)

The defense uses the metaphor of false testimony, describing the witness Gilmer as a "constitutional liar" whose testimony is so false that it would "fall of its own weight," and thereby interrelates the perceptions of falsity with probability. This linguistic strategy adds vividness to the story, which in turn draws the jurors into the reality of the story presented.

* * *

(Content)

Defense attorney Black concludes by again emphasizing that the defendants are not on trial for their individual beliefs and that their beliefs should not in-

Now, gentlemen, in conclusion, as I stated to you a moment ago, we do not intend to defend against Socialism, we do not intend to defend against Anarchism; we expect to be held re-

fluence the jurors' decision.

sponsible for that only which we have done, and to be held in the manner pointed out by law. Under the charge upon which these defendants are held under this indictment, we shall prove to you, and I hope to your entire satisfaction, that a case has not been made out against them. Whether they be Socialists or whether they be Anarchists we hope will not influence any one of you, gentlemen. Whatever they may have preached, or whatever they may have said, or whatever may have been their object, if it was not connected with the throwing of the bomb it is your sworn testimony to acquit them. We expect to make all this proof, and we expect such a result.

Evaluation of the Opening Statements

The opening statements of the prosecution and defense reveal some contrasts in form, content, and style. The prosecutor's story of the events that transpired includes portraying the defendants as conspiring maliciously to destroy property and person and endeavoring to make anarchy rule. The prosecution states further that while none of the defendants may have personally thrown the bomb, they each abetted, encouraged, and advised the throwing of it and, therefore, were guilty of conspiring to commit the "most fearful massacre ever witnessed or heard of in this country" (Transcript of Record, p. 25). Thus, the prosecution presents a persuasive narrative that is a one-sided statement about the evil motives, acts, and consequences for the crime that previews subsequent testimony and makes connections between the malicious acts and the evil behaviors of the accused.

In contrast, the story of the defense summarizes legal issues but adopts a conventional rather than a narrative form. The lawyers for the defense promote a story that the meeting at the Haymarket had been orderly, that none of the defendants had resisted the police, and that the defendants had assembled peaceably to exercise their First Amendment rights. This two-sided presentation, then, refutes the case of the prosecution and goes on to narrate a probable story for the defense.

The stories told by advocates in criminal trials can be assessed in two ways: by what effects the discourse has on the participants in the courtroom and by how the story of the opening statement frames the chain of reasons that evolve in the remainder of the trial. The effects depend upon the purpose, context, and audience of the trial. To achieve their purpose, advocates must tell a story that performs the following functions: clearly simplifies and emphasizes the issues, introduces and characterizes witnesses, establishes logical connections between acts and persons, and describes in detail the scene and motive of the alleged crime (Mauet, 1980, p. 39).

The context is the historical setting in which an alleged crime and the subsequent trial proceedings occur. This context embodies the prevailing public values and needs as well as commonly held prejudices and stereotypes. For example, contextual factors such as the communist hysteria of the 1950s entered into the decisions about Julius and Ethel Rosenberg and the mood of the nation during the Vietnam era affected the manner in which the Chicago Eight trial was conducted.

Whereas context reflects the public mood, the audience of the jury is the decision-maker that judges the trial. The audiences for opening statement consist of a primary audience of the judge and/ or jury (Campbell & Jamieson, 1976, p. 120), a secondary audience made up of the press and courtroom spectators (Campbell & Jamieson, 1976), and a universal audience consisting of all reasonable people (Perelman, 1963). These audiences hear, interpret, and judge the merit of the story. Moreover, advocates should adjust the form, content, and style to the audience they seek to convince.

Determining how the story works provides another mode of evaluation. Fisher (1984) suggests that narrative argument succeeds with an audience when it is consistent, accommodating, corroborated, and convergent with its audiences' experiences (pp. 7–8). Thus in a criminal trial, the story should describe persons and actions that are consistent with the facts of the case; establish the motives consistent with the credibility of those who testify; accommodate the story to the images and metaphors likely to represent the experiences of jurors; confirm the interests, values, and attitudes of jurors; and tailor the shape of the story so that it converges with the prevailing public mores and perceptions of justice. Thus jurors

61

decide verdicts by reflecting upon the competing stories of the defense and prosecution and choosing the narrative that they believe gives the most reasonable account of the action. For them, reasonable means that the narrative of the case presents a probable explanation that fits with the jurors' knowledge and experience of human behavior.

The purpose of the prosecution of the anarchists is accomplished by relating a story that reduces the issue of the case to one major claim—that the defendants are anarchists who conspired to commit murder. Other narrative facts that develop this argument are the prosecutor's detailed characterization of the proofs, his graphic depiction of the crime, and his presentation of a story that demonstrates that the accused had the motive and opportunity to commit the crime. The defense, on the other hand, achieves its purpose by labeling the issues and by challenging the opposition to prove the defendants were accessories to the crime of murder through story elements such as depicting the defendants as humanitarians and appealing to the constitutional rights of all Americans.

Additionally, the context of the trial and the jurors in the case are significant to the outcome of the trial. The context of the 1886 trial involves a polarized conflict between the capitalists and labor; deep resentment against political ideologies; fear of communism, socialism, and anarchism; and promotion of strong feelings about nationalism. All of these factors make it difficult for jurors to believe the opening statement of the defense.

More specifically, the jurors themselves were predisposed toward the case of the prosecution (Avrick, 1984, pp. 266–67). In the Chicago Anarchists' trial, the jurors consisted of twelve men ranging in ages from twenty-three to fifty-three. They represented a conservative, churchgoing, employed, and patriotic group. Among the jurors were no liberals, no union members, no immigrants. The occupations of the jurors ranged from stenographer to construction worker, farmer, and shipping clerk. Prior to the trial and during the *voir dire* process, ten of the twelve jurors admitted they had heard and read negative publicity and they had formed strong opinions of the case. Nevertheless, the judge allowed them to serve on the jury, because they said they would try not to let their opinions enter into their verdicts. Prior to his selection, one juror, George Adams, said, "the police ought to have shot [the defendants] down" and "if I was on the jury I would shoot the damned burglars" (Lum, 1969, pp. 48–66). Additionally, all but one juror admitted he held strong negative attitudes toward socialists, anarchists, and communists; yet all were allowed to serve on the jury for this case. Thus, in the Haymarket trial, the immediate audience of the jurors was predisposed to accept the story of the prosecution and to reject that of the defense enhancing the probability the trial verdict would be "guilty as charged."

As in many political trials, the guilt or innocence of the anarchist defendants was never clearly established; while technically the verdict was one of guilty, the actual guilt or innocence of the defendants continues to be debated today. The case is thought by many to have been beyond remedy, considering the state of public opinion and the judge's rulings and instructions. (See, e.g., David, 1936; Lum, 1969; Avrick, 1984.) However, with respect to this effect, the opening statement cannot be considered independently from the historical setting, the anxious mood of the times, and the nation's need for scapegoats.

As acknowledged by Kenneth Burke in developing his theory of scapegoat sociology, some overall human motives are likely to be present in all human associations: guilt, hierarchy, redemption, and victimage (Wilkie, 1981, p. 102). According to Burke, because persons participate in the social order and, by doing so, sanction the existing hierarchy, they share in the guilt over its divisions and imperfections. This guilt leads to the need for redemption through an appropriately fitting victim. To cancel society's guilt, the victim must be a perfectly fitting one—a representative of all society, and not of just one segment. In the court system of today, jurors may be out to define victims through rhetorical processes, in which case scapegoats are chosen to act as redeemers to purge a society of its evils. Through scapegoating, not only do the jurors make decisions on the basis of courtroom persuasion but the needs of the larger society are also addressed.

Thus, in political trials such as that of the Chicago Anarchists, the primary audience of the jury participates in the social order and shares in the guilt over its divisions and imperfections. This leads the jury to seek justice through the restoration of the social order and through an appropriately chosen victim. This victim can be found in the court system. In the Haymarket trial the mood of the audience was anxious and throughout the country the conviction prevailed that radical groups had been given excessive leeway, that these groups of anarchists now had to be repressed. Anarchists and socialists in particular, especially those of foreign birth, were made the scapegoats for mounting economic and social ills.

The defendants, in effect, were not being tried for murder or conspiracy to murder, as charged in the indictment, but for their social and economic beliefs. The state had failed completely to connect them with the bombing. What had been demonstrated, rather, was that they were anarchists who had denounced capitalism and government, agitators who had spoken and written against the prevailing order. That this was the real issue was made clear from the very outset, as evidenced by prosecuting attorney Grinnell's opening statement to the jury: "Gentlemen: For the first time in the history of our country are people on trial for their lives for endeavoring to make Anarchy the rule, and in that attempt for ruthlessly and awfully destroying life" (Transcript of Record, p. 24). The defendants had become the selected scapegoats of society, scapegoats that had to be eliminated.

Implications for Trial Practice

The Opening Statement as Persuasion

The opening statement functions in the trial process as persuasion by previewing the underlying story structure of the case, and thereby establishing the perceptual framework into which all subsequent trial persuasion will fit. The specific story of the opening statement previews, outlines, and directs the more developed story that emerges at the trial.

To achieve the purpose of the opening statement as defined by legal standards, the opening statement must clarify the issues, introduce the characters (witnesses and defendants), organize the facts logically, and tell a compelling story about the crime (how the crime occurred and the theory of the case). To do this persuasively, the opening statement must adhere to a storytelling framework. The opening statement tells a story about what the case and the evidence will reveal and, if developed effectively, serves as a systematic means of storing, bringing up to date, rearranging, comparing, testing, and interpreting information for the jurors (Bennett & Feldman, 1981). Because the story as presented in the opening statement is the framework into which all the remaining factors of the trial must fit, it should be considered a most important element in a jury trial. If the counsel does not present a comprehensive, credible story in which information can be stored and new information can be analyzed, the opening statement will not be effective.

The interpretive powers of stories take on special significance in the courtroom. The story of the opening statement entails mechanisms that allow jurors to determine the relevance of various court-room factors in any given case and provides a basis for transforming the inventory of trial variables into a theoretical framework. In order for the evidence introduced at a later time to be understood properly, it must fit within the developing story; thus, the story of the opening statement is the method used to explain and distinguish between the important and irrelevant aspects of the case.

The Opening Statement in Political Trials

The opening statement functions in political trials not only to address the forensic issues of the case, it also serves as a forum for the study of deliberative questions. When these issues become en-twined, the opening statement often addresses the broader questions of the nature of society and the social order, with such trials at-tempting to channel the acceptance and resolution of pressing so-cietal issues through the courtroom. Thus, the opening statement serves to do more than simply preview the story of the trial; it also allows the defendants and the attorneys to use the courtroom as a forum for communicating their world view.

This tactic, using the opening statement to address deliberative issues, was utilized in several of the trials presented in this volume. Nearly forty years after the Chicago Anarchists were brought to trial, another significant political trial occurred. On the rise since the late 1870s, political justice crested at well above flood stage during the period 1917–20, as first a world war and then a Red Scare added cases to those generated by the continuing struggle between business and workers. The most controversial case to arise out of the Red Scare was that of Nicola Sacco and Bartolomeo Vanzetti, Italian immigrants, tried and executed in Massachusetts for payroll robbery and murder. The opening statement of the Sacco-Vanzetti trial took advantage of this political climate. Today, Sacco and Vanzetti supporters remain convinced they were innocent vic-tims of political prejudice, convicted because of their commitment to anarchism and their wartime draft dodging.

Just as World War I brought on political trials like Sacco-Vanzetti, political trials increased again during the 1950s as the cold war came to an end with troops under the communist regime of the provinces of North Korea invading the Republic of South Korea. At the same time, Americans were concerned about the House Committee on Un-American Activities and federal prose-cutions under the Smith Act. It was in this atmosphere that Julius and Ethel Rosenberg were tried, convicted, and executed for stealing atomic secrets and passing them to the Russians. The prosecution conveyed an anticommunist world view during the opening statement in the Rosenberg trial; throughout the world, many people still regard the Rosenbergs as victims of anticommunist hysteria and political persecution.

The period of the Vietnam War is also associated with several political trials. Of particular note is the Chicago Eight trial. The Chicago Eight included representatives of the major antiwar groups, the youth counterculture, the campus protest movement, and the Black Panther party, making the trial a sort of microcosm of American political justice in the Vietnam era. Many contemporaries viewed the Chicago Eight case as the preeminent example of the period's political repression. The opening statement, indeed the entire Chicago Eight trial, was a forum for expression of the deliberative issues of the day.

In political trials such as the Haymarket, then, the opening statement typically addresses not only the primary audience about the legal issues but also the universal audience about the deliberative issues. When the universal audience is addressed with deliberative issues such as anarchy and communism, society often creates scapegoats. Seeking to correct the imperfections of the social order, the audiences may determine that scapegoats need to be identified and need to serve as victims to purge society of its guilt.

Therefore, because the audiences of political trials are likely to seek restoration of the social order through the courtroom situation, the attorneys need to frame their opening statements so that they address social needs. In order to be effective, the stories presented during the opening statement need to anticipate and refute the scapegoating theory as suggested by Burke, with the prosecution wanting to support and the defense seeking to deny the need for scapegoating.

The prosecution, for example, will want to emphasize the corruption of society, stressing society's imperfections and thereby necessitating redemption through a scapegoat. The defense attorneys, on the other hand, should create a message to address the overall human motives of hierarchy, guilt, redemption, and victimage. That is, the ideal form, content, and style for the defense in political trials might incorporate the following: the crime must be characterized as an act against an individual, not as a symptom of corruption in society as a whole; if the hierarchy is not present in the story, the audience will not share in the guilt of society's imperfections and will not need redemption through an appropriate victim. If the defendant is not allowed to appear both legally and ritualistically guilty, then a scapegoat situation may be avoided. In the Haymarket trial, the defense's opening statement does attempt to anticipate and refute the scapegoating strategy by emphasizing the defendants as individuals and stressing the charge was not anarchy. It seems, however, this appeal was unable to overcome the mood of the audience.

The Haymarket case has served as a vehicle to focus on the element of the opening statement, a phase of trial discourse often overlooked by theoreticians and practitioners alike. The most celebrated trial of the late nineteenth century, the Haymarket trial involved fundamental social as well as juridical issues; with its manifold effects, the trial was a major event in American legal history. As illustrated by this case study, the opening statement served as a forum for deliberative issues of the day and was effectively utilized by the prosecution in communicating its view to the world.

A Trial Lawyer's
and Trial Practice
Professor's Reaction

Thomas A. Mauet

The chapter on opening statements is consistent with and re-flects the current psychological and communication literature. The chapter's analysis is particularly appropriate on several points. First, it discusses the advantages and disadvantages of one-sided versus two-sided presentations. In the Haymarket trial, the prosecution used a one-sided argument, while the defense used a two-sided approach. The psychological and communication literature shows that the one-sided approach is more effective when listeners are predisposed toward that side's view from the beginning. The two-sided approach seems to be more effective where the opposing side has strong counterarguments and the listeners are undecided on how to decide an issue. In this trial, given the jury's predisposition toward the prosecution, both sides probably used the preferable presentational approach.

Second, the chapter's analysis focuses on the benefits of nar-rative and storytelling approaches in the opening statement. Ac-cording to modern research, these are effective approaches in opening statements, and the text does a capable job of pointing out their benefits. Third, the chapter's analysis focuses on the extent to which both sides used emotional appeals to persuade the jury by making extensive references to the social and political environment in which

Thomas A. Mauet is a Professor of Law and Director of Trial Advocacy at the University of Arizona College of Law. He has an A.B. degree from Dartmouth College, and a J.D. degree from Northwestern University School of Law. Before coming to Arizona, he was a State's Attorney for Cook County, Chicago, a United States Attorney for the Northern District of Illinois, and a trial attorney in private practice. He has taught trial practice for almost ten years at university law schools at Harvard, Chicago, Kent State, and Arizona, and is a teaching team member and Southwest Regional Director of the National Institute for Trial Advocacy. Professor Mauet is the author of *Fundamentals of Litigation Techniques, Fundamentals of Trial Techniques,* and several articles on trial advocacy.

the trial arose. This is probably the most notable feature of these particular opening statements.

Finally, the chapter's analysis of the opening statement focused heavily on labels, word choices, imagery, and repetition. It effectively pointed out how the lawyers used labels to characterize people and events. The prosecution continuously used such labels as "anarchy," "fearful massacre," and other pejorative terms. The defense in turn used other labels to paint the defendants in a positive light, such as "broad feelings of humanity," "better the condition of the laboring man" and "to have their fellow-men act and be as human beings." In the same vein, both sides used strong verbs and nouns to create an appropriate emotional atmosphere. Both sides also recognized the importance of imagery. The prosecution created an image of anarchists bent upon the destruction of the country's social and economic structure. The defense, by contrast, created an image of men working to better the social conditions of workingmen within the law. Both sides obviously realized the importance of creating images that would project each side's perspective of events involved in the trial. Finally, the opening statements relied heavily upon repetition. In this trial the prosecution was particularly skillful in repeatedly using pejorative labels such as "anarchists." Using labels, strong verbs and nouns, imagery and repetition are all recognized as significant persuasion techniques, and the chapter correctly emphasized their significance.

As a trial lawyer, what impressed me most about the Haymarket trial's opening statements is how different they are from those that prosecutors and defense attorneys present today. There are five differences that are particularly noteworthy.

First, the jury composition in this trial was significantly different from what it would be were the case tried today. The Haymarket jury was entirely male, primarily working or middle class men, who had no union membership, and were politically conservative. More importantly, many of the men expressed negative attitudes about unionism, the defendants, and the charges brought against them. Today many of those jurors would have been successfully challenged for cause, for having fixed opinions about the guilt or innocence of the defendants. In addition, the defense may have had the venue for this trial moved out of Chicago. Hence, the effectiveness of the opening statements in the Haymarket trial must be viewed in light of the jury that actually heard the case.

The second striking difference between the opening statements in the Haymarket trial and today's trials is the lawyers' styles. The

1890s in the United States were years in which formal oratory was a standard method of public speaking. This comes through loud and clear in these opening statements. Consider the prosecutor's style: "The State now and at no time hereafter will say aught to arouse your prejudices or your indignation, having confidence in the case that we present"; "this insidious, infamous plot to ruin our laws and our country secretly and in this cowardly way." The defense, while using less formal language, is still very oratorical by today's standards: "Under our forms of government every man has the right to believe and the right to express his thoughts, whether they be inimical to the present institutions or whether they favor them." By contrast, today's trial lawyers, while using proper English, are much more conversational, and try to engage the jury by talking with rather than at it.

A third interesting difference between the opening statements in this case and modern opening statements is the level of story-telling. The prosecution, for example, repeatedly referred to the evidence without expressly stating the fact: "He has said in public meetings—and the details of them I will not now worry you with—he has said in public meetings for the last year and a half, to go back no further—he and Neebe and Schwab and Parsons and Fielden have said in public meetings here in the city of Chicago that the only way to adjust the wrongs of any man was by bloodshed." The defense also summarized the evidence without expressly referring to admissible facts: "This evidence shows conclusively that they are men of broad feelings of humanity, that their only desire has been, and their lives have been consecrated to, the betterment of their fellow-men." By today's standards, of course, this is not factual storytelling. Today, trial lawyers directly use the facts, and "tell a story" using the actual evidence that they will present at trial. The theory is that using the actual evidence, rather than referring to the evidence in general terms, will present a more compelling case.

Fourth, a major distinction between the opening statements in this trial and modern trials is the level of emotional appeals. While such appeals may be consistent with psychological and communication studies, they are incompatible with today's evidence law. For example, the prosecutor constantly branded the defendants as anarchists, and used other pejorative labels. He called the incident "the most fearful massacre ever witnessed or heard of in this country." The prosecutor was using popular emotions against radicals of any kind in fanning the jurors' prejudices to obtain a guilty verdict. This approach forced the defendants' opening statement to be negative and defensive: "They are not charged with anarchy; they are not charged with socialism; they are not charged with the fact that anarchy and socialism is dangerous or beneficial to the community." In short, the prosecution's use of emotional terminology, and the defense's attempt to blunt it, while perhaps an effective technique, would simply not be permitted under today's evidence law.

Finally, perhaps the greatest distinction between these opening statements and modern opening statements is the degree of argument that was permitted. For example, the prosecutor referred to "the most fearful massacre ever witnessed or heard of in this country," and stated that what the defendants did was an "insult to the Father of our Country." By today's standards, these types of statements are obviously argument, and would be improper in an opening statement.

3
Narrative and Direct Examination: The Trial of Bruno Richard Hauptmann

The story prefaced by the advocates in opening statement is elaborated by the testimony presented in direct examination. This chapter analyzes direct examination by focusing on witness selection, ordering of testimony, and the goal of direct questioning—getting the witnesses to tell a coherent and probable story. The chapter investigates the advocates' persuasive strategies of definition, inference, and validation and the defenses' strategies of redefinition and reconstruction. This case study of direct examination shows that advocates on both sides of the case need to choose, order, and examine witnesses so that their testimony presents a corroborated, consistent, and probable story to jurors. A strong direct examination prevents a devastating cross-examination and, at the same time, verifies the story presented in opening statement. Direct examination as story creation is a preferred method for both historical and legal practitioners.

Charles A. Lindbergh flew the first transatlantic flight from New York to Paris. Five years after the flight, Lindbergh again took the public spotlight because of the tragic kidnapping of and the payment of ransom for his young son. The American people empathized with Lindbergh's tragedy and tried to show their support by offering money and information that would allow the police to find the criminal who had abducted and then killed the Lindbergh baby. Nearly two years after the kidnapping, police arrested Bruno Richard Hauptmann for the crime. A New Jersey court convicted the defendant and recommended the death penalty.

The Trial

Charles A. Lindbergh, Jr., the twenty-month old child of Charles and Anne Morrow Lindbergh, was stolen from his crib in the nursery of his parents' Hopewell, New Jersey, home on March 1, 1932. At this time, kidnapping was a relatively common type of crime. Alix (1978) reported that over two hundred kidnappings occurred in the decade from 1922 to 1932. However, the kidnapping and murder of the Lindbergh child, and the subsequent trial of a German immigrant carpenter made this a unique and sensational case for a number of reasons.

First, the case was called by journalists "the crime of the century" because of the fame of the child's parents. Ross (1976) explains: "Charles A. Lindbergh was one of the more adored, harried, photographed, and written about men in the world" (p. xi). He gained public adoration through his transatlantic flight from New York to Paris in 1927. By reason of her marriage to Lindbergh and her father's career as a United States senator and diplomat, the mother of the child was a national celebrity who endeared herself to the American public by her quiet and demure manner and by her gallant aeronautical assistance to her husband on his international flights.

Second, the case remained unsolved for over a year. During that time, Lindbergh, the police, mobsters, and public celebrities tried themselves to solve the case. Most notably, an eccentric retired Bronx college professor, John F. Condon, acted as a go-between and contact with the kidnappers. He delivered, with the assistance of Colonel Lindbergh, $50,000 in marked bills, including $20,000 in gold notes, to the kidnapper. Shortly afterward, the decomposed body of the dead child was found in a shallow grave on the Lindbergh property. The ransom payment, made without the approval of law enforcement agents, was directed by Lindbergh. Throughout the case, the investigation was jeopardized by interventions of untrained persons who wanted to help the Lindberghs. Finally, the defendant, Bruno Richard Hauptmann, was arrested, convicted, and executed for the crime even though he swore he was innocent.

The trial began on January 2, 1935, at the Herndon County Courthouse in Flemington, New Jersey. Judge Thomas Whitaker Trenchard, an experienced state trial court judge, presided. The Hearst newspapers paid the attorney's fees for the defense on the condition that Anna Hauptmann, the wife of the defendant, would grant exclusive interviews to them. This enabled the defense to hire a Brooklyn attorney of repute, Edward J. Reilly. He was assisted by New Jersey attorneys C. Lloyd Fisher, Frederick Pope, and Robert Roscranz. The state attorney general, David T. Wilentz, led the prosecution assisted by Anthony J. Hauck, Joseph Lanigan, H. Dobson Peacock, and George Large. The trial lasted six weeks. The jury returned a verdict of "guilty of murder in the first degree" and recommended no clemency. After over a year of appeals, Hauptmann was executed on April 3, 1936.

Before his execution, Hauptmann remarked: "They think when I die, the case will die. They think it will be like a book I close. But the book it will never close" (Scaduto, 1976, p. 484). And fifty years after the execution, the debate surrounding the case has not ended. In the fall of 1982, PBS television produced a documentary entitled, "Who Killed the Lindbergh Baby?" In 1985, Kennedy claimed that Hauptmann was framed by the zealous actions of Attorney General Wilentz, who encouraged the police to withhold evidence from the defense. In June 1986, Anna Hauptmann, eighty-seven-year-old widow of the defendant, urged authorities to reopen the case and to exonerate her husband. The book is still open as Hauptmann prophesied and the guilt or innocence of the carpenter continues to be debated. Whereas many of the early sources about the trial expressed certainty that Hauptmann was guilty (Whipple, 1937; Condon, 1936; Haring, 1937), other more recent sources argue that Hauptmann was framed because evidence was withheld from the jury (Scaduto, 1976; Kennedy, 1985). The most objective account of the trial (Siedman, 1977) concludes that the guilt of Hauptmann seems likely but it is clear that the defendant did not receive a fair trial.

This chapter does not attempt to demonstrate the guilt or innocence of the defendant; rather the study tries to explain how the communication of the direct examination led to the guilty verdict. In particular, the essay shows how the communication of this segment of the trial is story and how the individual testimony of each witness contributes to the overall persuasive effect of the narrative. To do this, the chapter (1) describes the narrative qualities of direct examination as a whole; (2) analyzes the recommended strategies for prosecution and defense in creating the stories of individual witnesses; and (3) evaluates the communication of the trial as narrative persuasion.

Narrative and Direct Examination

In our analysis of the opening statements of the Haymarket case, we explained how storytelling is the underlying form of a more complex genre of persuasive discourse. In this chapter, we view the narrative of direct examination as an extension of the story begun in the opening statement. Specifically, the opening statement resembles a preface or introduction to the entire trial narrative, and the direct interrogation of each key witness is a chapter of an entire account, which develops the actions of the characters central to the plot of the trial narrative. Jeans (1975), Heglund (1978), and Mauet (1980) recommend that direct examination should elicit testimony that sufficiently elaborates the facts so the advocates can prove their theory of the case as it was outlined in opening statement.

Narrative in a broad sense includes "the words and/or deeds—that have sequence and meaning for those who live, create, and interpret them" (Fisher, 1984, p. 2). Applying narrative to a trial situation, the term means words and actions that relate to the disputed issues of the case. Scholes and Kellogg (1966) note that narrative requires "no more or no less than a teller and a tale," a storyteller and a story. In direct examination, each side of the case has a story to tell—its theory of the case; and this story is jointly told by the attorneys and their witnesses. More specifically, the narrative of direct examination involves sharing of a common function, careful selecting of witnesses, deliberate ordering of testimony, and logically establishing connections between the stories of those who testify.

Function

The general function of direct examination is for advocates to elicit stories from their witnesses. Mauet (1980) explains that direct interrogation is "a creative art" that permits attorneys to "tell a story to a jury" in a way that is most advantageous to their side of the case. Tanford (1983) identifies direct examination as "the most important part of the trial" because this process draws out the facts of the story. Because jurors draw conclusions from these narrated facts, it is essential that the stories witnesses tell are "clear, logical, and persuasive" (p. 329).

Bennett and Feldman (1981) conclude that story is useful both to the storytellers, attorneys and witnesses, and to the jurors who are expected to believe the narrative. For the witness, the story conveys "selective interpretations," provides a logical sequence of information to explain the action, and focuses attention on persons and actions. In turn, the stories told by witnesses facilitate jurors' understanding about the facts and issues of the case by enhancing their ability to organize large amounts of information and by placing that data into coherent perceptual categories (pp. 8–11).

The Federal Rules of Evidence give broad discretion to judges in the way they oversee direct examination. Rule 611 identifies three general judicial guidelines about how advocates should conduct interrogation: direct examination should "ascertain truth," avoid "needless consumption of time," and "protect witnesses from harassment."

In a general sense, the function of storytelling was carried out in the Hauptmann trial by the development of theories of the case for each side. Because the State of New Jersey lacked a strong legal statute against kidnapping, the prosecution could not indict on that charge. Instead, the state decided to indict Hauptmann for first degree murder. The advantage of the murder charge was that, if convicted of the crime, Hauptmann would get the death penalty. The disadvantage of the indictment was that the state had only circumstantial and hearsay evidence to link the accused with the murder of the child. To prove the indictment, the prosecution needed to contrive a story that would show the defendant willfully killed the child while he was in the process of burglary—stealing the child from the Lindbergh home.

The defense's theory of the case was that Hauptmann had nothing to do with the crime. Although Hauptmann admitted possession of over $14,000 of the marked bills from the ransom money, he claimed he was taking care of the money for a former business partner, Isidor Fisch, who died suddenly on a visit to Germany. The defense's story was that Hauptmann discovered the money in 1933 when he opened a box Fisch had left with him. Hauptmann decided to spend the money because Fisch owed him thousands of dollars for business loans. The direct examination of witnesses elaborated both of these stories of the case.

Witness Selection

In a typical criminal trial, advocates select from a wide variety of potential witnesses. The primary witnesses for the prosecution are the victim or the close associates of the victim, and the primary witness(es) of the defense is, or are, the accused. The testimony of the primary witnesses is often the basis for the theory of the case, therefore the primary witnesses are expected to present a thorough account of the actions, scene, and persons involved in the case. The stories of the primary witnesses are elaborated and corroborated by expert, records, occurrence, and reputation witnesses. In the Lindbergh kidnapping trial, the primary witnesses for the prosecution were Charles Lindbergh, the father of the victim, and John F. Condon, the intermediary who talked to the kidnapper and delivered the ransom money. The primary witness for the defense was Hauptmann. Both sides introduced dozens of corroborating witnesses.

A second type of witness is the expert witness, defined by Federal Rule of Evidence 702, as someone who has specialized knowledge of a scientific or technical nature who can assist jurors to understand the evidence or to determine facts pertinent to the case. Experts have special "knowledge, skill, training, or education" to qualify as this category of witness.

In the Hauptmann case, the prosecution relied on experts to link the defendant to the crime through comparisons of his handwriting samples with the ransom notes and through linking the wood in the ladder to wood purchased by the defendant and wood taken from his home. Because expert witnesses often command high fees for their testimony, attorneys secure the type of experts that they can afford. Scaduto (1976) and Kennedy (1985) explain that the Hauptmann defense could not afford expert witnesses, so they called persons to testify about handwriting and wood that had credentials significantly inferior to the experts of the prosecution. And the defense called fewer experts than the prosecution. For example, John M. Trendley offered his testimony free of charge to the defense after seeing handwriting samples of the defendant in the newspaper. He examined fifty documents for two and one-half hours and then concluded the ransom notes were not written by Hauptmann. Additionally, the defense featured the testimony of Ewald Mielke, a mill worker who had worked with wood but had no technical training.

A third type of testimony comes from records witnesses, who explain the contents of travel, work, bank, and investment records. The prosecutors of Hauptmann used records witnesses to interpret the complicated financial transactions of the defendant's work and payroll records. A government bank auditor extrapolated the banking assets and liabilities of Hauptmann by scanning the bank and stock market deposits and withdrawals over a five-year period. Another prosecution records witness, an employer, claimed the defendant had not come to work on the day of the kidnapping and that he quit the day after the crime. The defense did not present any records witnesses; rather they relied on Hauptmann to explain his financial transactions. The defendant claimed that large sums of money, not accounted for by salaries of either Richard or Anna Hauptmann, came from money given him by Isidor Fisch. Throughout his three days of testimony about money transactions, Hauptmann denied the conclusions of the records witnesses presented by the prosecution.

A fourth category of witnesses are called occurrence, meaning they are persons who "saw, heard, or did anything pertinent to the case" (Mauet, 1980, p. 98). Occurrence witnesses support the story line of the primary witnesses by verifying the facts about the events others have reported and by heightening or sharpening certain aspects of the story for jurors. One occurrence witness differs from another in persuasiveness depending on his or her confidence, ability to make precise statements, and reputation and trustworthiness. In most criminal trials, the largest percentage of witnesses for both sides are of this type.

Among the many occurrence witnesses called by the state in the Hauptmann case were: John Wallace, a sergeant in the New Jersey State Police, who arrested Hauptmann; Walter Lyle, a service station attendant who accepted a ransom bill from Hauptmann for five gallons of gas; and William Mulligan, an employee from a stock investment company who did business with the defendant. The defense introduced a number of occurrence witnesses to prove that Hauptmann was at the bakery where his wife worked at the time of the kidnapping. Among these witnesses were: August Van Henke, who talked to Hauptmann about a dog that evening; Paul Vetterle, who was at a birthday party with Hauptmann when the ransom money was delivered; and Louise Wollenburg, who knew of Fisch and Hauptmann's business partnership.

A fourth type of testimony comes from reputation witnesses, who testify about the character traits as well as the truth or veracity of the statements of other witnesses. Generally, the defense calls more reputation witnesses because, even though the defendant is presumed innocent, jurors often trust the witnesses of the state more than those of the defense (Sannito, 1981). The prosecution calls corroborating witnesses to verify judgments given by other witnesses whose testimony lacks technical or scientific validation. For example, the prosecution called several witnesses to verify the testimony of the major handwriting expert of the state, Albert Osborn, Sr., Eldrige Stein, Hildegarde Alexander, Herbert J. Walter, Harry Cassidy, William Souder, and Clark Sellers corroborated Osborn's testimony saying that they observed similarities among the ransom notes and Hauptmann's handwriting, such as the defendant did not dot i's or cross t's and misspelled the same words—"singnature" for signature, "boad" for boat, "where" for were, "ladder" for later, "anyding" for anything, and "someding" for something. The reputation witnesses called by the defense testified about the reputation of Fisch and his relationship to Hauptmann. Among the defense witnesses used for this purpose were: Oscar John Bruchmann, Gustave Miller, Auguste Hile, and Gerta Henkel. All knew both Fisch and Hauptmann, and they corroborated Hauptmann's story that Fisch left a shoe box with him on the night before he left for Germany. However, all these reputation witnesses were impugned by Prosecutor Wilentz because they were German friends of the Hauptmanns. The defense did not call independent character witnesses, such as employers, neighbors, or colleagues from work situations. As a result, the story of Hauptmann's credibility was never fully told in the trial.

Advocates should choose a variety of different types of witnesses and emphasize the testimony of credible witnesses so they can develop the narration previewed in opening statement in a plausible way. Since jurors often base their decisions on the credibility of the witnesses (Kalven & Zeisel, 1966), those who testify are important to the narrative of direct exam. In this case, the prosecution had a superior quality of expert and records witnesses and as a whole their testimony was more credible than that offered by the defense. The defense presented less technical information and their witnesses had weaker credentials. In his cross-examination, Wilentz impugned several of the defense's occurrence witnesses by showing one to be a former mental patient, another a former convict, another a professional witness, and still another a bootlegger. Scaduto (1976) and Kennedy (1985) admit the inferiority of the defense witnesses and blamed this on several factors: Reilly was not interested in the case and did not work to find credible witnesses; the defense lacked the money needed to pay expert witnesses; and the prosecution intentionally withheld evidence from the defense, thus prohibiting them from securing some important witnesses.

Ordering of Testimony

Hughes and Duhamel (1962) note that effective oral and written narratives should establish "a clear and single effect" (p. 65). Because trial narratives are a series of stories with varying degrees of relevance and importance, the task of advocates is to impose on this conglomeration of description a coherent narrative order that highlights the important evidence, de-emphasizes the secondary, and eliminates the irrelevant. To do this, advocates should order their testimony so the primary witnesses tell stories that focus and unify the whole sequence of witness narratives.

More specifically, Sannito (1981) recommends that advocates structure their witnesses according to three principles. The first principle is the need to develop a thematic order; that is, each story segment of a witness should point to the same conclusions as those of other witnesses. A good theme establishes a thread of common meaning that runs through all of the testimony. The second principle is the adoption of a serial-position order, which places the most important witnesses first and last. This order is grounded in social science research, which concludes that arguments in a controversy presented first and those presented last enter most prominently into the decisions of audiences (Lund, 1925; Asch, 1946; Luchins, 1957). Sannito (1981) summarizes how advocates should determine order: "Put emotional evidence first to get the primacy effect"; place "factual evidence last to gain the recency effect"; and insert your best evidence "first on each separate day of the trial" (p. 32). The final principle is the *Von Restorff Effect*, that is, a method of interjecting "unique or novel events" so they "stand out and are virtually unforgettable" (p. 32). The novelty effect can be achieved by an unusual theme, striking evidence, or unexpected changes in the content of witnesses' testimony.

In the Hauptmann trial, the prosecution developed their story by clustering together the testimony of occurrence, expert, and records witnesses so that it confirmed the information of the primary witnesses, Lindbergh and Condon. After a very short appearance by his wife, Lindbergh was the second witness called. He testified about the circumstances inside and the scene outside of his home on the night of the kidnapping, and he identified the presence of ransom notes and the ladder. Condon verified the authenticity of the ransom notes and identified scenes where the contacts between him and the kidnapper had occurred.

The clustering of testimony around the evidence introduced by the key prosecution witnesses is depicted in Table 1. The common theme of the prosecution was that a German committed the crime, extorted the ransom, and spent the money. Charles Lindbergh's appearance at the beginning of the trial provided the emotional evidence to achieve the primacy effect; and Arthur Koehler, the wood expert, who traced the wood samples to a lumber yard where Hauptmann purchased wood and the ladder brace to the defendant's house, put the strongest factual evidence last for a recency effect. Although the prosecution did not have a novel theme, they did feature Condon, an eccentric and colorful character, in the middle of their testimony. According to the standards for ordering the trial narrative, the prosecution presented their narrative in a clear and persuasive way.

Table 1. Prosecution Witnesses

Lindbergh's Testimony
Reported circumstances inside of the house on the night of the crime and this data corroborated by: Betty Gow, the child's nurse; Anne Lindbergh, the child's mother; and Elsie Whately, the Lindberghs' cook.
Reported scene outside of the house on the night of the crime and this data corroborated by: state troopers Frank Kelley and Nuncio De-Gaetana; wood expert Arthur Koehler; and Newark policeman John Sweeney.
Identified ransom notes and this data corroborated by: police at the scene of the crime, John Condon, and Lindbergh's friend Henry Breckenridge.

Condon's Testimony
Identified ransom notes and this data corroborated by: Henry Breckenridge; Condon's daughter Myra Condon Hacker; police officers Thomas Ritchie and James Finn; and handwriting experts Thomas Sisk, Frank Wilson, Albert Osborn, Sr., Albert Osborn, Jr., Eldridge Stein, Herbert Walter, Harry Cassidy, William Souder, and Clark Sellers.
Identified pictures and events related to the transfer of ransom to the kidnapper and this information corroborated by: John Perrone and James O'Brien, taxi cab drivers who were involved with the ransom notes; and Milton Gaglio and Alfred Reich, friends of Condon who drove him to meet the kidnapper.

In contrast, the defense did not develop their story through a clear arrangement of testimony. Reilly's examination of forty-nine witnesses took place in a random sequence. The defendant was the first witness called, and his testimony was then interrupted by the insertion of the testimony of both Christian and Katie Fredricksen, owners of the bakery where Anna Hauptmann worked on the day of the crime. They testified that Mrs. Hauptmann came to work and was picked up by her husband that evening. Hauptmann returned as the primary witness, and his testimony continued for five days. Table 2 chronicles the appearance of the remainder of the defense witnesses.

The synopsis in Table 2 shows that the defense switched from one set of evidence to another, mixed expert witnesses with reputation testimony, and for the most part did not cluster witnesses so they corroborated the story of the primary witness.

Several facts explain the lack of coherent order for the defense in their presentation of witnesses. Quite clearly, Reilly did not schedule witnesses ahead of time because Judge Trenchard repeatedly warned the defense that their witnesses must be ready to testify. Several times during the trial, witnesses unexpectedly appeared and the person testifying was asked to step down and the unexpected witness took the stand. The defense recalled prosecution witnesses, apparently to fill time until one of their other witnesses showed up, and that testimony did not relate to the defense's theory of the case. Reilly showed his desperation about insufficient witnesses by soliciting testimony through the local newspapers prior to the trial. Five witnesses answered his ads and appeared at the trial. All of these witnesses were impugned by Wilentz, indicating the defense had not properly interviewed or prepared the witnesses prior to their appearance in the courtroom.

The theme of the defense was not really a theme but merely a denial that the defendant committed the crime. To achieve the primacy effect, the defense presented Hauptmann, their most emotional witness. However, their final witness was a mill worker, without technical credentials in wood analysis, who failed to offer the strong factual testimony needed for the recency effect. Perhaps the persistent denials of the defendant and outbursts by him and his wife in the courtroom achieved some novelty but overall the defense's theme, evidence, and witnesses failed to create the *Von Restorff Effect.*

The testimony of the defense had at least three clusters of ideas that could have been arranged in a more logical order in the direct

Table 2. Defense Witnesses

Hauptmann's Testimony

Gave his personal background including his criminal record in Germany and this information was corroborated by Anna Hauptmann.

Explained how he received the ransom money from Fisch and this information was corroborated by several witnesses who appeared at the end of the trial.

Interpreted his financial transactions and noted that Fisch gave him the money that could not be accounted for by his or his wife's salary; this information was not directly corroborated by anyone.

Order of Appearance of Other Defense Witnesses

Three witnesses said they saw Hauptmann on the day of the crime.

Lou Harding saw a man with a ladder on his car but it was not Hauptmann.

John Trendley, a volunteer handwriting analyst, said the ransom notes were not written by Hauptmann.

Peter Sommer saw Fisch and a woman with a child the night of the crime.

Sebastian Lupica saw a car near Hopewell, but Hauptmann was not the driver.

Hans Kloeppenburg saw Fisch bring a shoe box to Hauptmann's house in December 1933.

Anna Bonestell saw Violet Sharpe, a maid of the Lindberghs who later committed suicide, at her restaurant the evening before the crime.

James Dott and Carl Jeorg saw Fisch and a woman with a baby on the dock the evening after the crime.

Paul Vetterle was with Hauptmann so he could not have spent gold notes on a particular date.

Thomas Sisk, previously called by the prosecution, said he took footprints of the kidnapper after the exchange of ransom money.

Officer Schwarzkopf, previously called by the prosecution, said he did an experiment with a duplicate ladder to prove its instability.

Philip Moses, a taxi driver, saw three men the night the ransom was exchanged.

Maria Mueller, niece of Hauptmann, saw him at home on one of the days when marked ransom money was passed.

Ten witnesses testified about Fisch and his relationship to Hauptmann.

Three witnesses said that prosecution witness Whited had a reputation for lying.

Four witnesses gave conflicting testimony about the wood and the ladder used in the kidnapping.

examination. In retrospect, a more coherent arrangement of testimony would have been: begin with Hauptmann; follow his testimony with all of the witnesses who could corroborate Hauptmann's story of Fisch; use both occurrence and reputation witnesses; show that Fisch was the criminal by using expert, reputation, records, and occurrence witnesses; and deny the story of the prosecution's case by using occurrence witnesses and records witnesses. Reclustering and reordering of the witnesses could have produced a more coherent order and hence a more persuasive defense narrative.

Connections Between Stories

Jeans (1975), Mauet (1980), and Tanford (1983) advise advocates to link the narratives of diverse witnesses together so they connect logically to one another. The preceding section shows that when advocates arrange testimony according to similar evidence, the direct examination is more coherent. Other ways to connect testimony are to link witnesses by exhibits, personal and professional relationships, shared contexts, and common experiences.

Exhibits are artifacts related to the case that can be perceived by jurors, such as photographs, diagrams, models, summary charts, recordings, and business records. Advocates typically introduce an exhibit with the testimony of the witness who has the most knowledge about the exhibit. After the exhibit has been introduced into evidence, it can be referred to many times by other witnesses.

The prosecution introduced over 250 exhibits in its attempt to convict Hauptmann. Some of these exhibits, such as the ransom notes and the wood samples from the ladder, were referred to throughout the trial. Moreover, Wilentz used the ransom notes to connect Lindbergh's testimony with that of Condon, police officers, and handwriting analysts so all of the testimony of the prosecution's witnesses appeared to fit together. The defense introduced less than ten exhibits and did not use any of them to connect the witnesses' stories. Curiously, Reilly repeatedly used prosecution's exhibits for his witnesses to deny verbally the meaning of those exhibits.

A second strategy for linking the testimony of witnesses is through personal and professional relationships and associations. Persons who testify can be associated because they are from the same family, live in the same neighborhood, belong to the same social group, or eat at the same restaurants. Attorneys can also connect testimony through professional relationships, such as banker-customer, seller-buyer, doctor-patient, teacher-student, employer-employee, or counselor-client.

Many of the 150 witnesses called in the Hauptmann case were related to one another. Advocates make these relational links through the content of the questions they ask in direct examination and later through their interpretations of the testimony in closing arguments. The existence of relationships is a way of corroborating testimony, impugning testimony, logically connecting testimony, or deciphering the credibility of a witness. Advocates can use relationships to build the coherence of the story by showing how testimony fits, or they can intentionally leave out references to relationships when these connections imply collusion between witnesses.

In the Hauptmann case, both the prosecution and defense drew relationship connections to promote the veracity of the testimony. For example, Wilentz established the relationships between the Lindberghs, their servants, and the child. In contrast, the prosecutor omitted links between handwriting analysts so their testimony would appear to be independent. For the defense, Reilly emphasized the friendship between Hauptmann and his German associates, his relatives, and the associations of all the witnesses to Fisch. However, Reilly downplayed the relationships between the defendant and the records witnesses so the testimony would seem more objective.

A third link between witnesses occurs when persons do not know each other but share knowledge about a time, setting, or area pertinent to the disputed issues of the case. Even though many occurrence witnesses do not know each other, they have separate information about the same context. As an illustration, several witnesses for both the prosecution and the defense had knowledge about the cemetery where Condon delivered the ransom notes to the kidnapper. Additionally, several witnesses on both sides reported knowledge about cars traveling the road to the Hopewell residence on the night of the kidnapping. By placing the testimony of these witnesses together in the direct exam, the jurors gained a composite description of the context in which the alleged crime occurred.

Finally, advocates fit the testimony of one witness with another through their common experiences of persons, groups, events, or actions. Even though persons testifying neither know each other nor share information about the context, they may have common experiences and perceptions that unify their narratives in the trial. For example, a number of police witnesses, called by the prosecution, came from different law enforcement agencies, jurisdictions, and states, but they shared common duties and found similar evidence. Also, several witnesses for the defense held common negative perceptions about a prosecution witness, the man who testified he saw Hauptmann in the vicinity of the crime on March 1, 1932. By reporting the same negative perceptions, the witnesses drew a composite conclusion that this prosecution witness should not be believed.

Making connections between witnesses who testify for one side of the case has the broad advantage of adding cohesiveness to the overall story of the case. These linkages add a singular point of view to the story, verify the testimony of the primary witnesses, emphasize the evidence essential to conviction or acquittal, provide grounds for the refutation of the oppositions' story, and point to the motives for the disputed actions in the case. Advocates are likely to leave out or down play connections that imply lack of objectivity, suggest collusion, or establish inappropriate familiarity between witnesses. When advocates establish inappropriate connections, the opposing counsel often uses these links to impugn that witness in cross-examination.

The function of the story through direct interrogation is the elaboration of the theory of the case. To accomplish this function, advocates need to select a variety of credible witnesses, order the witnesses in a logical way, and connect the testimony of the witnesses to each other. The direct examination of both the prosecution and defense elaborates the narrative of opening statements, and each of the stories of the witnesses combines to form the entire defense or prosecution narrative.

The Stories of Witnesses

Tanford (1983) claims that direct examination is often done poorly because: each witness knows only part of the whole story; the questions asked by counsel are too narrow to elicit the complete narrative; the rules of evidence "defy common sense" and make testimony different from normal conversation; objections from opposing attorneys disrupt the sequence and logic of the story; and the cross-examination introduces irrelevant and inconsistent information into the story (p. 329). Tanford's criticism points to the fact that direct examination demands a great deal of skill and planning on the part of the interrogators.

Extracting a cohesive, relevant, and believable story from each witness calls for advocates to be competent communicators. Effective strategies for direct examination of the prosecution include definition, inference, and validation. Effective strategies for the defense include redefinition and reconstruction. This section defines and illustrates the prosecution strategies using the testimony from Lindbergh, and then defines and illustrates the defense strategies using testimony from Hauptmann.

Prosecution Strategies

Definition. Most prosecutors try to "elicit particular definitions of evidence from witnesses" (Bennett & Feldman, 1981, p. 118). To do this, they ask restrictive questions that require concise and particular responses. Answers of this type tend to be narrow explanations of evidence that directly fit with the prosecution's theory of the case—the kidnapper killed the child in the process of committing burglary. To prove this claim in the Hauptmann case, Wilentz tried to establish through Lindbergh's definitions that the ladder broke when the kidnapper came down with the child. The questioning of Lindbergh about the ladder used the following definitional strategy:

W: Did you see any objects coming down past that window or in the vicinity of that window?
L: I did not. . . .
W: Well, some time during that night did you hear some sort of noise or crash?
L: Yes, I did.
W: About what time was it and where were you?
L: Sitting on the sofa in the living room during ten or fifteen minutes after we had come into the living room. At that time, I heard a sound . . . like an orange box, the slats of an orange box falling off a chair, which I assumed would be in the kitchen.
W: That is sort of like the falling of a crate, a wooden crate?
L: The slats of a crate. . . .
W: Was it the sort of a noise that would come with the falling of a ladder?
L: Yes it was, if the ladder was outside. [Transcript of Record, pp. 80–81]

This definition of the noise and the possible sources of that noise were essential testimony to the prosecution because this information connected the kidnapper to the death of the child. Lindbergh was the only witness who could associate the broken ladder

87

directly with the time when the kidnapping occurred. Lindbergh defined the noise with the assistance of these questions by Wilentz. This excerpt illustrated how advocates can shape and focus the content of the story with the cooperation of a witness such as Lindbergh. In this case, the advocate succeeded in transforming "bits of evidence [the noise, the ladder, the time] into language terms that fit" the story of the prosecution (Bennett & Feldman, 1981, p. 125).

Inference. By itself, definition does not produce conclusive evidence to support a story. Definition needs to be followed by inferences about the meaning, relation, and/or significance of the definition. Bennett and Feldman (1981) explain that in most cases, the inference from the definition to the story of the case requires "blatant innuendo" (p. 126). In other words, the inference, made jointly by the advocate and witness, asks the jurors to make leaps from a definitional fact to the meaning of that fact to the story of the case.

Wilentz' direct questioning of Lindbergh led the witness to report hearing a sound resembling the cracking of wood and to conclude that the cracking was the sound of the ladder breaking. Then Wilentz encouraged Lindbergh to conclude the broken ladder had been used by the kidnapper and the break probably resulted in the fracture of the skull and eventual death of the baby. This segment of the direct examination showed how Wilentz extended the definition about the noise into an inference that the kidnapper killed the child when the ladder broke. The following excerpt shows how the prosecution attempted to prove the indictment:

W: Colonel, you stated, too, that some time during the evening through the flashlight of one of Hopewell's officers, you could see the ladder used in the distance?
L: Yes.
W: Eventually that ladder was brought into your home, was it not, that evening?
L: Yes it was. Whether it was before midnight on the evening or not, I am not sure, but during that night it was brought in. . . .
W: And will you tell us whether or not the ladder was strange to your premises . . . ?
L: It was a ladder I had never seen before. [Transcript of Record, p. 98]

Wilentz continued the questioning by asking him whether he saw a chisel and a dowel pin near the ladder. The conclusion to this sequence of questioning would not have been clear had it not been immediately preceded by these conclusions to the story in opening statement:

> He came there with the ladder, placed it against the house. He broke into and entered at night the Lindbergh home with the intent to commit battery on that child. . . . Then, as he went out that window and down that ladder of his, the ladder broke. He had more weight going down than he had going up. And down he went with the child. In the commission of that burglary that child was instantaneously killed. [Transcript of Record, p. 9]

In this segment of the direct examination, the meaning of the inferences thus becomes very clear. Lindbergh's job as a witness was to verify the relation and significance of this evidence to the prosecution's story of the case.

Validation. Whereas both definition and inference strategies establish the overall fit between the evidence in the case, validation refers to "the completeness, consistency, and plausibility" of each witnesses' story (Bennett & Feldman, 1981, p. 132). Completeness means that witnesses report all the information they know. Consistency refers to the internal fit of the evidence, and plausibility means the logical sense of the information presented. Advocates seek to elicit stories that possess these narrative qualities so that jurors will believe the testimony they hear. Attorneys can assist the completeness of testimony by questions they ask, and they can affect consistency and plausibility by interviewing the witnesses ahead of time, preparing them to testify, and using exhibits to refresh their recollections.

Wilentz asked very concise questions that aided the completeness of Lindbergh's testimony. Clearly, Lindbergh's testimony about the ladder was incomplete because he did not have empirical information to link the ladder to Hauptmann. However, Wilentz filled in these gaps by calling police investigators who reported the construction and strength of the ladder, and a wood expert who said the ladder came from the attic of Hauptmann's home. The completeness of any one witnesses' testimony depends on available information. When this information is limited, other witnesses need to complete the story with additional information.

Lindbergh's story seemed internally consistent because he recounted it in a clear chronological sequence according to precise time recollections. Lindbergh told the jurors he arrived home at

8:25, finished supper at 9:00, heard the wood-cracking noise at 9:15; and discovered the baby was missing at 10:00 (Transcript of Record, pp. 79–85).

The plausibility of Lindbergh's story was likely affected by the reputation of the storyteller, the well-known, respected, and revered American hero. Although some aspects of his testimony would not be credible if reported by an ordinary person, because Lindbergh said them they were believable. For example, Lindbergh claimed that he could positively identify Hauptmann by hearing two words "Hey Doc" over two years after he heard those words from a distance of sixty feet. Nonetheless, this quite remarkable identification seemed very reasonable to the jurors (Scaduto, 1976). At several points in his testimony, Lindbergh did not remember the chisel by the ladder, did not see other footprints in the mud below the child's window, and did not recall who was present the night of the crime. These omissions might have weakened the plausibility of most testimony but because of Lindbergh's reputation and the traumatic nature of the crime, the story seemed quite plausible to jurors and the public ("Who Killed the Lindbergh Baby?" 1982; Kennedy, 1985).

The storytelling of each witness is one small part of the narration of direct examination and even a smaller segment of the story of the trial as a whole. Each prosecution witness is still important to the trial because the jurors are instructed to render a verdict of guilty only when they are convinced "beyond a reasonable doubt." Therefore one inaccurate definition, ambiguous inference, or statement that leads jurors to believe the testimony is incomplete, inconsistent, or improbable might jeopardize the desired verdict.

Defense Strategies

The goal of the defense in direct interrogation is twofold; they must develop a coherent story of their own and, at the same time, cast doubt on the stories told by the prosecution. The major risk of direct examination is for the defense to spend too much time refuting and too little effort on the development of a narrative alternative to the story of the prosecution. Jeans (1975) and Mauet (1980) recommend the defense develop their own narrative in direct exam and refute the story of the prosecution primarily through cross-examination and closing argument. In direct questioning, the defense strategies are redefinition and reconstruction.

Redefinition. In order for the defense to introduce a plausible story of their own, they need to identify a story element from the prosecution that is sufficiently ambiguous so that it creates doubt. An advocate creates doubt by exploiting an obvious gap or hole in the prosecution's theory that will permit an alternative interpretation of the contested issues relating to the indictment (Bennett & Feldman, 1981). Redefinition strategies are likely to fail when the prosecution's story lacks ambiguities or gaps, the redefinition does not fit with the contested issues of the indictments, and the alternative theory is incomplete, inconsistent, or not plausible.

Even though the prosecution's story implicating Hauptmann was based primarily on circumstantial evidence, the preceding analysis shows that the definitions, inferences, and credibility were carefully crafted into a cohesive story. Clarence Darrow, one of the most famous lawyers of the era, publicly commented that he believed Wilentz had insufficient evidence to prove a murder charge against Hauptmann, although there might be sufficient evidence to prove extortion (Scaduto, 1976; Kennedy, 1985). Instead of pursuing the lack of evidence for murder, the obvious gap in the prosecution's story, and redefining the indictment into a lesser charge, Reilly chose a different tack. In their pretrial depositions, several witnesses had claimed that more than one person was involved in the kidnapping. However, the prosecution intentionally ignored these references to other persons that had appeared in the ransom notes, the depositions of Condon and of two taxi drivers, and the statements of several occurrence witnesses for both sides. Thus, Reilly's tack was to redefine the kidnapping as a conspiracy involving several persons. Later Reilly redefined some of the key evidence.

The defense's redefinition of the nature of the crime was cast in two parts: first, Reilly showed that Hauptmann was not at the scene of the crime; and next, he claimed that the crime was likely committed by more than one person. Hauptmann's alibi, recounted in this excerpt, served as the justification for redefining the crime as a conspiracy involving several people. Reilly established the alibi in the following questions to Hauptmann:

R: What time did you go back and call for Anna?
H: I was there around 7 o'clock.
R: Well, tell us what you did there that night.
H: When I came down, I usually got my supper first. I took the police dog [belonging to the owners of the bakery] out . . . on the street sometimes for half an hour. . . .

91

R: You remember meeting a man that talked to you about that dog?

H: I do.

R: On March lst?

H: Yes.

R: At about what time of the night?

H: I would say it would be between eight and half past eight.

R: What did you do? Did you bring the dog back to the restaurant?

H: Oh yes.

R: What time did you and your wife leave there? . . .

H: It was after 9 o'clock. I can't remember the exact time. [Transcript of Record, pp. 2453–54]

In this excerpt, the defense laid the foundation for an alternative story, one that would overtly contradict the narrative of the prosecution. Reilly presented four witnesses, immediately following the testimony of Hauptmann, who confirmed the possibility of a conspiracy. One witness claimed he saw a car with a ladder on top, traveling to Hopewell with two men inside. Another testified there were several sets of footprints beneath the window of the Lindbergh home. Still another witness said the ladder revealed several sets of fingerprints. Finally, a passerby remembered three men at the cemetery on the night when the ransom notes were passed. The conspiracy theory redefined the crime but the evidence was not sufficiently complete to make the story credible since only four witnesses confirmed the story compared to dozens of others who denied this story.

Reilly's second strategy was to redefine the key evidence presented by the state that seemed to verify that the ransom notes were written by Hauptmann. In this segment of testimony, the defense tried to show that the misspellings in samples of Hauptmann's writing secured in the interrogation were not spontaneous, but that instead these statements were dictated by the police:

R: Now, in the station what did they do to you if anything?

H: The first thing they required the request writing.

R: Yes, now in writing did you spell the words of your own free will or did they tell you how to spell the words?

H: Some of them words they spell it to me.

R: How do you spell "not"?

H: N-o-t.

R: Did they ask you to spell n-o-t-e?

H: I remember very well they put an "e" on it.
R: How do you spell "signature"?
H: S-i-g-n-u-t-u-r-e.
R: Did they tell you to spell s-i-n-g?
H: They did.
R: N-a-t-u-r-e?
H: They did.
R: So when they were dictating the spelling, that was not your own free will in spelling, was it?
H: It was not. [Transcript of Record, pp. 2526–27]

The jurors' belief in this redefinition depended on whether they would accept Hauptmann's version of the interrogation or that of the police.

The redefinition of the defense did respond to a gap in the prosecution's story, and they used that gap to build an alternative narrative that related to the indictment. However, as a competing explanation, the redefinition lacked completeness and plausibility. The conspiracy narrative was validated by the same four witnesses, persons whose credentials were severely impugned by Wilentz' cross-examination. The spelling dictation was not corroborated by other defense witnesses and was denied by several officers who were present at the interrogation and testified for the prosecution. For these reasons, the redefinition did not produce a believable alternative story to that presented by the state.

Reconstruction. The reconstruction of the prosecution's story by the defense should place "the central action in the context of an entirely new story to show that it merits a different interpretation" (Bennett & Feldman, 1981, p. 104). During Hauptmann's six days of testimony, the reconstruction of the story developed in three segments of approximately equal length—the Hauptmann biography, the guilt of Fisch, and the role of Fisch in Hauptmann's financial transactions.

Reilly curiously began the reconstruction by focusing on Hauptmann's biography. This is an unorthodox method of reconstruction for several reasons. The testimony emphasized the defendant's German background at a time when Hitler had risen to power in Germany and when Americans held anti-German feelings. The testimony also accentuated Hauptmann's criminal record, information that seemed to implicate rather than absolve him of involvement in the kidnapping. Finally, the testimony stressed the sporadic work history as well as the financial instability of the defendant. The following segment illustrates these incriminating biographical details:

93

R: Now, during the period of reconstruction in Germany, about 1919 and 1929, you were convicted of some offense there, is that correct?

H: I was. . . .

R: And as a result of that did you serve any sentence?

H: Yes.

R: Where?

H: Beuthen, Beutthen.

R: And afterward, you were paroled?

H: Yes. [Transcript of Record, p. 2400]

The defense probably elaborated Hauptmann's biography to inoculate the jury, that is, to give jurors a weak dose of the arguments they had heard in the media and then explain those charges. However, by introducing these facts into direct examination, the defense established the subject matter as part of the legitimate scope of questioning, thus the content could be brought up by Wilentz in his cross-examination of Hauptmann. Reilly's reconstruction strategy had two distinct disadvantages as trial narrative. The information was presented first in Hauptmann's direct examination generating a primacy effect, that is, this information would be more likely to be remembered by the jury than had it appeared in a different order in the interrogation process. Additionally, the negative biographical data harmed rather than helped the credibility of the subsequent testimony that Hauptmann was to give over the next five days.

Reilly's reconstruction of the central action, the kidnapping and murder implicating Fisch, was a more conventional strategy. Several facts of the prosecution story could be recast by the implication of Fisch: this theory could explain the ransom notes since Fisch was a German; account for the German accent of the kidnapper heard by Condon and Lindbergh; provide an explanation of the kidnap ransom money found in Hauptmann's garage and spent by him; and give reasons for the large stock transactions made by the carpenter when he was receiving a small salary. However, the story could not account for the ladder, the wood in the ladder, the death of the child, or offer a motive for crime.

The defense's narrative reconstruction began in this segment of the direct examination of Hauptmann:

R: Well, before he [Fisch] sailed did he leave anything with you to take care of while he was in Europe?

H: Well, he left two suit cases.

R: What else?
H: Four hundred skins, Hudson seals.
R: What else?
H: And a little box. . . .
R: Now this little box . . . what kind of box was it? . . . carton, cardboard?
H: Yes.
R: Now will you describe to the jury what circumstances it was he left this shoe box with you . . . ?
H: Well, of Mr. Fisch request it was he was throwing a party when he left for Chermany. . . . We invited a couple of friends . . . Fisch came out and got a little bundle under his arm. . . . He came out and we went in the kitchen and he said, "I leave it . . . if you don't mind, keep care of it and put it in a tight place." [Transcript of Record, pp. 2447–48]

Hauptmann continued with the story placing Fisch in the major role involving the disputed issues of the case. Hauptmann explained that he took the money, placed it on the top shelf of his broom closet, and forgot about the box until a rain storm came and leaked on the box. When he found the box rain soaked, the defendant said he opened it up and realized it contained $15,000 in gold notes. By the time he found the money, he had learned of Fisch's death in Germany. Because Fisch owed him several thousand dollars, Hauptmann decided to spend the money because he had no knowledge it was ransom money. The connection with Fisch also explained the many large bank deposits and stock market transactions made by Hauptmann when he was not working.

Just as with the story of the prosecution, the reconstructed story of the defense needed to define facts, connect these facts to issues by inferences, and present a credible story that was complete, internally consistent, and plausible. Although the Fisch reconstruction attempted to meet these standards, it failed on several counts. Hauptmann could define the fact of his relationship with Fisch but no other witness could verify his definition that the money really came from Fisch. If jurors were to accept the story, they would have to make some huge inferences from the established fact that Fisch was a business partner who gave him the box to the conclusion that Fisch was also the kidnapper and the man who killed the child. These inferences were not logical ones for jurors to make because the story of the defense was incomplete, not corroborated by a significant number or quality of witnesses, and lacked internal consistency. Wilentz pointed out the inconsistency of the story when, in cross-examination, he got Hauptmann to admit he told no one about the money, lied about the money when he was arrested, and buried the money in his garage. If Hauptmann had innocently come by the money, Wilentz reasoned, why did he make such deliberate efforts to conceal it. In this way, Wilentz seemed to create reasonable doubt about the reconstructed narrative of the defense.

Evaluation of Narrative Persuasion

Not all narratives are equally persuasive. In addition to the points already discussed, several additional factors are likely to distinguish between narratives that are likely to persuade jurors from those that are not persuasive.

First, stories "serve a screening function" (Bennett & Feldman, 1981, p. 148); that is, the narrative includes some data and excludes other information. In particular, stories can exclude some essential information. For example, in the Hauptmann case, neither side produced a murder weapon, identified the time of the murder, or directly implicated the defendant to the murder. Because the prosecutor made more believable inferences than the defense, the jurors convicted the defendant on a charge of first degree murder.

Stories can also include extraneous material, not related to the indictments but part of the narrative, such as the ethnic background and social status of the characters involved in the central action. These extraneous factors enter into jurors' decisions when they are relevant to the disputed issues of the case. For example, Reilly developed the following character description of the defendant: He came to the United States illegally as a stowaway on a ship; was convicted of burglary and served time in prison; worked sporadically; engaged in questionable business ventures; and spent time with another woman while his wife was in Europe. Because these biographical factors made Hauptmann a suspect burglar and an untrustworthy person, jurors likely had little difficulty concluding that he probably committed the crime.

Second, Fisher (1984) notes that in order for stories to work persuasively, they must meet the standard of narrative fidelity, that is, fit with the beliefs and commonsense understanding of listeners. In a criminal trial, a story may be accurate, but if it does not "ring true" with the experiences of jurors they will not be persuaded. Considering that 1934 was part of the Great Depression, marked by the rise to power of Hitler, the prosecution's story about a convicted burglar and illegal immigrant who was an out of work carpenter committing the crime made more sense than the competing story of the defense. And for the jurors living in the depression, the story of someone discovering thousands of dollars in a shoe box, burying the money, and spending it without telling anyone the source of the bills, must have lacked fidelity. Rather than fitting with their commonsense understandings, the story more likely resembled fantasy.

Third, Kalven and Zeisel's (1966) research on jurors provides guidelines about what narrative factors enter into jurors' decisions. They discovered that a previous conviction for a similar offense increases the likelihood of conviction and that defendants whose victims were perceived as "good people" by jurors often received more severe sentences. Both of these features were part of the stories of the Hauptmann case. Hauptmann was previously convicted of burglary, part of Wilentz' verbal allegations against him in opening statement, and Lindbergh was held in very high esteem by Americans in general and presumably these jurors as well. Moreover, the state seemed to recognize the mystique that Lindbergh had with the jury because they insisted that he sit at the prosecution table during the entire case. This fact may well have sustained the public feeling that a good man had suffered at the hands of the defendant. Even though this research on juror decisions postdates the trial by thirty years, it still offers clues about how the stories likely were interpreted by the jurors in the case.

Finally, much of the popular literature on trial advocacy (Keeton, 1973; Kelner & McGovern, 1981; Mindes & Acock, 1982) suggests that the attitude and image of the storyteller affects how the story is evaluated. These sources give the following advice: Storytellers (attorneys and their witnesses) should appear well prepared, convey a strong belief in the stories they tell, show a sincere attitude, and recount the story in an orderly and logical way. Although the transcript does not provide information about these factors, both film clips from the trial and observers suggest how the storytellers acted. Whipple (1937) reported that Defense Attorney Reilly was a flashy dresser, had an aggressive manner, and expressed an arrogant attitude, which alienated the rural New Jersey jurors. Whipple's view is confirmed by Ethel Stockton, the only living juror from the trial, in an interview for PBS television ("Who Killed the Lindbergh Baby?" 1982). Stockton says that the jury disliked Reilly because he was aloof and boastful. She claimed he was unprepared and sometimes came to court drunk. In contrast, she said Wilentz was articulate, well-prepared, and convincing.

Stockton also remarked that jurors felt compassion for Lindbergh and disdain for Hauptmann. Thus, according to Stockton, the key storytellers of the prosecution were more persuasive than those of the defense.

Our analysis of the storytelling of direct examination has considered the Hauptmann case, yet the theory is equally applicable to other trials in this volume, and to contemporary trials. The perspective explains how direct questioning should be conducted, how the prosecution and defense should construct the stories, and why some stories are more persuasive for jurors than the competing narratives.

Specifically, this chapter explains how storytelling works as the preferred mode of communication in direct examination. First, the story of the case prefaced in the opening statement should be a brief scenario of the story each side of the case upholds and elaborates through direct examination. Second, advocates can enhance the cohesiveness of their story by their selection of a variety of competent witnesses, a carefully planned arrangement of testimony, and a logically connected cast of witnesses. Third, the strategy of the prosecution features definition, inference, and validation strategies; whereas the defense uses redefinition and reconstruction. Finally, stories are persuasive when they intentionally screen out factors that they cannot substantiate with evidence, and introduce extraneous evidence, implicating the guilt or innocence of their client, that ring true with the experiences of jurors, incorporate juror-sensitive data into the stories, and establish witness credibility.

Storytelling is both an art and a skill of trial advocacy and the practice is best illustrated by the way attorneys and witnesses jointly create or fail to create persuasive stories through direct examination.

A Legal Scholar's Reaction

Kenneth S. Broun

The Hauptmann trial and the more than fifty years of controversy that it has engendered serve as an example of the limitations inherent in any judicial system. No trial can guarantee that the truth will emerge. The best of trials can only achieve a rational solution to a dispute. When a case has achieved the notoriety of the Hauptmann case, we can be certain that the truthfulness of the result will be questioned for as long as the incident piques the interest of scholars and journalists. The important question is whether a rational result was achieved.

Under the Anglo-American adversary system, we seek to achieve a rational solution by calling on each party to present its best case to the trier of fact. The effectiveness of the system depends upon the effectiveness of the advocates in presenting their cases. An advocate cannot act as a seeker of truth. The system depends on a controlled partisanship. An advocate must serve as the playwright, producer, director, and principal actor in a play designed to persuade the trier of fact that his or her view should prevail. When both sides make the most dramatic, most persuasive presentations possible, the adversary system works at its best.

The advocate as playwright creates the questions and thus the answers that will make up the presentation of each witness. Although he or she must take the facts as they exist, the advocate must make sure that all available facts are discovered and that the witnesses present those facts in a manner likely to make the most impact on the jury. Just as the playwright orders the acts and scenes, the advocate determines the order of witnesses and the order of the

Kenneth S. Broun is Dean and Professor of Law at the University of North Carolina. He was engaged in the private practice law in Illinois before joining the faculty at the North Carolina, where he currently teaches courses in civil procedure, evidence, and trial and appellate practice. Professor Broun is the author of several law books including: Charles T. McCormick's *Handbook on Evidence* (co-author); National Institute for Trial Advocacy, *Problems and Cases* (with James H. Seckinger); *Evidence*, Black Letter Series (with Walker S. Blakey). He also has been a Team Teaching Leader and Director for the National Institute for Trial Advocacy.

testimony for each witness. As noted in this chapter, the concepts of primacy and recency are important factors, but secondary to the more basic tenet of understanding. Most good lawyers will stay as close as possible to chronological order in their examinations of witnesses. Juries understand things better in orderly time sequences. They cannot be persuaded by what they do not understand.

The advocate is also the producer; he or she must find the resources to gather witnesses and information for presentation. When resources are limited or unbalanced between the sides, greater ingenuity is needed. Counterattacks need to be waged against expensive expert witnesses called by the other side. In criminal cases, court funds may be available for the calling of experts. The services of other experts may be obtained by appealing to a sense of duty.

No matter how much money is available to one side or the other, the basic resources—the facts and the fact witnesses—are a given. Unlike the playwright, the advocate is bound by reality. The witnesses in the Hauptmann case, even for the defense, were a cut above the drug-pushers and police informants typically found on both sides of a 1980s criminal prosecution. However, the contrast between the two sets of witnesses in the Hauptmann case presented a reality that was at least a hurdle and at a worst a fatal flaw in the defense case. The Lindberghs on one side and the immigrant, low-life German in the time of Hitler was a contrast that would have presented a challenge for the best and the most diligent of advocates. Yet, from the facts presented in the chapter, it seems that the defense counsel lacked either the skill or the diligence to begin to solve his problem. The extent of the direct examination concerning Hauptmann's background exacerbated the defendant's dilemma. Defense counsel will often decide to bring out a harmful conviction on direct examination in order to minimize the sting of a dramatic disclosure on cross-examination. However, as in this case, the decision is sometimes a bad one that leaves the jury with more of a recollection of the conviction than of the forthrightness of the defendant/witness. The object of a direct examination is as much to build up the credibility of a witness as it is to have him or her testify to the facts. Unless the disclosure of a conviction will, on balance, add to credibility, it should be left out of direct examination.

The advocate is also bound by the rules of the trial—the law of evidence. The prescribed structure of questions, the liability to interruption by objection, and the whims of the trial judge all serve to make a presentation of a case at law a very different kind of drama. The lawyer who best knows the rules is obviously at an advantage. The time to worry about evidentiary problems is not when an advocate or an opponent is asking a question or getting an answer. Rather, as part of the preparation, questions must be framed in a way not only to be understandable and thus persuasive to the jury, but also to be the least likely to evoke an interruption by way of an objection. At times, however, the rules of evidence will bend, if not break. In Wilentz' direct examination of Lindbergh concerning the noise of the ladder breaking, the key question was: "Was it the sort of a noise that would come with the falling of a ladder?" The question was clearly leading and objectionable. For advocacy and evidentiary reasons, it is ordinarily better to let a witness tell his own story without leading. Yet, the insertion of a leading question at a critical point such as this may be the turning point in the trial. Examining counsel must use the leading question judiciously; his opponent must be alert to stop it if he or she can.

As in the Hauptmann trial, the job of defense counsel is often far more difficult that that of the prosecution. To be sure, a prosecutor must be organized, thorough, and imaginative. But often, the prosecutor will have the case ready for trial just by reference to the police or investigator's report. In most instances, the *prima facie* case is obvious. The defense, on the other hand, must always make a more subtle decision—to attack or to reconstruct the events. Most often defense counsel seeks only to attack. Their case depends more upon cross-examination and summation than on the presentation of their own witnesses. Theoretically at least, the burden of proof is on the prosecution to prove the defendant guilty beyond a reasonable doubt. If some doubt can be cast, the defendant may come away victorious. To the extent that any direct evidence is introduced at all, defense counsel may simply call a series of witnesses whose testimony is more calculated to divert the jury from the actual facts than to present a coherent alternative theory of the case. Sometimes the "sand in the eyes" approach is used out of desperation; the defendant has no real proof. Sometimes it is used out of sloppiness or poor preparation. Where the defendant actually seeks to redefine the prosecution's case, actually to present his own version of the events, he takes a significant risk. Unless he or she can present a story that is at least as coherent as that of the prosecution's, he or she runs the risk of losing by comparison. Thus, in the Hauptmann trial, the attempts of the defendant to reconstruct the events fell short and ultimately cost the defendant dearly. As stated in the chapter's analysis, the prosecutor was able to create "reasonable doubt about the reconstructed narrative of the defense." Thus, despite the fact that the law always requires the prosecution to prove its case beyond a reasonable doubt, an attempt by the defense to reconstruct the events may result in those tables being turned.

In addition to being the playwright and the producer, the advocate is also the director and the principal actor. Witnesses must be prepared to give their best stories in the form most favorable to the client. For example, it is not inappropriate for counsel to direct a witness to look at him or her or at the jury when giving a particular response. Similarly, counsel must recognize that one's client may be judged by what the jury thinks of counsel. Where a client is particularly attractive, counsel tends to fade into the background. Wilentz had an easy job representing a national hero. Reilly's job was infinitely more difficult, but he apparently let his own personality interfere with his client's case rather than help it.

The adversary system depends on the skill and diligence of advocates to achieve rationality. We all have different skill levels. It is preparation that is the great equalizer. The chapter on the Hauptmann case suggests that preparation may have been the difference in life or death to Bruno Richard Hauptmann, just as it has been to countless other men and women.

4
Reshaping the Stories of the Adversary: Cross-Examination in the Sacco-Vanzetti Case

In contrast to the direct examiner who creates the story, the cross-examiner refutes and reshapes the narrative accounts presented by the adversary. The Sacco-Vanzetti case is an exemplar of positive and negative approaches to cross-examination. This chapter explains the recommended approaches to interrogation, showing how the advocate should reshape the story of the case through the functions, strategies, and refutative methods. The chapter also outlines how advocates can be more persuasive by adopting communicative tactics such as postures, rules, and maneuvers. Finally, the chapter shows how the cross-examination process can be abused through issue, procedural, and semantic diversions.

The arrest and trial of Sacco and Vanzetti took place during the Palmer raids, the Red Scare, and the deportation of hundreds of aliens under the Alien and Sedition Acts. Sacco worked as a shoemaker and Vanzetti as a fish peddler, and both men actively participated in anarchist groups. The two men were indicted for the murder and payroll robbery of a paymaster and guard of a shoe factory in Braintree, Massachusetts. After the verdict, the trial became a celebrated example of the martyrdom of innocent immigrant workers for the labor movement. The case rallied the international and national labor groups in support of the Sacco-Vanzetti Defense Fund. The verdict also resulted in thousands of laborers joining together to protest against what they claimed was an unjust verdict based only on circumstantial evidence. Despite the vehement protests, Sacco and Vanzetti were executed.

Just as the Haymarket defendants, Sacco and Vanzetti embraced principles of anarchism, participating in demonstrations and distributing literature of this radical group. Most scholars believe the defendants were arrested, not because of any solid evidence, but because they were anarchists, appeared to be unpatriotic, and were considered "dangerous" alien influences. The trial of Sacco and Vanzetti was not as blatantly ideological as the Haymarket case. In fact, the case evolved into a rather typical murder trial until the twenty-seventh day, at which time the prosecutor cross-examined Sacco.

The Trial

Nicola Sacco and Bartolomeo Vanzetti were arrested on May 5, 1920, for the murders of Fredrick A. Parmenter and Alessandro Berardelli, the paymaster and security guard at the Slater-Morrill Shoe Factory in Braintree, Massachusetts. The victims were murdered and robbed as they left building number two carrying a payroll of $16,000.00. Three weeks after the crime, Sacco and Vanzetti were arrested at a garage where they had gone to pick up a vehicle that police had identified as the getaway car from the murder. At the time they were taken into custody, the defendants carried guns and possessed papers identifying them as anarchists. In fact, Sacco's gun was of the same type as the weapon used in the murder of Berardelli. When the defendants were first interrogated by police, they lied about their actions on April 15, the day of the crime.

The murder trial of Sacco and Vanzetti opened on May 31, 1921, in Dedham, Massachusetts. Frederick G. Katzmann led the prosecution team for the Commonwealth of Massachusetts. His assistants included Harold P. Williams, William F. Kane, and George E. Adams. Jeremiah J. McAnarney and Thomas F. McAnarney acted as defense attorneys for Vanzetti; Fred H. Moore and William J. Callahan served as the advocates for Sacco. The Sacco-Vanzetti Defense Fund, organized after the arrest of the defendants, hired and paid the defense attorneys. Judge Webster Thayer presided at the trial.

After deliberating for five hours on July 14, 1921, the jurors returned a verdict of "guilty of murder in the first degree" for both Sacco and Vanzetti. Even though the trial itself moved quickly to its completion in five weeks, the appeal process took six years. On August 22, 1927, both men were executed. The death of the defendants, however, did not close the debate surrounding the trial of Sacco and Vanzetti. Forty years after the trial, Justice William O. Douglas (1969) characterized the case in this way:

> The Sacco-Vanzetti trial was a highly sophisticated affair. The judge, honest and dedicated, was fiercely partisan. The jury was picked as a "hanging jury." The community was saturated with fear of foreigners. . . . The trial itself was infected with extraneous, irrelevant, and highly prejudicial testimony. [Transcript of Record, p. xv]

In fact, the case has been continually retried and reanalyzed by historians and legal experts in over a dozen books and scores of essays. These sources seek an answer to the question: Did Sacco and Vanzetti commit the crime? Some sources say no (Fraenkel, 1931; Musmanno, 1939; Joughin & Morgan, 1948; Frankfurter, 1960; Ehrmann, 1969; Feuerlicht, 1977; Young & Kaiser, 1985). Other sources acknowledge the guilt of Sacco but question the involvement of Vanzetti (Sinclair, 1928; Montgomery, 1960; Russell, 1971).

The purpose of this essay is to investigate the methods of cross-examination and to show how interrogation is used to refute and reshape the story of the case presented by the opposition. To accomplish this purpose, the essay (1) summarizes the historical background of the Sacco-Vanzetti case; (2) explicates approaches to the content of cross-examination according to its function, strategy, and refutation methods; (3) explains the persuasive strategies used to embellish the content, including postures, rules, and maneuvers; (4) illustrates negative aspects of interrogation by showing how the prosecution's cross-examination of Sacco diverted the trial into political arenas; and (5) shows implications of the study for other trials.

Historical Background

Although sixty years have elapsed since the Sacco-Vanzetti trial, this case remains interesting because of the social and political circumstances surrounding the event, including the Red Scare, the Palmer raids, the labor unrest, and the Alien and Sedition Acts.

Between 1919 and 1920, the American public became "completely preoccupied with the Bolshevik menace" (Levin, 1971, p. 52). The signs of this menace appeared in the form of 1,400 labor strikes occurring nationwide between March and August of 1919. This unrest took place during the Red Scare, the period of national hysteria resulting from Americans' fears about communists, anarchists, and Bolsheviks. Murray (l964) explains this labor unrest created polarization between strikers and nonstrikers and between aliens and nonaliens. Moreover, the press encouraged this polarization and intensified the fears of the public about foreign dissidents. The press' attacks on the strikers were particularly vehement in the Boston area, close to the homes of Sacco and Vanzetti.

Feuerlicht (1977) believes the Red Scare was part of a "national nervous breakdown" brought on by the increase in left-wing groups—communists, socialists, anarchists, and syndicalists; the flu epidemic that killed 500,000 Americans; the frequent labor strikes; and the economic slowdown caused by reduced production after World War I. During this time, thousands of immigrants arrived in the United States from Eastern and Southern Europe; many were Italians, including Sacco and Vanzetti.

These internal changes resulted in the development of laws restricting the activity of immigrants and aliens. In 1918, the Sedition Act made it illegal to "utter, print, write, or publish" any information using "disloyal, scurrilous or abusive language" about the United States government and to advocate "curtailment of . . . product or products necessary or essential to the prosecution of the war" (198 Amend., 40 Stat. 553 [1918]). The Deportation Act of 1918 legalized the expulsion of any alien who believed in anti-American ideas or belonged to anti-American groups. Nearly two-thousand persons were prosecuted and hundreds deported under these acts (Chaffee, 1969), and others were arrested on criminal charges because of their beliefs.

The Alien and Sedition and the Deportation Acts together became the legal basis for massive raids on the homes and workplaces of noncitizens. The United States attorney general, A. Mitchell Palmer, conducted these raids, made many arrests without warrants, denied counsel to those arrested, and forced confessions from them (Feuerlicht, 1977, p. 58). A few months prior to the jailing of the defendants, Palmer took credit for the arrest of four thousand radicals, including some Italian anarchists who were close associates of Sacco and Vanzetti. Young and Kaiser (1985) conclude that many of the tactics of the Palmer raids were used in the arrest of Sacco and Vanzetti.

Because the legal and political climate spawned the Red Scare, the tough anti-alien laws, and the Palmer raids, it is not surprising that two Italian immigrants, active in anarchist causes, were suspects for an unsolved crime in the vicinity where they lived and worked.

This climate of opinion has led legal commentators such as Justice Douglas (1969) to conclude that Sacco-Vanzetti was "an ideological trial that took place behind the facade of a legal trial" (p. xlvii). Our analysis of the case reveals that a large part of the trial was not overtly ideological; the case became political, however, when the defendants gave their testimony. Frankfurter and Jackson (1960) support this opinion: "Up to the time Sacco and Vanzetti testified to their radical activities, their pacifism and their flight to Mexico to escape the draft, the trial was for murder and banditry; with the cross-examination of Sacco and Vanzetti, patriotism and radicalism became the dominant emotional issues" (p. 345).

Despite the fact that the interrogation of the defendants was blatantly political, most of the trial record exemplified skillful and thorough cross-examination by advocates on both sides. In the following segment, the chapter explicates the approaches to the content of cross-examination using illustrations of effective inter-rogation from both the prosecution and defense in the Sacco-Van-zetti case.

Approaches to the Content of Cross-Examination

In most criminal trials, advocates develop their theories of the case in narrative form. Our analysis of the Haymarket case demonstrates how the opening statement outlines the story, and our study of the Hauptmann trial shows how direct examiners extract the various parts of the story from their witnesses. Here we emphasize how advocates pursue cross-examination to refute the story of the opposing counsel by discrediting the witnesses who are storytellers and disputing the facts essential to the development of the story, thereby raising doubts about the probability and fidelity of the opponents' theory of the case. This first part of the analysis of cross-examination, in terms of content, includes the function, strategy, and refutative methods.

Function

The function of cross-examination is explained in various ways. Mauet (1980) associates successful questioning with two functions: it elicits testimony favorable to one's own theory or story of the case and discredits the credibility of the witnesses of opposing counsel. Using the language of storytelling, we may say that cross-examiners reinforce their own narrative by corroborating facts essential

107

to their own story while, at the same time, they try to destroy the credentials of the storyteller-witnesses, identify gaps in the accounts of witnesses, and thereby dispute the credibility of each witness' narrative.

Rather than conceiving of cross-examination as the destruction of a segment of opposing counsel's theory or story, Lannuzzi (1981) conceives of interrogation as the reshaping or retelling of the narrative. Specifically, he explains: The function of cross-examination is to reshape "adversaries' evidence into pieces, which by the end of the trial will fit together with the advocate's own evidence," forming a "mosaic of fact" that supports the case (p. 8). Both Lannuzzi and Mauet agree the function of the interrogation is to recast the story of witnesses so their responses support, elaborate, or verify one's own theory or story.

The competing stories of the prosecution and defense in the Sacco-Vanzetti case are suggested by the summaries of the opening statement presented by both sides of the case. Prosecutor Williams crafted his tale of murder and burglary into scenes. He described how Parmenter and Berardelli received the payroll in the presence of two short, stocky Italian men who waited for them, seized the money, and shot the paymaster and guard in broad daylight with many witnesses present. Then the assailants disappeared in a large, dark, getaway car. This car was concealed for twenty days in a private garage until Sacco and Vanzetti went to retrieve the car and were arrested for the crime. According to Williams, several witnesses identified the defendants as two of the men who had been at the scene of the crime at the Slater-Morrill Shoe Factory. Williams further claimed that Sacco and Vanzetti lied at the time of their arrest and that these lies were evidence of the guilt of the defendants (Transcript of Record, pp. 2325–34). This story was pieced together by fifty-nine prosecution witnesses.

Defense attorney Callahan chronicled a quite different story in the opening statement of the defense. His narrative began with biographical sketches of the defendants and an explanation of their activities on April 15, the day of the crime. He described Vanzetti as an immigrant who was a conscientious but unskilled laborer who made his living selling fish. Sacco, on the other hand, was a skilled craftsman who made shoes. Callahan claimed that both men closely identified with their Italian heritage and that their actions could be explained by their cultural loyalties. On the day of the crime, Sacco was in Boston seeking a passport to return to Italy to visit his sick mother, and Vanzetti was selling fish in an area close to his home in Plymouth, Massachusetts. Callahan concluded his story by summarizing how the defense witnesses would demonstrate that persons with very different appearances from the defendants committed the crime. Furthermore the defense inferred that because the prosecution witnesses had changed their stories so many times prior to the trial, they lacked credibility. Additionally, the defense claimed the defendants lied at the time of their arrest because they feared being deported for their radical beliefs (Transcript of Record, pp. 2760–65). The defense called ninety-nine different witnesses to piece together their story.

Strategy

Whereas the function refers to the goal of cross-examination, the strategy focuses on who should be questioned and the extent to which the questioning can refute or reshape the story of the opposition. Since the direct examiner selects the number and order of witnesses and controls the scope of the examination, the cross-examiner's choices are limited to the selection of those who will be examined and the extent and focus of the interrogation.

The decision of who should be examined depends on several factors. Bailey and Rothblatt (1971) claim, first, that only witnesses who damage an advocate's theory or story should be interrogated. The only circumstance for examining a witness who has not rebutted the opposition's story is when the witness knows additional facts that were not brought out in direct examination. Second, advocates should examine witnesses who have a central role in the case because of their proximity to the crime, their ability to give eyewitness accounts, their victimage, the accusations against them, or the unique information they have about the circumstances of the crime. Third, advocates should interrogate witnesses whose responses on direct examination are flawed, that is, whose answers are inconsistent with their depositions, other witnesses, or pretrial records. Finally, advocates should seek to discredit witnesses on grounds that their stories are biased, inaccurate, or otherwise incredible. This means that advocates should interrogate most witnesses, although the method and the focus of questioning will change from witness to witness.

Mauet (1980) describes the extent of questioning as either brief or thorough. A brief interrogation occurs when advocates wish simply to meet the expectations of jurors that all witnesses should be questioned. In this case, advocates either conduct a brief line of

109

inquiry that elicits facts favorable to their own theory of the case, or they attempt to refute one particular fact presented by the witness. In contrast, thorough examinations are extensive efforts to refute the facts of the case or the credentials of the storyteller and thereby reshape the narrative of opposing counsel.

Because of the function and strategy of cross-examination, certain types of witnesses are likely to receive very brief, and others very thorough, interrogation. For the prosecution, occurrence and expert witnesses are often the key storytellers. Cross-examiners often are most concerned with occurrence witnesses, who identify people, objects, locations, or other facts essential to the introduction of exhibits and the depiction of the details of the alleged crime.

Both the prosecution and the defense call expert witnesses to explain the technical details relevant to the actions and effects of the alleged crime. Advocates for both sides interrogate and discredit the experts of the opposition in order to verify their own story of the case. Expert witnesses vary depending on the facts of the case and may range from police to forensic pathologists, ballistics experts to handwriting analysts, and psychiatrists to physicists.

Key witnesses for the defense verify the alibis or the reputation of the defendants. Alibi witnesses often conclude that the defendants were in a location different from the one in which the crime occurred, or they were occupied in activities prohibiting them from committing the crime or both. The testimony of alibi witnesses is used directly to contradict the information of the occurrence witnesses called by the prosecution. Reputation witnesses, on the other hand, testify about the background and character of the defendants.

Of the ninety-nine witnesses called by the defense, fifteen were alibi witnesses (ten testifying for Sacco and five for Vanzetti). The defense called eight reputation witnesses. Nearly all of the other defense witnesses rebutted the testimony of the occurrence witnesses of the prosecution. The following two segments of testimony illustrate the difference between brief and thorough examination. In the first example, defense attorney Callahan called Angelo Guidabone as a reputation witness for Vanzetti. Guidabone testified he had known the defendant for six and one-half years; had seen him at about a quarter past twelve on April 15; and had received some codfish from Vanzetti for his lunch. The witness explained that he remembered the day because he had undergone an appendicitis operation on April 19 (Transcript of Record, p. 3025).

Katzmann followed with this brief examination to discredit the witness about the facts related to time:

K: I take it Mr. Guidabone, that the fact you were operated on
        on April 19th makes you remember you bought some fish on
        the 15th. Is that it?

G: Yes.

K: And that is the only thing that makes you remember it?

G: Well, the operation and that, because I was very careful what
        I was eating.

K: Do you think the codfish caused the appendicitis?

G: No, No, No.

K: What is the connection between your operation the 19th and
        your buying codfish on the 15th?

G: It had nothing to do with it. . . .

K: Did you have a pain on the 15th?

G: No sir, I did not. On the 17th, I did. . . .

K: But you remember codfish on the 15th day, is that right?

G: Yes.

K: Now being operated on the 19th for appendicitis, you could
        have bought codfish just as well on the 14th, couldn't you?

G: . . . On the 15th I got the fish in my hand and I had it.

K: Could you have bought the fish on the 13th and been oper-
        ated on the 19th?

G: Well you want me to buy the fish months before and eat it
        months after— . . .

K: Well how can you say it was the 15th and not on the 13th
        [that] the fish was put right in your hand and you had it?

G: Because it was not so. Because it was not so. [Transcript of
        Record, pp. 3025-26]

In this brief interrogation, Katzmann emphasized only one fact, the
date of the purchase of the fish. He demonstrated the witness could
not pinpoint the date and thereby discredited the testimony. This
discrediting also refuted the story of the defense that Vanzetti was
selling fish in Plymouth on the day of the crime.

The defense conducted a thorough cross-examination with Lewis
Wade, purported to be the star witness of the prosecution prior to
the trial. Katzmann's direct examination showed that Wade was
working at the entrance of the shoe factory at the time of the crime,
saw the gunmen shoot the paymaster and guard, observed the stealing of the money box and the getaway, called the police, and attended to Berardelli, who was still alive after the shooting. Despite
Wade's close proximity to and involvement with the crime, he failed
to identify either Sacco or Vanzetti in a definitive statement. Katzmann tried to secure the identification of the defendant in this
segment of direct examination:

111

K: And will you tell the jury if the man you . . . saw who did the shooting that day, is in the courtroom?
W: I would not say for sure.
K: What is your best judgment?
W: Well he resembles, . . . looks somewhat— . . .
K: And which is the man you say "he resembles—"? . . .
W.   The man on my left in the cage. . . .
K: Point him out, the one you mean.
W: The man with the black hair. . . .
K: As you are looking now, which man in the cage do you say?
W: The man with the black hair on the end of the cage.
K: Do you know what his name is?
W: Sacco. [Transcript of Record, p. 2373]

Defense attorney J. McAnarney and Prosecutor Williams continued the interrogation of Wade. The goal of the defense was to impugn the witness because he had changed his mind. Prosecutor Williams wanted to get the witness to recall his testimony; therefore he stressed Wade's recollections of what he had said to the defense attorneys at the Brockton police station when Prosecutor Katzmann was present. The interrogation follows:

WL (Williams):   Do you recall the first occasion that I talked with you in regard to this case in this court house?
W (Wade):   When was that? . . .
WL: Did I ask you at the time if Sacco was the man who did the shooting? . . .
W: Yes, sir.
WL: Did he [Katzmann] ask you if Sacco was the man who did the shooting? . . .
W: Yes, sir.
WL: What did you tell him?
W: I told him, yes. [Transcript of Record, p. 2375]

The prosecutor got Wade to admit that he had identified Sacco. Later the defense's cross-examination demonstrated that four weeks subsequent to the interrogation Wade changed his mind because he saw a man at a barbershop who closely resembled the gunman at the Slater-Morrill Shoe Factory. Katzmann followed with this re-direct examination:

K: Did you then answer . . . "He [Sacco] looks like the man in every description"?
W: I must have said that.

112

K: Have you any doubt you said that?
W: No. [Transcript of Record, p. 2375]

Defense attorney McAnarney concluded with re-cross-exami-
nation, getting Wade again to admit that he had made a positive
identification of Sacco but now was retracting it. The defense's
interrogation of Wade impugned his credibility as a believable storyteller and refuted his role as an eyewitness who could connect Sacco
with the murder. Moreover, the interrogation helped shape the
defense's theory that a gang of bandits committed the crime and
these bandits were still on the streets (perhaps even going to the
local barbershops).

Refutative Methods

Examiners achieve their functions and carry out their strategies
by developing effective refutative methods. These methods center
on refuting the story content of the testimony. During cross-examination, the advocates' skills as arguers are most evident. Bailey
and Rothblatt (1971) claim "cross-examination is the most vital
part of your defense. In many cases it is your only defense" (p. 17).
Even though historians have emphasized the unfairness of the interrogation in the Sacco-Vanzetti case, the trial record reveals many
examples of skillful refutation from both the prosecution and the
defense. Refutation is of two types: attacking the truth of the statement and attacking the lack of consistency of the argument.
Attacking Truth. In a classic nineteenth century study, Schopenhauer (1942) points out that refutation can take two major tacks.
The first tack is to attack the truths as presented. In legal cases, the
truths refer to the facts of the case outlined in opening statement
and developed through the corroboration of witnesses on one side
of the case. Thus, the refutative attacks made against witnesses by
interrogators involve discrediting witnesses by pointing out bias,
prejudice, self-interest, lack of common sense, or inaccuracies.
Another method of attacking the facts in cross-examination is
to refute directly the internal logic of witnesses' stories. An interrogator can do this in several ways. First, the questioner can make
the argument appear to be non sequitur, that is, show that the
inference or the conclusions do not logically follow from the factual
data. Second, the interrogator may reveal that the reasoning is
circular, meaning that the evidence is true because the conclusion
is true, and the conclusion is true because the evidence is. A third

113

avenue for refutation of facts occurs when questioners point out that witnesses have made hasty generalizations from observations that are unrepresentative or ambiguous. Finally, cross-examiners may refute purported facts presented by witnesses by questioning the reasonableness of the inferences or the implied connection between a stated fact and a conclusion drawn from that fact by the witness.

Attacking Inconsistency. Schopenhauer's (1942) second tack is to refute a message on the grounds of its inconsistency. In a trial setting, advocates try to show inconsistency by impugning the witness, that is, showing a prior statement made by a witness is inconsistent with later testimony. Advocates can also demonstrate inconsistency when they force witnesses to admit that stated conclusions conflict directly with reports of other witnesses. A final method of showing inconsistency occurs when advocates force witnesses to eliminate alternative explanations for some action or event and thereby accept a new explanation. In argumentation theory, this is called a method of residues (Jensen, 1981).

The examination of Louis Pelser by the defense illustrates several of the characteristics outlined above. Pelser became a controversial witness because he presented a story to the prosecutors prior to the trial different from the one he gave during the trial. Pelser's testimony was important to the prosecution because he was the only witness who definitely and consistently had identified Sacco as the gunman who shot Berardelli. Defense attorneys McAnarney and Moore took nearly four hours to interrogate this witness. The interrogation began by questioning the witness on the grounds of self-interest:

M (Moore):   Mr. Pelser, you have no interest in the outcome about this case at all, have you?
P (Pelser):   Any interest?
M: Other than to see to it that due and proper justice is administered between the parties?
P: I don't know what you mean.
M: I say, you have no interest in this case other than to see to that justice is administered in this court?
P: Yes, sir.
M: By this jury?
P: Yes, sir. [Transcript of Record, p. 297]

At the beginning of the interrogation, Moore got the witness to admit he had no self-interest in the trial, but after further interrogation the defense showed that in fact Pelser did have a self-interest because he felt he could be a celebrity by being the only witness to identify Sacco.

Next, Moore refuted Pelser on grounds that his story violated the principles of common sense, since the closed windows in the room from which he observed the crime prohibited the witness from seeing what he said he had observed. This excerpt shows Moore's line of questioning:

M: Now, those windows in that building on that floor are opaque, are they not, that is, you can't see through the window?

P: Yes, sir. You can't see through the windows.

M: So that the windows have to be opened to see anything, is that correct?

P: Yes, sir.

M: At the time this affair started, what was the condition of that window or those windows where you were?

P: Well, there was a little window open about that much.

M: About three to four inches?

P: Yes. . . .

M: And the crack that you say was in the window—

P: It was open.

M: About that much?

P: Yes, sir.

M: And your statement to the jury is that you saw out through there and saw bodies lying in the street?

P: Yes, sir.

M: Inside of what would be the gutter line, or outside street line?

P: Well, he was lying right in the middle of the sidewalk. . . .

M: And that was the body of Mr. Berardelli?

P: Yes, sir. [Transcript of Record, p. 297–98]

After showing it would have been exceedingly difficult for Pelser to see the victim from the small opening in the window, Moore tried to impugn the witness by showing the inaccuracy of his testimony. Pelser's original statement to the defense was that he did not see the shooting and that he only saw the body of Berardelli after the shooting. Moore read the witness' original statement from the record and then followed with this line of questioning:

M: Was that a true statement of the fact?
P: Well, yes, it was.
M: What?
P: It was.
M: It was? This is a correct statement of what you told Mr.
       Reid?
P: That I told Mr. Reid, yes, sir.
M: Now, is it a true statement of what you saw?
P: No, sir.
M: Why was it that you didn't tell Mr. Reid the facts?
P: Because I didn't want to tell my story.
M: Why?
P: Because I didn't like to go to court.
M: What has happened between now and then that you should
       tell to one side in this lawsuit one set of facts, and tell the
       other gentlemen in this lawsuit another set of facts? What has
       happened?
P: Well, I didn't know them well enough.
M: You knew them on March 26th just as well as you know
       them today, did you not?
P: Yes, sir.
M: Why then didn't you tell them what the facts were?
P: I didn't think I had to tell my story.
M: Did you tell Mr. Reid a falsehood in order to avoid being
       called a witness in this case?
P: Yes, sir.
M: In other words, you think so lightly of your word that, in or-
       der to avoid being called a witness, you deliberately told a
       falsehood, representing it to be the truth?
P: Yes, sir. [Transcript of Record, p. 300]

In this segment of the trial, Moore not only impugned the witness
by showing that he lied but he also demonstrated the witness lied
because of self-interest.

Moore then attacked Pelser's testimony because the witness
made hasty generalizations based upon ambiguous and limited information. The refutation of Pelser's reasoning follows:

M: Now you don't pretend or claim that you ever saw either of
       the men previous to this date, do you?
P: No, sir.
M: And you want the jury to believe that you stood in that win-
       dow with the bullets flying in your direction—
P: I didn't say that.

116

M: And carefully inspected the man that was firing below to the point of being able to state that he had a pin in his necktie?
P: I didn't say he had a pin in his necktie.
M: Or pin in his collar. And the first time you ever told anybody these facts, or what you claim to be facts, is on this witness stand?
P: Yes, sir.
M: And you haven't any explanation to give to this jury for telling an entirely different story, without coercion, without any pressure or any force, in the sanctity of your own home, surrounded by you own family—you haven't any explanation to give for telling an entirely different story, except that you didn't want to be a witness?
P: No, sir. [Transcript of Record, p. 306]

In this segment, Moore summarized the problems with Pelser's testimony: it showed self-interest, violated common sense, was contradictory, and contained a hasty generalization. McAnarney completed the interrogation forcing Pelser to admit the difficulty of describing the gunman and taking down a license number through a small crack in a window during the course of a few seconds.

The defense's examination provides an example of skillful refutation of the logic of Pelser's testimony. The defense severely discredited the witness, the only person who definitively identified Sacco as the murderer.

The Persuasive Tactics of Interrogation

Our focus so far has been on the content of the cross examination, that is, how advocates establish issues and provide evidence to support those issues. The function, strategy, and refutation methods all assist advocates to develop the content of their examination of witnesses so the interrogation will refute the story of the opposition. However, content in itself does not create successful cross-examination. Bailey and Rothblatt (1971), Heglund, (1978), Givens (1980), and Mauet (l980), acknowledge the importance of the second aspect of successful interrogation, the persuasive tactics. Tactics focus on the way the questions are communicated by the advocate. In other words, tactics are methods used by the questioner to make the questions and answers more central to their narrative accounts and more destructive to the stories of the opposition. Tactics include postures, rules, and maneuvers.

117

Postures

Postures refer to the attitudinal orientation of advocates toward the interrogation process. Bailey and Rothblatt (1971) identify several postures they believe contribute to effective interrogation. The first is to be courteous and considerate. Because jurors believe witnesses are at an unfair advantage as the target of the questions of a professional, they "are quick to sympathize with a witness" who is ridiculed or drilled by an attorney (p. 169).

To maintain a calm and unemotional attitude is a second recommended posture. In most circumstances advocates should retain a composed questioning posture, stressing deliberateness and intensity. Advocates should not yell at the witnesses, berate them, coerce them, or in other ways show anger or disrespect.

Third, advocates should frame their questions so that they lead logically toward the objectives of the interrogation. Bailey and Rothblatt (1971) recommend the following sequence of questioning: Start with the most innocent or neutral questions, ask leading questions that focus directly on the facts that advocates want the witness to report, and phrase questions carefully so the witness answers questions in an order that fits with the logical interpretation the advocate wishes to establish.

A fourth posture points to the fact that advocates should control the witnesses' answers by forcing them to respond directly to the interrogation. Moreover, the advocate should dominate the questioning so that witnesses' stories are gradually attacked. This gradual destroying of a witness' story occurs when the sequence of questions and responses shows that the testimony of direct examination is inconsistent, prejudicial, different from pretrial interrogation, or inaccurate.

A final posture is that advocates should know when and how to object. An objection is legitimate when questions are improper or when the answers to questions are likely to harm one's own clients. Attorneys commonly object during cross-examination when they perceive the following conditions have occurred (Ehrlich, 1970):

—The question is incompetent, because the witness lacks the knowledge or personal observation to answer the question.

—The question is irrelevant; no relationship exists between an item of evidence and an attempt to prove a fact.

—The question is immaterial; evidence does not relate to the issues of the indictment.

—The question calls for a conclusion, the witness is asked to interpret rather than report information.

—The questioner argues with a witness, confronts or challenges what the witness says.

—The question calls for hearsay evidence, based on reports of others rather than the witnesses' own knowledge;

—The respondent provides information beyond what the questioner asks.

—The questioner asks the respondent to give self-incriminating testimony.

—The question lacks a foundation, the assumptions behind the question are not developed by the questioner.

—The questions are unclear, complex, compound, unintelligible.

In the Sacco-Vanzetti case, some of the postures are evident in the transcript, but attitudinal postures are difficult to discern. Scholars writing about the trial of Sacco-Vanzetti after it occurred characterized the attitudinal postures of the advocates in similar ways. Joughin and Morgan (1948) note that Katzmann conducted a ruthless cross-examination of Sacco, and that Moore was harsh and threatening in his interrogation of Pelser, Goodridge, and Andrews. Ehrmann (1969) described Katzmann as an exceedingly skillful examiner who used interrogation ruthlessly and was permitted to do so by Judge Thayer. Feuerlicht (1977) stressed the devastating cross-examination of both Sacco and Vanzetti. Our analysis reveals a strongly adversarial sentiment throughout the trial. Moreover, the interrogation of the defendants by Katzmann was antagonistic and Moore's questioning of Pelser, Goodridge, and Andrews was aggressive.

The following segments of the trial record show how the advocates directed questions, controlled answers, and objected to opposing counsel's tactics on appropriate grounds. The testimony of defense witness James E. Burns, ballistics expert, illustrates these tactics. The defense called Burns to refute the testimony of the ballistics experts of the prosecution. Burns claimed the bullets taken from the victim could not be certified as coming from Sacco's gun. The objective of Katzmann was to show that Burns' testimony neither affirmed nor denied that the bullet was fired by Sacco.

119

Throughout the examination, Katzmann controlled the witness by asking yes-no questions such as those illustrated in this segment:

K: Does the double marking at the upper end of those grooves on the bullet indicate anything to your mind?
B: Yes.
K: What?
B: A worn lead.
K: Anything else?
B: A neglected gun.
K: Anything else?
B: No, sir.
K: Does it indicate anything else as to the matter the bullet took the lead?
B: Not plumb. . . .
K: That is it did not jump the rifling perfectly? That is what it means, doesn't it?
B: It did not go straight into the lead, perfect center. [Transcript of Record, pp. 1433–34]

The controlling tactics of Katzmann led him to the crucial question about whether the bullet taken from the victim was fired from Sacco's gun. A positive answer to the question would have been devastating; therefore defense attorney McAnarney objected to the following:

K: You are talking and predicting your opinion, are you not that this bullet . . . was not fired through the Sacco gun?

McAnarney objected apparently on grounds that the question lacked a proper foundation saying: "This witness has not said that that bullet was not fired by the Sacco gun" (Transcript of Record, p. 1439). The testimony of Burns included a number of objections.

Rules

In addition to the postures of the interrogator, a second set of persuasive tactics is grounded in the rules developed from the codes governing the court and the norms of trial communication. Givens (1980) outlines several of these principles applicable to interrogation. First, cross-examiners should not ask for explanations, because these type of inquiries permit the witnesses to justify responses.

Second, interrogators should ask leading questions to keep control of the witness. Third, questioners should include in the question itself the substance of the facts, including time, dates, names, and statements from depositions. Fourth, questions should be selected on the basis of the vulnerability of the witnesses, such as their contradictions, prejudices, or inaccuracies. Finally, nearly all literature on trial advocacy warns interrogators never to ask questions to which they cannot predict the answer.

In the following excerpt, Moore asks leading questions, controls the witness, and includes facts within the questions. The interrogation severely harms the credibility of Lola R. Andrews. Andrews purportedly saw Sacco under a car on the day of the crime. She was walking to the shoe factory on her way to an interview. She claimed she observed a parked car with one man inside and the other underneath the car. On direct examination, she identified the person under the car as Sacco. During cross-examination in this trial segment, Moore tried to show that Andrews never saw the face of the person she had identified as Sacco:

M: Why, Mrs. Andrews, did you speak to that man, directing your attention again to the man down underneath this car, rather than to the other man who was standing doing nothing at a point no farther removed from you than I am at this moment?

A: You mean, why I spoke to him rather than the other man?

M: Yes.

A: Simply because I was standing there talking and I directed my conversation to him to ask him that question, instead of going back. . . .

M: Yet you couldn't see even the face of the man you were directing the questions to?

A: Why sir, I saw his face when he got up.

M: You had to call him up before you were able to see his face at all, didn't you?

A: He was getting up when I spoke, getting up from the auto. . . .

M: At the time you asked him the question, he was down on the ground under the car?

A: His head and shoulder was under the car. . . .

M: Mrs. Andrews, on the date that I talked with you, did you in any way, form or manner identify Nicola Sacco as the man that you saw, or claim to have seen, on April 15, 1920?

A: You mean, did I recognize him as the man? No, sir, I didn't tell you that way. [Transcript of Record, pp. 2482–87]

121

Moore's inclusion of the fact within the question and leading questions allowed him to control the witness so that she gave the answers he expected to elicit from his interrogation of her.

Maneuvers

In addition to postures and rules for interrogation, a third interrogating tactic consists of verbal maneuvers that assist advocates to persuade jurors that the story told by the witness probably is flawed. These maneuvers consist of asserting false premises, using tag questions, and eliciting "I don't know" responses.

The first maneuver occurs when advocates phrase leading questions so that an uncertain or a false premise is asserted and the witness is asked to verify that assertion. For example, in Katzmann's cross-examination of Burke, he included an uncertain statement within the question: "You got there about . . . twenty minutes past two, didn't you? (Transcript of Record, p. 2782). This was not the time stated by the witness and in fact the witness was unsure of the time but agreed that the advocate's statement was probably true. Swann, Guiliano, and Wegner (1982) explain why these questions work for interrogators. They believe that jurors apply their understanding of conversational rules to infer that the advocates must have a foundation in evidence to substantiate the premises they use in cross-examination and therefore they accept these assertions as factual when they may not be.

A second kind of verbal maneuver is to add "tag questions" to a yes or no question. Tag questions are simply questions added on to the original question. In interrogation, tag questions are assertions of fact followed by a question. These types of interrogatives appear frequently in the Sacco-Vanzetti transcript in the following types of inquiries: "You didn't see them, did you?" "You don't remember, do you?" "You mean to earn money, don't you?" Loftus (1980) found that tag questions are usually answered in line with the response implied by the tag question.

A final maneuver occurs when advocates try to elicit "I don't know" answers. When interrogators try to discredit witnesses, they often are met with the response "I don't know." According to Dunston (1980), when witnesses start to say "I don't recall," they usually continue this response because they believe the response adds consistency to their testimony. During Moore's cross-examination of Pelser, Goodridge, and Andrews, large segments of their responses were answered with statements stating they did not know.

This sample of Moore's interrogation of Andrews exemplified the maneuver of eliciting "I don't know" responses:

M: What did you see about the car? . . .
A: It was a large car. . . .
M: Bright, clean, shiny?
A: I would not say.
M: Or dirty or grimy?
A: I could not answer that.
M: The make of the car. . . .
A: I do not know the names. [Transcript of Record, p. 2452]

In sum, then, interrogators add to the content of the functions, strategy, and refutation by choosing persuasive tactics that present positive postures, follow rules, and adopt verbal maneuvers. The interrogation tactics are the methods used by advocates to add persuasiveness to their story and to refute the story of opposing witnesses. Skillful cross-examination involves both a focus on the content of interrogation and a choice of persuasive tactics that will embellish the content and add to the believability of the testimony.

The interrogation process explained thus far shows how advocates can follow the standard practices of cross-examination and achieve their goals in shaping their narrative accounts and refuting the story of the opposition. In the Sacco-Vanzetti case, the interrogation of the defense and the prosecution proceeded with skill until the defendants took the witness stand. The adversarial duel was marked by the severe impugning of three occurrence witnesses by Moore and two of Vanzetti's alibi witnesses by Katzmann. Prior to the interrogation of the defendants, the weight of the testimony appeared to favor the defense because the eyewitnesses of the prosecution could not identify the defendants as the gunmen. Thirty-three eyewitnesses were called by both sides. Only seven of these could identify the defendants in the vicinity of the crime before or after it occurred. Only the witness Pelser, who was impugned by the defense for changing his story, identified Sacco as the gunmen. The testimony of ballistics experts was not decisive for either side.

Why then did the defense lose the case? Scholars (Musmanno, 1939; Joughin & Morgan, 1948; Ehrmann, 1969; Feuerlicht, 1977; Young & Kaiser, 1985) argue the reason for the verdict is that the defendants incriminated themselves during direct and cross-examination by recounting their political beliefs and activities. For this reason, the interrogation of the defendants marks a crucial event in the trial. Our analysis of cross-examination, up to this point, focused on the skillful approaches to the content and persuasion that fit the standards usually associated with the questioning of adversarial witnesses. However, the trial is noteworthy for the negative cross-examination of Sacco and for the unorthodox persuasion used by prosecutor Katzmann. The next segment of the chapter explains this negative approach and indicates how this part of the trial contributed to the verdict against the defense.

Negative Approaches to Cross-Examination: Diversions in the Interrogation of Sacco

Ehrmann (1969) judges the interrogation of Sacco as one of the "most extraordinary cross-examinations in a capital case that ever took place in a courtroom" (p. 307). Feuerlicht (1977) contends that the trial turned from a criminal charge of murder into an ideological charge of heresy during the questioning of Sacco. Quite clearly, Katzmann's questioning of Sacco made the defendant appear to be both a liar and a hypocrite. The prosecutor's unorthodox refutation derived from his ability to divert the witness and the court proceeding away from the issues of the indictment and to restructure the procedural norms to accomplish this diversion through carefully selected semantic maneuvers. Even though many of these diversions violated the accepted norms of procedure and introduced many ideological issues, the defense did not frequently object. In cases when the defense voiced legitimate objections, Judge Thayer often overruled these objections. The testimony of Sacco also shows that his command of English was marginal and that many times during the interrogation Sacco misunderstood what was asked, and at other times, he gave responses filled with semantic and syntactic errors.

"Diversions" refer to strategies of interrogation that draw the attention of the jurors, judge, and witnesses away from the normative approaches of cross-examination. In other words, the examiner changes the course or deflects the witness into a different story line than has thus far been introduced in the trial. Because of the rhetorical choices of the advocate, this diversion seems legitimate and relevant to the facts of the case and the issues of the indictment, and the judge and jury may not notice that it is aberrant or irrelevant to the legal charges. Our judgment is that these diversions violate the standards for cross-examination and eventually enter into the reasoning given by jurors for a verdict. In fact, the appellate briefs for the Sacco-Vanzetti case mention some of these diversions as the legal grounds for overturning the verdict.

Issue Diversion

Katzmann's most overt diversion was away from the charges of the indictment of murder and toward the issue of political ideology. Katzmann successfully diverted the focus of the case from the murder charge to Sacco's lack of patriotism, his involvement with anarchist groups and causes, and his reading of radical literature. In fact, throughout the two days of the prosecutor's interrogation of Sacco, Katzmann persistently and repeatedly confronted Sacco about his radical beliefs and associations. At the beginning of the interrogation, Katzmann began this diversion by focusing on Sacco's lack of patriotism:

K: Did you say yesterday you love a free country?
S: Yes, sir.
K: Did you love this country in the month of May, 1917?
S: I did say,—I don't want to say I did not love this country. . . . If you, Mr. Katzmann, if you give me that,—I could explain—
K: Do you understand that question?
S: Yes.
K: Then will you please answer it?
S: I can't answer in one word. . . .
K: Did you love this country in the last week of May, 1917?
S: That is pretty hard for me to say in one word, Mr. Katzmann.
K: There are two words you can use Mr. Sacco, yes or no. Which is it?
S: Yes.
K: And in order to show your love for this United States of America when she was about to call upon you to become a soldier, you ran away to Mexico? [Transcript of Record, p. 1867]

During this sequence of questions, the defense made no objections to the testimony despite the fact that the questioning seemed immaterial, argumentative, and self-incriminating. The explanation seems to be that the defense had inquired about Sacco's going to Mexico to avoid the draft in direct examination and therefore had opened up this line of questioning to the prosecution. In retrospect, this defense strategy seems to have been an extremely poor choice.

Katzmann discredited Sacco by reason of his disloyalty to the United States, his evasion of military service, and his unpatriotic statements about American education. Sacco had asserted earlier in the cross-examination that poor children could not receive the same educational advantages as children from wealthy families. The prosecutor continued his diversion of the defendant's testimony from issues related to the indictment to issues of ideology:

K: Do you remember speaking of Harvard University?
S: Yes, sir.
K: Do you remember saying that you could not get an education there unless you had money? I do not mean you used those exact words. I do not contend you did, but, in substance, didn't you say that?
S: They have to use money in the rule of the Government.
K: No. You don't understand. . . . Did you say in substance you could not send your boy to Harvard?
S: Yes.
K: Unless you had money. Did you say that?
S: Of course.
K: Do you think that is true?
S: I think it is.
K: Don't you know Harvard University educates more boys of poor people free than any other university in the United States of America? [Transcript of Record, p. 1789]

The defense repeatedly objected to this line of questioning, to no avail. Judge Thayer allowed the questions without explaining the reasons for doing so saying: "The question may stand and the answer as well."

Katzmann's diversions of the issues continued by his focus on ideological ideas, such as the type of literature the defendant read and possessed at the time of his arrest on May 5, 1920. This segment illustrates the continuation of issue diversions:

K: What papers did you read?
S: I read *Boston American* every night.
K: What other papers?
S: Some papers from Italy, too. Some other Socialist papers from Italy.
K: Some other Socialist papers from Italy?
S: Yes.
K: Were all those papers except the *Boston Globe* and the *Boston American*, copies of them, in your house—

126

S: No. . . . They all used to destroy when I finished reading.
K: . . . What papers did you have on May 5th in your house?
S: You mean books? . . . Just the papers?
K: I mean papers, newspapers, or periodicals?
S: I got some [of] every kind literature.
K: All these kinds you have mentioned, *Le Mortello?*
S: Yes.
K: *Cronaco Soverseva?*
S: Yes.
K: The papers from Italy?
S: Yes.
K: Were they Socialist papers?
S: Yes, sir.
K: [Were] [t]hey Anarchistic papers? [Transcript of Record, p. 1883]

The defense objected to this line of questioning but Judge Thayer permitted the questions and responses.

The line of questioning continued, showing that Sacco knew anarchists who had been deported by the government for their illegal activities. Katzmann pursued the ideological diversions more persistently in this excerpt:

K: Did you know Fruzetti of Bridgewater, who was deported, you did?
S: Yes.
K: Did you know him personally?
S: Yes, sir.
K: Been to his house?
S: I met him lots of times.
K: In Boston?
S: In conference.
K: Talked with him about anarchy, haven't you?
S: Certainly.
K: Did you know his views on anarchy? [Transcript of Record, p. 1885]

Subsequent questions by Katzmann to the defendant aligned Sacco with other known anarchists such as Orcciani, Boda, Salsedo, and Elia. All of these men were considered dangerous radicals. Thayer allowed this line of questioning on the grounds that it pertained to the credibility of the witness.

The issue diversions altered the prosecution's story of the case by showing that one of the leading characters, Sacco, was unpatriotic and disloyal because he had embraced the doctrine of anarchy, which promoted the overthrow of the government of the United States. By diverting the issues from facts related to the charge of murder to facts related to the defendant's political beliefs and associations, Katzmann implied that Sacco was capable of murder and also refuted the defense's story that Sacco was a grateful American and a trustworthy citizen.

Procedural Diversions

In addition to the shift from legal issues to ideological ones, Katzmann's interrogation forced procedural shifts in the trial such as shifting the burden of proof from the prosecution to the defense and shifting the roles usually associated with one set of trial participants to others.

Shifting the burden of proof means the defendants are expected to prove their innocence rather than the prosecution prove guilt. An example of shifting the burden of proof occurred in the way Sacco was interrogated about a cap found near the scene of the crime. Appellate attorney Ehrmann (1969) explains how the evidence resulted in shifting the burden of proof from the prosecution to the defense. The background of the cap as evidence is chronicled in this scenario: the cap was found after the crime was committed on Pearl Street in the vicinity of the Slater-Morrill Shoe Factory; no eyewitness mentioned the cap in pretrial depositions; the cap that was found was never introduced into evidence, but a cap from Sacco's home was introduced and presented as if it were the cap found at the scene of the crime; the investigating officers did not find the cap until a day after the crime; and hundreds of workers wore caps like the one found near the scene of the crime. Katzmann asked Sacco to try on the cap from his home during this segment of cross-examination:

K: Mr. Sacco, do you know anything about that cap?
S: That is my cap.
K: When did you buy that?
S: Last March?
K: In 1920? [Transcript of Record, pp. 1851–52]

Then Katzmann asked Sacco to model the cap for the jury and to state again that this was his cap. As the jury observed this activity, they assumed that he was modeling the cap found on the street

128

rather than the one taken from his home. In this way, the prosecution shifted the burden of proof to the defense to prove this was not the cap found on the street near the site of the crime.

Besides shifting the burden of proof, the prosecutor shifted the normative roles of the trial participants. These shifts occurred as the result of the focus on ideological issues. One shift of roles happened when the judge began interrogating defense attorney McAnarney after an objection to the ideological focus of the prosecutor's questions. This trial segment illustrates a role shift in which McAnarney is examined by Judge Thayer as if he were the witness:

M: That claim is not presented in anything tantamount to the language just used by the Court, and in view of the record as it stands at this time I object to this line of inquiry.

T: Is that not your claim, that the defendant, as a reason that he has given for going to the Johnson house, that they wanted the automobile to prevent people from being deported and to get this literature out of the way? Does he not claim that that was done in the interest of the United States, to prevent violations of the law by the distribution of this literature? I understand that was the—

M: Are you asking that as a question to me?

T: Yes. . . .

M: I am going to make whatever claim that is legitimate.

T: I want to know what that is [that] you are going to claim in the argument—

M: I am going to claim this man and Vanzetti were of that class called Socialists. I am going to claim that a riot was running a year ago last April, that men were being deported, that twelve to fifteen hundred were seized in Massachusetts.

T: Do you mean you are going to offer evidence of that?

M: We have witnesses which we may introduce here. I do not know whether we will introduce them or not.

T: Are you going to claim that what the defendant did was in the interest of the United States?

M: Your Honor please, I now object to your Honor's statement as prejudicial to the rights of the defendants and ask that this statement be withdrawn from the jury.

T: There is not a prejudicial remark made that I know of and none were intended. I simply asked you, sir, whether you propose to offer evidence as to what you said. [Transcript of Record, 1873–74]

Judge Thayer interrogated McAnarney in front of the jury. Thayer assumed the role of storyteller rather than following his designated role of story listener and courtroom umpire.

Another procedural shift occurred when Katzmann allowed the defendant Sacco to address the jury directly about his political views during the cross-examination. In this shift, Sacco seemed to try to persuade jurors of his political beliefs. The response by Sacco followed an open-ended question by Katzmann, an inquiry characteristic of direct examination: "What did you mean yesterday when you said you loved a free country?" (Transcript of Record, pp. 1875–77). The long narrative response revealed Sacco's political beliefs and also showed his lack of command of the English language. A part of Sacco's long soliloquy follows:

> I was a Republican, so I always thinking [that a] Republican has more chance to manage education, develop, to build some day his family, to raise the child and education, if you could. But that was my opinion; so when I came to this country I saw there was not what I was thinking before, but there was all the difference, because I been working in Italy not so hard as I been work in this country. I could live free there just as well, work in the same condition, but not so hard, about seven or eight hours a day, better food. I mean genuine. Of course, over there is good food, because it a bigger country. When I been started work here very hard and been work thirteen years, hard worker, I could not been afford much a family the way [I] did have the idea before I could not put any money in the bank. I could no push my boy some to go to school and other things. I teach over here men who is with me. The free ideas gives any man a chance to profess his own idea, not the supreme idea, not give any person, not to be like Spain in position, yes, about twenty centuries ago, but to give a chance to print and education, literature, free speech, that I see it was all wrong. I could see the best men, intelligent, education, they been arrested and sent to prison and lied in prison for years and years without getting them out, and Debs, one of the great men in this country, he is in prison, still away in prison, because he is a Socialist. [Transcript of Record, p. 1876]

The half-hour long response added a great deal of information, demonstrating Sacco lacked patriotism and held politically radical views. Despite the fact that this information did not pertain to the indictment of murder, none of the defense attorneys objected to the response.

This diversion is an example of how Katzmann succeeded in

focusing the interrogation on political issues. This lengthy political narrative showed how Katzmann deviated from controlling the witness, a practice associated with cross-examination, and let the witness tell his own story in an uninterrupted manner. Later, Katzmann attacked Sacco vehemently for the remarks made in this statement. These shifts of procedure changed the roles normally attributed to the judge, cross-examiner, and witness. These changes permitted Katzmann to extract a politically incriminating story from Sacco, which the prosecutor then used as the straw man argument to attack the defendant in subsequent questions.

Semantic Diversions

In addition to shifts of roles, the case also revealed procedural diversions of a semantic form. Semantic diversions refer to the ways interrogators use language to construe the meaning of the cross-examination. Katzmann's cross-examination of Sacco illustrated several examples of this type of diversion of meaning in the form of misleading analogies and strategic repetitions.

Misleading Analogies. An analogy is a form of inference based on the assumption that if two things are known to be alike in some respects, then they must also be alike in other respects. A misleading analogy occurs when the likenesses are inferred from a common word, rather than similar relationships (Jensen, 1981). Katzmann tried to compare "love" of country with "love" of spouse in the following excerpt:

K (Katzmann):   Did you love your country when you came back from Mexico?
S (Sacco):   The first time?
T (Thayer):   Which country did you say? You said—
K: United States of America, your adopted country?
S: I did not say already. . . .
K: You still loved America did you?
S: I should say yes.
K: What is your idea of showing your love for this country?
S: (no response)
K: Is that your idea of showing your love for America?
S: Yes.
K: And would it be your idea of showing love for your wife that when she needed you, you ran away from her?
S: I did not run away from her. [Transcript of Record, p. 1868]

131

Katzmann attempted to infer that the responses to one's country and to one's wife are similar, an obviously misleading analogy.

Strategic Repetitions. Katzmann used a second type of semantic diversion, repetition of emotional words. Given the context in which the crime appeared, words such as "radical," "draft-evader," "socialist," or "anarchist" held extremely negative connotations for the public at large and presumably for the jurors in the trial who represented the public. All of these terms were in Weaver's sense (1953) "devil terms," that is, terms of repulsion that designate enemies and evils in a culture. Katzmann added more devil terms to the conclusions he drew in the interrogation about the credibility of Sacco, such as "concealment," "falsehood," and "lying." In the following segment, Katzmann associated Sacco with two sets of devil terms—anarchy and lying:

K: Do you remember my asking you then: "Did he see and talk with Bartolomeo?" And your reply: "No, he doesn't know Bartolomeo?" Did you tell me that?

S: Yes, sir.

K: That was falsehood, wasn't it?

S: It was false.

K: What did you mean by telling that falsehood?

S: It is the same question, the Radicals—

K: Well, the only hope you had by telling these falsehoods, was it not, was to avoid arrest of your friends?

S: Certainly. . . .

K: Then, how would concealment of that fact that Vanzetti knew Orcciani help avoid arrest?

S: (no answer).

K: Can't you answer that?

S: I gave the answer already, same question, about Radicals.

K: You knew that had nothing to do with Radicalism, didn't you?

S: You didn't?

K: Radicals? . . . You did not know that?

S: Yes.

K: The Radicals had nothing to do with it. You knew that.

S: Yes.

K: Did you know a single one of those persons?

S: No, sir.

K: Had you ever given any Radical literature to any of them?

S: No, sir. [Transcript of Record, pp. 1920–22]

Katzmann's connection of falsehood to radicalism helped to affirm the prosecution's theory of the case that the defendants lied because they were "conscious of their own guilt" and their lying was a cover-up of guilt.

The procedural diversions used by the prosecutor contributed to claims by critics of the trial that Katzmann was vicious in pursuing the techniques, Thayer was prejudicial in allowing such diversions, and the defense attorneys were negligent in failing to object to some of these tactics. Certainly these unorthodox methods did reinforce the story of the prosecution and cast doubt on the credibility of Sacco as a storyteller. In combination with the issue diversions that focused the case on ideological rather than legal indictments, the procedural diversions overtly introduced credibility factors into the trial so that jurors were likely to use these factors as grounds for a decision. The procedural diversions must have suggested Thayer's hostility to defense attorneys and his favoritism toward the prosecution. Despite the fact that Thayer warned jurors not to make their decision on political grounds in three or four sentences in his jury instructions, the hours of content of testimony about political factors must have entered into the grounds for decision, particularly when the country was so immersed in issues of radicalism.

Implications of the Cross-Examination for Trial Practice

Each chapter of this volume illustrates how one segment of a trial can be decisive in the outcome of a case. In the Sacco-Vanzetti case, the interrogation of the defendants is a decisive point in the trial because it reshaped the story of the defense and added credibility to the prosecution's issue about the defendants consciousness of their own guilt. Three conditions contributed to the centrality of cross-examination in this case.

The first condition relates to a fit between the ideas of the interrogation and the perceptions of the jurors. The successful diversion of the cross-examination into political ideology results when jurors are predisposed to make connections between the information elicited from the interrogation and a new story line that provides an alternative rationale for a guilty verdict. This condition was present in Sacco-Vanzetti. The political focus seemed pertinent due to the climate of opinion of the era. Because of the new Alien and Sedition Acts and the subsequent arrests and deportations of anarchists, the political activities of the defendants were likely interpreted as a motive for the crime and a reason to render a guilty

133

verdict. In fact, one argument on appeal was that the foreman of the jury, Walter Ripley, openly admitted the defendants should be hanged for their disloyalty and their anarchist activities. Even though the indictments against the defendants were not based on the Alien and Sedition Acts, Judge Thayer's association of anarchy and criminality in his jury instruction (this point is stressed in the appellate briefs for the case) and Katzmann's declarations that Sacco's dishonesty, anarchy, and crime were all causally connected reinforced this line of reasoning for jurors opposed to radicalism.

This same condition occurred in the Chicago Anarchist, or Haymarket, case. In fact, most of Haymarket jurors admitted they held strong feelings against labor in general and anarchists in particular (Lum, 1969; Avrick, 1984). In the Haymarket case, as in Sacco-Vanzetti, the defendants testified in their own behalf, admitted their radical goals, and even expressed their belief in violence. As a result, the defendants were subjected to a hostile and vigorous cross-examination by the prosecution, focusing on their radical beliefs.

In the Rosenberg case, Julius and Ethel were called in their own defense, but both refused to testify on grounds of self-incrimination. The Rosenbergs invoked the Fifth Amendment in response to questions about their communist beliefs and affiliations. The defendants refusal to testify on grounds of self-incrimination helped the prosecution to raise the ideological issues. However, the Rosenberg case differed from the Haymarket and the Sacco-Vanzetti cases because the Rosenberg defense was ill-conceived and poorly prepared in all stages of the trial.

The defendants in the Chicago Eight case subverted the cross-examination so that they overtly called attention to their motives and ideology and, in doing so, altered the expected norms and procedures associated with interrogation.

A second condition contributing to the persuasive effect of the diversions of cross-examination occurs when the judge sanctions the practices, and opposing counsel through neglect or prejudice is unable to stop the diversions. In the Sacco-Vanzetti case, the diversions succeeded. From the trial record, it appears that Judge Thayer frequently overruled proper objections by the defense. This indicates the defense could not halt the diversions through the legitimate channels of the court. Some sources fault the defense for insufficient objections; the record however shows the defense frequently objected, without success. Because the transcripts do not record all conversations in chambers or with the bench, historical observers are unlikely to know the extent and skill with which the objections were presented.

Our study of other trials where political ideology is a concern demonstrates the defense has a very difficult time with most of the judges in getting favorable rulings to objections made during the cross-examination of defendants. The problem seems to be handled differently by different attorneys. In the Haymarket case the defense was repeatedly overruled by the judge, just as in the Sacco-Vanzetti case. In the Chicago Eight case the defense argued with the judge, sometimes to the point of contempt. In the Rosenberg case the defense rarely objected.

A third condition when cross-examination is likely to be decisive is in cases in which the real evidence is contradictory or nonexistent and thus the advocates have to rely on circumstantial proof. When this condition is present, the cross-examiner often focuses not on the facts of the crime itself, but instead on the motives for the crime. In some of the cases discussed in this volume, the political motive was the dominant focus of the interrogation. In the Haymarket case, no one in the trial argued that those charged with murder threw the bomb that killed the officer whose death was the focus of the indictment, but most witnesses claimed the defendants supported violence and disliked police. In Sacco-Vanzetti, only one of the 155 witnesses claimed Sacco fired the gun that killed the paymaster and guard, but Katzmann's cross-examination showed Sacco was capable of violence. In the Rosenberg case, the denial of the defendants' story constituted the entire defense so the impugning of the credibility of Julius and Ethel on political grounds damaged the case as a whole.

The climate of opinion in which the case is tried, the predispositions of participants, and the absence of evidence enter into the interrogations of defendants. These conditions probably contributed to the verdict against Sacco and Vanzetti; a verdict that appeared to go against the weight of evidence in the case. Considering the trial as a whole, the transcript offers numerous examples of skillful interrogation on the part of advocates on both sides of the case. This skillful examination shows how advocates refute and reshape the stories of their adversary according to traditional standards for interrogation. The case also shows how Katzmann's unorthodox diversionary maneuvers in the interrogation of Sacco supported the prosecution's story, emphasizing consciousness of guilt, and refuted the theory of the defense, that Sacco and Vanzetti were law abiding citizens who lacked criminal motives.

A Communication Scholar's Reaction

Ruth McGaffey

Janice Schuetz and Kathryn Snedaker have written an interesting essay about a famous historical trial. I doubt if the trial of Sacco and Vanzetti is very important in any legal sense. Its importance lies in its illustration of the American tendency to make association the prime "proof" of guilt during times of national stress. Most of the trials discussed in this book illustrate that point. Perhaps the trial of Sacco and Vanzetti keeps our interest more than most because we still don't know the truth about the guilt or innocence of the defendants. In addition the many famous names associated with their defense have given the trial a lasting place in history.

The authors' stated purpose is to "investigate the methods of cross-examination and to show how interrogation is used to refute and reshape the story of the case presented by the opposition." The most important part of this purpose seems to be to "illustrate negative aspects of interrogation by showing how the prosecution's cross-examination of Sacco diverted the trial into political arenas."

The authors really discuss two trials. The first is a murder trial in which the methods of cross-examination were fairly conventional. In their discussion of this trial, the authors present a clear explanation of the purpose, strategy and refutation methods of cross-examination. In most cases they provide examples from the trial to illustrate their points. While the conclusions drawn from the examples do not always appear obvious, it is perhaps difficult to present excerpts of sufficient length to clearly illustrate a point.

The first trial seems to have been won by the defense. The

Ruth McGaffey is currently Assistant to the Chancellor at the University of Wisconsin-Milwaukee. Professor McGaffey has taught at Boston College, Concordia College, and the University of Wisconsin-Milwaukee. She has a B.A. degree from St. Olaf College, a M.A. degree from the University of Nebraska, and a Ph.D. degree from Northwestern University. Professor McGaffey has taught a variety of communication courses, such as public speaking, argumentation, debate, free speech, and communication and law. She has a particular interest in First Amendment topics, has published extensively in issues related to communication and law, and has served as editor of the *Free Speech Newsletter*.

136

prosecution was not able to show very convincingly that Sacco and Vanzetti committed the crime of which they were charged. One can not help but wonder what would have happened had the defendants not taken the stand in their own defense. For when they took that stand, the second trial started—the political trial, which Sacco and Vanzetti clearly lost, and which cost them their lives.

Two statements in the book's introduction are important in setting the scene for discussion of the cross-examination of Sacco and Vanzetti. The authors state that "our purpose is not to discern the guilt or innocence of the parties involved. Instead we seek to understand how the public opinion of the era enters into the trial, and to identify how the communicative practices work." Later the authors paraphrase Chaim Perelman who "recommends that the law be interpreted in terms of rhetorical choices that incorporate the values and understandings of the audiences addressed by the litigation." Public opinion and rhetorical choices geared to the values and understandings of the audience appear to have been crucial in this trial.

These values and understandings are not hard to determine. The authors have described the political climate of the Red Scare. From my study of First Amendment history during this time, I know they are, if anything, understating the public hysteria. This was a time, for example, when most states had laws prohibiting the display of a red flag or banner of any kind. Massachusetts did not, but only because the law had been hastily repealed when someone realized that it would prohibit the display of Harvard's crimson banners.

From Schuetz and Snedaker's essay, we know little of the makeup of the jury in the Sacco-Vanzetti case except that the foreman had stated that the defendants should be hanged for their disloyalty and their anarchist activities. If we add to this the not unreasonable assumption that the jury probably reflected the general fear of socialists and anarchists, we have an audience "predisposed to make connections between the information elicited from the interrogation and a new story line that provides an alternative rationale for a guilty verdict."

Into this setting come Sacco and Vanzetti to testify in their own behalf. We do not know what they said in direct testimony, nor do we know what the defense strategy was in having them appear. The prosecution clearly attempted to identify Sacco and Vanzetti with the bad guys—anarchists and socialists—and did it successfully enough to win.

There are three questions to be asked here. Was this an intel-

137

ligent strategy? Was it an ethical strategy? Why didn't the defense counter it more effectively? Let us consider each one briefly.

If the objective in a trial is to win, the strategy was an intelligent one. The prosecution apparently did not have a strong case. Their witnesses were not convincing, and seemed at times contradictory. That being the case, probably any trained public speaker would consider his or her audience and attempt to identify himself or herself with the values of that audience and identify his or her opponents with values diametrically opposed to those held by the audience. Such a "common ground" strategy is explained and recommended in most public speaking textbooks as well as in most textbooks of trial practice. Judged by its result, it worked.

The question of ethics, however, is not as simple. Unless the only obligation of the prosecutor is to achieve a guilty verdict, the methods used in the cross-examination of Sacco and Vanzetti were not ethical. Almost any argumentation book that discusses the "ethical use of argumentation," exhorts students to draw only those conclusions that are warranted from the facts. Argumentation writers tell us to avoid hasty generalizations, bandwagon techniques and ad hominum attacks. Writers on the ethics of communication tell us that honesty in communication is vital, and that appealing to the worst instincts of your audience is unethical. Even by the tenets of either utilitarianism or Kant's categorical imperative such a practice is not ethical. Putting innocent people away and letting the guilty go free if crowd feelings dictate certainly can not provide the greatest good for the greatest number. Nor does it seem reasonable to say that such strategies are good not only in this instance but also in every similar situation, which would qualify it as ethical in the Kantian sense. If the higher ethic in this society is that the innocent shall go free and the guilty shall be punished, attempts to establish guilt by association cannot be considered ethical. The adversary system does assume that each of the participants in a trial will try his or her best to win. The legal system itself has tried, however, to make sure that not "anything goes." The rules of ethical communication should go even further than that.

Why didn't the defense counter the prosecution's strategy more effectively? The authors of this essay seem to think that they could not because the judge continually denied their objections. To a great degree that may have been true. In the case of the cross-examination of Sacco, however, there was apparently no objection raised. Since both the authors and common sense point out that the long discussion by Sacco of his anarchist beliefs must have had an effect on the jury, the lack of an objection here seems especially strange. Perhaps by this time the attorneys for the defense had been frustrated so often by both the prosecution and the judge that they had given up objecting. Such a decision, while understandable, certainly is not justifiable.

In addition, the defense should have been able to figure out what the strategy of the prosecution would be. If that is true, one can question the decision to put Sacco and Vanzetti on the stand. It is true that a jury may assume that any defendant who does not testify is guilty. Considering the extremely volatile nature of the subject, however, and the particular opinions of the defendants as well as their lack of understanding and poor use of the English language, I question the wisdom of the defense's actions.

Because the authors focus so much on the actions of the prosecution in the second phase of this trial, it is hard to understand what the defense was doing. Did they have a counterattack? Did they also have some strategy to associate their opponents with the bad guys? If so, what bad guys were they talking about and how did they proceed? It appears that they did a reasonably competent job during the first part of the trial. One wonders what they did in the second part where once again Americans looked at individuals on trial and found them guilty by association.

5
Participatory Persuasion in Closing Arguments: The Trial of Julius and Ethel Rosenberg

In closing argument, the advocates rebuild the story of the trial to enable the jurors to arrive at a verdict in accordance with the most consistent, corroborated, and probable narrative account. This chapter focuses on the closing arguments delivered in the Rosenberg trial and investigates how the final speeches of advocates are an important phase of the litigation process. The chapter identifies participatory persuasion as the theoretical basis for effective closing argument and considers how the elements of form, content, and style contribute to the persuasiveness of this final message to the jury. By isolating the communication strategies underlying effective closing argument, including the narrative or story elements, the argumentative structure and content, and the linguistic embellishment, the chapter shows how closing argument simultaneously validates the story presented in opening statement and developed in direct exam and refutes the theory of the opposing counsel. The chapter illustrates how lawyers can enhance the content of their closing arguments.

The trial of Julius and Ethel Rosenberg marked the first time accused spies received a death sentence from an American civil court for their conviction of conspiring to communicate, deliver, and transmit documents to the Soviet Union. In this case, the prosecution alleged that Julius Rosenberg's passing of documents about the A-bomb prior to the end of World War II hurt the American war effort. Although the crime was alleged to have occurred in the 1940s, the trial was held at the beginning of the McCarthy era, a period that resembled the Red Scare of the 1920s when Sacco and Vanzetti were arrested and convicted. The press called for execution of the spies; many people throughout the world, however, regarded the Rosenbergs, alleged members of the Communist party, as victims of anticommunist hysteria and political persecution. The actual guilt or innocence of the Rosenbergs continues to be debated even today. Our analysis shows the defense attorneys did not present a probable story in developing the case, and therefore could not produce an effective closing argument.

The Trial

On June 25, 1950, Americans saw the end of the cold war as troops under the communist regime of the provinces of North Korea invaded the Republic of South Korea. Americans were, at the same time, alarmed over the spectacles created by the House Committee on Un-American Activities, to which, because they were committed in the sacred cause of preserving the nation, nobody could be totally indifferent. Many Americans thought that the committee was the only way to protect the common security; that it was time to recognize that communism was not politics but a criminal movement; and that the radicals of the depression era may well have become traitors, and it was better to destroy a few doubtful ones than to allow a real one to survive. In addition, federal prosecutions under the Smith Act had begun and anybody who had been in a position of Communist party leadership could expect, if arrested, to be convicted. There could be little doubt that America was relieving its frustrated fury over the cold war in the tangible prosecution of communists at home.

Julius and Ethel Rosenberg, in July and August 1950, were arrested and charged with conspiring to communicate, deliver, and transmit to the Soviet Union documents, sketches, and information relating to the national defense of the United States, in violation of the Espionage Act of 1917. The charge evolved from a complicated series of arrests and confessions.

In February 1950, a former scientist at the Los Alamos atomic test facility, Klaus Fuchs, announced that he had been a spy who transmitted secrets about the atomic bomb to the Soviet Union (Wexley, 1977, p. xvii). Fuchs implicated Harry Gold, who then confessed that he had been a courier for carrying secrets from spies at Los Alamos to a Soviet counsul, Anatoli Yakolev (Wexley, 1977,

p. xvii). Gold's confession led to the arrest of David Greenglass, a former army soldier stationed as a security guard at Los Alamos. Greenglass confessed that he had drawn replicas of plans that described the production of the bomb and delivered them to Gold, who in turn passed them on to Yakolev. However, Greenglass blamed his brother-in-law, Julius Rosenberg, for his espionage claiming that Julius planned and organized the operation and paid for the duplicated plans and other secrets. Ethel Rosenberg was also implicated as a coconspirator in Julius' plan. Ultimately, Julius and Ethel Rosenberg were indicted and charged with conspiring to violate the Espionage Act of 1917.

On March 6, 1951, the trial of Julius and Ethel Rosenberg began before Judge Irving R. Kaufman in the federal court for the Southern District of New York. The attorney for the prosecution was Irving Saypol; the Rosenbergs were defended by Emmanuel and Alexander Bloch. Less then one month after the opening of the trial, on March 29, 1951, the jury returned their verdict. Both Julius and Ethel Rosenberg were found guilty; Judge Kaufman sentenced them to death, making them the first accused spies ever to receive the ultimate penalty from an American civil court (Goldstein, 1975).

Their convictions were upheld by the Second Circuit Court of Appeals in February 1952. In the fall of 1952, the Supreme Court declined to review the case. In December of that year, the District Court denied a motion to reduce the death sentence and for a new trial. On June 14, 1953, the Supreme Court declined for a third time to review the case and refused to stay the execution. Although three days later, Justice Douglas granted a temporary stay of execution, on June 19th the whole court vacated the stay by a vote of six to three, Justices Frankfurter, Black, and Douglas dissenting (Wexley, 1977, p. xxii). Hours after this final decision, President Eisenhower refused to grant the Rosenbergs executive clemency; they were executed almost immediately at Sing Sing state prison in New York.

The Rosenbergs were native New Yorkers—the children of Jewish immigrants. They had been active in the Young Communist League and in various professional societies espousing communist doctrine. It likely was believed (though never proven) that they were members of the Communist party proper. Many other people throughout the world, however, regarded the Rosenbergs as victims of anticommunist hysteria and political persecution. The actual guilt or innocence of the Rosenbergs continues to be debated today.

The purpose of this chapter is to investigate how the closing argument of a trial serves as a key phase of the courtroom persuasion process. The essay posits that an effective closing argument contains two separate, but related, forms of discourse: narration and argumentation, with participatory persuasion theory underlying both forms. Thus, this investigation seeks to understand how the two forms of discourse are effectively developed—how they are different and how they relate. Further, the study considers how participatory persuasion strategies are central to full development of both forms of discourse.

To achieve this end, the essay (1) examines the importance of the closing argument in the trial process; (2) identifies participatory persuasion as the theoretical basis underlying effective closing argument; (3) considers how the elements of form, content and style contribute to the development of a persuasive closing argument; (4) analyzes the closing argument of the defense and prosecution in the Rosenberg trial according to each of these elements; and (5) suggests the implications of the investigation for trial practice.

Audience Involvement as Persuasion: Closing Argument

Legal Procedure and Norms

Closing argument is the last opportunity for the trial advocate to address the jury. Moreover, it is the psychological culmination of the trial. For these reasons, successful trial practitioners emphasize the importance of the closing argument and argue that the value of the closing argument cannot be overestimated (Busch, 1963, pp. 411–12; McCullough & Underwood, 1980, p. 647). More specifically, Stryker (1954) claims the closing argument is the highpoint in the art of advocacy and an opportunity to "rescue a lost cause" (p. 111).

During closing argument, more so than at any other time of trial, an attorney is an advocate in the purest sense of the word. Counsel's function is to organize and emphasize favorable evidence, present the position the jury is to adopt, rebut the allegations of the opposition, suggest ways the jury should resolve conflicting testimony, explain the law, and demonstrate how the evidence mandates a favorable verdict (Mauet, 1980, p. 295; Tanford, 1983, p. 133). In the interest of promoting this function of advocacy, attorneys are given great latitude in the presentation of the closing argument. In fact, the law surrounding closing argument has fewer specific rules and limitations than are found relating to opening statements. The few limitations that exist in relation to the closing argument fall within one of two general categories.

The first limitation on the closing argument is a procedural limitation. There are three procedural rules to which the closing argument is subject. First, the court generally has discretion to decide the order in which the parties will present the closing argument. The most common practice is to allow the plaintiff or prosecution to give the first argument, the defense is then permitted to reply, and finally, the plaintiff or prosecution has the opportunity to reply in rebuttal. Some jurisdictions, however, limit the parties to one argument each, in which case the defendant usually goes first and the party with the burden of proof last (Tanford, 1983, p. 139). The second procedural rule limits the number of attorneys for one party who may participate in the closing argument, even if one party is represented by a number of attorneys (Tanford, 1983, p. 140). Finally, the court has broad discretion to set a reasonable time limit for the closing argument. The length of time set typically depends on the complexity of the case and the number of parties per side (Tanford, 1983, p. 140).

The second limitation on the closing argument deals with the scope and content of the argument itself. In general, the closing argument is properly confined to the record developed during the earlier portions of the trial. Specifically, counsel is restricted to arguing the applicable rules of law that control the case (as long as fairly presented), the testimonial evidence adduced from the witnesses, the exhibits admitted into evidence, and the inferences that may reasonably be deduced from the testimony and exhibits (Stein, 1985, sec. 12, p. 23). Counsel may also properly argue and comment on matters of common knowledge, even though not developed in the trial record (Stein, 1985, sec. 19, p. 48). Additionally, in making closing arguments, counsel is permitted to use visual aids to help communicate the argument—to clarify a dispute, emphasize certain facts, or calculate damages. Thus, new exhibits may be prepared if they are based on the evidence or fair inference from the evidence even though not introduced during the trial (Tanford, 1983, p. 141). Finally, counsel is not permitted to appeal directly to the jurors' sympathy (Stein, 1985, sec. 22, p. 57), or to play on the emotions and prejudices of the jurors (Stein, 1985, sec. 21, p. 54). For example, it is improper to ask jurors to put themselves in the client's position and evaluate the case from that perspective, or to comment on the financial condition of the parties, or to ask jurors to base their decision on broad social issues, or to address a single juror by name (Tanford, 1983, pp. 146–47).

The rebuttal argument, if allowed, is limited in scope and properly confined to issues which were raised either in the plaintiff's or prosecution's first argument or the defense's reply argument (Tanford, 1983, pp. 141–42; Stein, 1985, sec. 23, p. 59). Provided that no completely new issues are raised, however, it is proper to bring up new lines of argument, expand or reiterate issues raised in the first argument, introduce new illustrations and exhibits, and provide additional details.

As the culmination of the trial, closing argument presents an excellent opportunity for counsel to explore the full realm of logic, eloquence, and persuasion. The advocate's goal is to persuade jurors how they should vote in the jury room, and the closing argument is the last opportunity for the advocate to address the jurors before they retire to deliberate. Specifically, this portion of the trial serves to provide those jurors who have already made up their minds with enough ammunition—logic, facts, explanations, and solid arguments—to persuade other jurors who are undecided and change the minds of those who would vote adversely. Thus, identifying strategies of persuasive argumentation is critical to understanding elements of effective closing argument.

Communicative Features of Closing Argument

Effective closing argument is premised on a participatory persuasion theory. Carl Hovland, Irving Janis, and Harold Kelley conceive of participatory persuasion as persuasion that involves the listener; making the listener participate in the argument is the goal (1953, pp. 215–40). This persuasive approach adheres to the theoretical premise that recipients of a message hear, understand, and are more susceptible to persuasion by that message if they are active in the receiving process. Receiver involvement boosts attention, facilitates understanding, and, consequently, enhances persuasion (Hovland et al., 1953, pp. 215–40; Sannito, 1981, p. 30). Thus, communicating in ways that stimulate thought, mental activity, and sensory involvement is the primary technique of participatory persuasion.

Participatory persuasion is the theoretical basis underlying the effective closing argument. Yet analysis of closing argument reveals the genre is more complex. As earlier developed in chapter 2 on

145

opening statement, genre analysis is a method of classifying discourse according to its type or kind. This type of analysis allows the critic to identify the norms of the particular discourse and organize the linguistic and organizational features for those who may wish to develop similar discourse in future situations. Closing arguments constitute a genre of discourse because there are a limited number of ways for counsel to achieve a rhetorical purpose when legal constraints and contexts are similar. Elements of genre consist of form, content, and style.

Form. Form is the connective structure that gives a pattern and shape to the discourse. In closing argument, the discourse takes on two separate forms, each with its own separate function. Specifically, one underlying form found in closing argument is that of narration; a second form of closing argument is argumentation. Effective closing arguments contain both forms of discourse and develop both functions.

The narrative form essentially parallels the opening statement; it functions to provide a basic, logically organized review of the facts and evidence using a narrative approach (Mauet, 1980, p. 306). Because the evidentiary portion of a trial may appear disjointed, confusing, and contradictory to jurors, attorneys in closing argument are given the opportunity to bring the case back together into a logical relationship, weaving the testimony, documents, and other evidence into the cohesive story presented originally in opening statements. The purpose of this form of discourse is to lay a foundation upon which counsel subsequently will argue the case for the jury.

The second category of form is argumentation. In the argumentative portion of the discourse, counsel selectively argues the important evidence, witness by witness, exhibit by exhibit, to support the position taken on the issues in the trial. This portion of the closing argument functions as argumentation in the traditional sense; it uses only those witnesses, exhibits, inferences, and techniques which will persuade the jury to resolve the disputed issues in the manner desired (Mauet, 1980, p. 306). The attorney in this section seeks to corroborate the testimony and exhibits favorable to the theory being promoted, question the testimony and exhibits of the opposing theory, refute the contentions of the opposition, summarize the key jury instructions (such as burden of proof and elements of the cause of action) and relate them to the evidence, and argue damages or verdict (McCullough & Underwood, 1980, pp. 654–60; Mauet, 1980, pp. 314–22; Tanford, 1983, pp. 154–60).

Content. Whereas form is the underlying structure of the discourse, content consists of the elements of discourse itself. The content of closing argument is dictated by the particular form of discourse and its corresponding function. That is, when arguing in the narrative form, the discourse functions to review the parties, scene, instrumentalities, issues, theory and basis of liability/nonliability or guilt/innocence in a narrative fashion (Mauet, 1980, pp. 306–14). Thus, the content of the narrative portion of the argument generally reviews the story of the case as introduced in opening statement and developed in the evidentiary portion of the trial. Specific strategies of the narrative form include such devices as ingratiation and reiteration of the theme.

The content of the narrative form deserves further explanation. The story of the case includes reviewing such items as the parties, the issues, and the theories. In the Rosenberg case, for example, the story of the prosecution was that the Rosenbergs had conspired to commit espionage for the advantage of the Soviet Union. In contrast, the defense promoted a story that the Rosenbergs were kind and gentle people, the victims of anticommunist hysteria and political persecution who never conspired to communicate, deliver, or transmit information to the Soviets.

A second element of the narrative form is ingratiation. Ingratiation theory suggests that at the beginning of closing argument, attorneys should give some expression of appreciation to the jurors for having fulfilled their function (Starr, 1983, p. 424). At least one effective advocate, however, warns that attorneys should not "compliment [the jurors] too profusely or they will feel you are trying to curry favor with them—a flowery speech about the glorious task they have done will do more harm than good" (Morrill, 1971, p. 86). Morrill warns of what is referred to as the "ingratiator's dilemma": this strategy can backfire when the ingratiation is obvious (Jones & Wortman, 1973).

Finally, the theme of the case must be reiterated in the narrative portion of the closing argument. A theme broadens the participatory potential of the closing argument by injecting a simple rationale that explains the essence of the theory; it provides a comfortable viewpoint from which the jury can assess all the evidence. The theme itself should be plausible, aligned with the jurors' knowledge of the way the world works, and congruent with the listeners' values (Brosnahan, 1979, pp. 250–52; McElhaney, 1981, p. 6). The theme should be introduced initially during the opening statement and then be woven throughout the closing argument. The theme of the prosecution in the Rosenberg case, for example, was one of communist conspirators seeking to harm the United States. The defense theme, on the other hand, was that the Rosenbergs were victims of anticommunist hysteria and political persecution.

In contrast to the narrative form, the argumentative portion of closing argument functions as traditional linear argument and seeks to argue only that evidence deemed most important, most persuasive. The content of the argumentative form of discourse includes such tactics as factual persuasion, order of presentation, and tactics to induce resistance to persuasion such as commitment and anchoring strategies.

Specifically, factual persuasion involves articulating and strategically sequencing specific facts or reasons before the general points that they support. Such development is also a participatory strategy in that developing detail by detail the factual premise before providing the conclusion coaxes the listener to reach the conclusion first, which in turn provokes listener participation (Goldberg, 1982, p. 196; Lundquist, 1982, p. 23). Properly developed factual persuasion should go beyond the facts and include details about how the listener should interpret the evidence. Specific suggestions regarding witness credibility, inferences, reasoning options, counsel's theory of the case, and the applicable law should be included. The key, however, is to provide the detail that enables the listener to draw his or her own conclusion; the activity and attention enhances persuasion.

A second element of the argumentative form is order of presentation. Order of presentation itself involves two separate, but related, concepts. The first concept is that of one-sided versus two-sided communications. One-sided communication limits the message content to entirely supportive material, while two-sided communication prepares for opponents' arguments and speaks to those issues as well. Two-sided arguments, arguments that present and then refute an anticipated counterargument, are effective as persuasion because they provoke critical perspectives and resistance rationales that listeners can use against counterpersuasion (Lawson, 1970, p. 579). Of specific importance in the jury situation, effective two-sided arguments provide friendly jurors with ammunition to use against the counterpoint during deliberation.

There is also a collateral psychological factor of which the trial advocate must be aware—that of the psychological function of primacy as opposed to recency. Primacy-recency studies investigate whether the strongest persuasive element should come first (primacy) or last (recency) in the message. In essence, primacy relates to the intensity of belief, while recency relates to the ability to remember. The principle of primacy, briefly stated, is that people tend to develop strong beliefs, highly resistant to change, upon first impression (Lund, 1925, pp. 174–96; Costopoulos, 1972, pp. 384–409). Thus, the strongest argument should be given first (Sannito, 1981, p. 30).

The final component of the argumentative form, tactics to induce resistance to counterpersuasion, involves two strategies: commitment and anchoring. The strategy of commitment or immunization is effective for inducing resistance to persuasive techniques that might be employed by the opposition (Miller & Burgoon, 1973, p. 28). Research in this area indicates that forcing a person publicly to commit himself or herself to a belief is an effective way to increase resistance to subsequent persuasive appeals. Thus, for example, if jurors commit themselves during *voir dire* to follow the law, to be fair in their review of the facts and in their deliberations, and to overcome their particular prejudices and biases that concern case issues, they are less likely to go against these commitments once they have been publicly made. Accordingly, in closing argument, counsel should remind the jurors of the commitments made in the earlier *voir dire* portion of the trial.

A related strategy is the technique of anchoring (McGuire, 1969). Anchoring involves the linking of beliefs that the attorney uses as support for the case issues to beliefs already held by the jury. Anchoring differs from commitment strategies in that no public commitment from the jurors is sought; the attorney simply advances arguments that appeal to the beliefs he or she perceives exist within the community or within the personality types present on the jury panel. By appealing to known juror values, the receiver is more attentive and, therefore, a more active receiver.

Style. The third element of genre is style—the linguistic embellishment of the discourse. From a participatory persuasion perspective, counsel should actively select linguistic devices that involve the listener and encourage the listener to participate in the argument. Examples of participatory linguistic devices include use of analogy, visualizing techniques, language choice, and rhetorical questions.

One linguistic technique of participatory persuasion is analogy. Analogies are a powerful persuasion tool in that they provide the equal sign between something strange and something familiar. One effective trial advocate acclaims the analogy as the "greatest weapon" in persuasion's arsenal because nothing moves jurors more convincingly than "an apt comparison to something they know from their own experience is true" (Spangenberg, 1977, p. 13).

Analogies are persuasive because they first provoke and then reward the listener's intellectual pride. By engaging the audience in the story of analogy, the activity and attention enhances persuasion. An analogy skillfully done lets the audience reach the conclusion before the speaker does, and jurors who reach their own conclusions tend to hold them more firmly than those they have been told to develop (Stryker, 1954, p. 125; McElhaney, 1979, p. 37). Later counterarguments then often alienate listeners because they hear them as assaults on their own ideas. As a legal matter, analogies are exceptions to the rule limiting argument to the evidence adduced at trial because they stem from matters of common knowledge and understanding. In the Rosenberg case, the prosecution uses the following analogy to explain the nature of a conspiracy:

> A conspiracy in operation, such as the conspiracy we have here, is in many ways familiar to the structure of a business enterprise, with a number of partners. All of the partners and employees of the firm do not do the same thing at the same time. While one partner talks to a customer, another may be negotiating with another prospect. While one employee is traveling, selling merchandise, so another employee may be in another city, buying merchandise, but the act of each partner and each employee is not an individual, isolated act performed only for the benefit of the actor. Each act by each party, by each employer in the course of business is an act performed for the benefit of the firm and for the benefit of his fellows. [Transcript of Record, p. 1513]

Visualizing techniques—visual evidence that involves the eyes— are powerfully persuasive because they take advantage of the fact that most people learn more and faster through their eyes than through their ears (Sannito, 1981, p. 31; Strawn & Munsterman, 1982, p. 444). Visualizing techniques include use of demonstrative aids such as diagrams, charts, photographs, documents (Smithburn & Seckinger, 1983, p. 33), or writing key words on a blackboard or large flip pad (Singer, 1977, p. 19; Head, 1980, p. 29; Crane, 1982, p. 18). Use of such techniques can be very persuasive because they visually involve the fact-finder; this visual participation contributes to the persuasive process.

Language choice—use of imagery, choice of vivid adjectives—can contribute to participatory persuasion. Wise word choice stimulates visually by creating images that help listeners see points in their minds. Moreover, concepts delivered with language that creates visual mental images are more easily understood and remembered (Goldberg, 1982, pp. 199–200). Vivid words are dramatic and persuasive by provoking visual participation. In the Rosenberg case, for example, the prosecution uses imagery in describing the involvement of Julius Rosenberg in the alleged conspiracy as follows: "Imagine a wheel. In the center of the wheel, Rosenberg, reaching out like the tentacles of an octopus" (Transcript of Record, p. 1513). The prosecution effectively uses this figurative language to produce a mental image of Rosenberg's overreaching involvement in the conspiracy.

Another participatory linguistic strategy is the use of rhetorical questions (Smith, 1978, pp. 1–32 to 1–33). By posing the rhetorical question, the juror then answers the question for himself or herself. When this happens, the statement ceases being the questionable argument of the advocate; instead, the thought becomes one that the juror believes to be his or her own. Once this happens, the juror is not easily dissuaded from this opinion by others in the jury room. In this way, the rhetorical question can be a most effective technique in the adversary process.

Thus, the closing argument functions as speech in one of two ways: narration and argumentation. Effective closing arguments contain both functions. Additionally, persuasive closing arguments include the use of specific persuasive strategies. Such persuasive strategies may be included in the content of the closing argument as well as the linguistic development of that content.

Analysis of Participatory Persuasion in Closing Argument

In an effort to delineate clearly the qualities of genre—form, content, and style—and their impact on enhancing participatory persuasion in closing argument, the defense's argument and the prosecution's argument will each be examined in turn. In the Rosenberg trial, the parties were each limited to one argument, with the defense going first and the prosecution last. Accordingly, the closing arguments will be examined in that order.

The Defense's Closing Argument

Rather than presenting a probable narrative explaining the events from the defendants' perspective, the defense's strategy in the Rosenberg case was one of refutation of the prosecution's story and vilification of the prosecution's witnesses. Thus, in closing argument, the defense chose to argue that the Rosenbergs were victims of anticommunist hysteria and political persecution and that the prosecution witnesses were not to be believed (Transcript of Record, p. 1452).

(Narrative Content)
Defense begins its closing argument with ingratiation, expressing appreciation to the jurors for having served as jurors.

Closing Argument for the Defense. [Transcript of Record, pp. 1452–93]

Mr. E. H. Bloch: May it please the Court, ladies and gentlemen of the jury, it is usual when you come into a house to say good evening, and it has sprung up in court that there are certain social amenities, certain preliminaries, certain graces that one goes through before one gets into the facts of a case, and I would like to say to the Court on behalf of all defense counsel that we feel that you have treated us with the utmost courtesy, that you have extended to us the privileges that we expect as lawyers, and despite any disagreements we may have had with the Court on questions of law, we feel that the trial has been conducted and we hope we have contributed our share, with that dignity and that decorum that befits an American trial.

* * *

(Argument Content)
Defense uses commitment strategy to induce resistance to persuasion. Jurors are reminded that during voir dire, *questions were*

Now I want to take your minds back, ladies and gentlemen, to something you were asked on your *voir dire* examination, to something that you were *asked and commitments were made regarding each individual's ability to view the case impartially and with an open mind. Defense now reminds the jurors of the commitments they made during the earlier* voir dire *portion of the trial.*

(Narrative Content) Ingratiation strategy is utilized again in this portion of the closing argument. This time, however, the flattery is obvious and thus the ingratiation much less effective as compared to defense's first attempt. The two attempts at ingratiation in this closing argument clearly demonstrate the notion of "ingratiator's dilemma" where the strategy is thought to backfire.

asked by me and I think as well by other counsel when you took your seats in the jury box: We were all very careful, very meticulous, the Court and counsel on both sides, to get a jury, a body of American men and women who would come to this case with an open mind and who would decide this case on the evidence that was presented in this courtroom in this court from this witness chair that is now silent, but which was so eloquent for many, many days. And we wanted that because if a juror comes in to try somebody, to determine his guilt or his innocence in a criminal case, and this would be true in any case, if he or she should not come in with a preconceived notion or a preconceived judgment or impression which would make it impossible or very difficult to decide the case on the facts as presented and on the law as the Court will give it to you later after the summations of all counsel.

The fear that an impartial jury could not be secured was particularly important in this type of case. Now, all of you are New Yorkers or you come from the environs of New York. We are pretty sophisticated people. People can't put things over on us very easily. We are fairly wise in the ways of the world and the ways of people and we all know that there is not a person in this world who hasn't some prejudice, and you would be inhuman if you didn't have some prejudice. But we ask you now as we

153

asked you before, please don't decide this case because you may have some bias or some prejudice against some political philosophy.

* * *

(Narrative Content)
The content of the narrative portion of closing argument should review the parties, the issues, and the theories. Here, defense clearly sets forth the narrow issue for the jurors' consideration. The defense, however, stops short of completing the narrative form, of developing an alternative characterization of the parties, events, and theories in a plausible story form.

(Narrative Content)
Instead of developing a plausible alternative of the events from the defendants' perspective, the defense again reverts back to ingratiation strategy. The defense, by complimenting the jurors so profusely may have alienated the audience, doing more harm than good.

There is one question for you to decide, just one: Did these defendants agree and confederate with each other and with others to transmit information relating to the national defense of the United States to the Soviet Union with that intent or reason to believe that that information so transmitted would be advantageous to the Soviet Union?

* * *

I am confident, I am confident that when you took your oaths, you meant what you said and you swore to. I am confident you are going to analyze, scrutinize, most carefully probe every piece of evidence that has been introduced into this case and begin to weigh and begin to evaluate and say to yourselves, "What is the probability here?" And "What is the probability there?" Because in the last analysis you, sitting here in this jury box, constitute the bedrock of American justice, which is founded upon the concept that this is the average man and woman that has the wisdom to decide what is a fact and what is not a fact. You are all intelligent people. I say again, you are developed people; you are fortunate in living in a big city like New York, where ideas percolate and are exchanged, and in the course of that we become

154

wiser people. People can't put things over on us easily.

* * *

(Narrative Form)
The narrative form in closing argument functions to provide a logically organized review of the facts and evidence using a story approach. Its purpose is to bring the case back together into a logical relationship by weaving the testimony, documents, and other evidence into a cohesive story. In contrast to the persuasive narrative form, defense in this case merely lists the Government's exhibits, one by one, and dismisses each exhibit as unimportant without explanation. The defense goes through each of thirty-two exhibits in this same manner, one by one. Each exhibit is dismissed as not relating to the defendants, yet no logical explanation is given for so finding; no probable alternative explanation is advanced.

Now, what are these exhibits?. *[sic]* Here is Government's Exhibit 1. Government's Exhibit 1 is a true copy of the security regulations at the Los Alamos Project. Is there any dispute that this is a bona fide document? Is this exhibit in the handwriting or has it been manufactured by or is it a product of the work of the defendants Julius Rosenberg and Ethel Rosenberg? Is there any doubt that it is not?

Government's Exhibit 2 is a sketch. Whose sketch is that, ladies and gentlemen? Is it Rosenberg's sketch? Is it Ethel Rosenberg's sketch? Or is that a sketch that was drawn by David Greenglass? Any doubt about that? I think not.

Government's Exhibit 3 is a picture of Mike and Ann Sidorvich. Is that Rosenberg's making? Is that Ethel Rosenberg? These are friends or were friends of the Rosenbergs. Any dispute about that? No dispute.

* * *

And of course I know you are going to be honest with yourselves and admit very readily—not out loud, but very readily that there isn't one piece of documentary evidence in this case to tie the Rosenbergs up with this conspiracy.

* * *

(Narrative Content)
Defense here reiterates their theme that there is no evidence that the Rosenbergs committed espionage. Counsel asserts that the Government's documentary proof has failed completely to implicate the Rosenbergs and suggests that if they are to be convicted, the jurors must be convinced by the oral testimony. Thus, counsel turns to the oral

These are the exhibits in this case. There are no other exhibits. This is the complete documen-

155

evidence proffered against the
Rosenbergs.

(Argumentative Form)
In the argumentative portion of
the closing argument, counsel selectively argues the important
evidence witness by witness to
support the defense's theme that
the State has failed to implicate
the Rosenbergs and that they
have been the subject of political
persecution. Here, the defense
sets up the issue as a credibility
question—either the Greenglasses or the Rosenbergs were
telling the truth.

(Argumentative Content)
Defense's first argument attacks
prosecution witness Greenglass.
The order of presentation of the
defense's argument is somewhat
unique. Typically, a one-sided
argument limits the message to
supportive material while two-
sided arguments present supportive material but go on to present and refute anticipated
counterargument. Here, the defense adopts a one-sided communication consisting entirely of
refutation and vilification strategies; no supportive material is
advanced.

tary evidence adduced by the
Government to tie the Rosenbergs up with this case.

* * *

Now this case, therefore,
against the Rosenbergs depends
upon oral testimony.

* * *

Now, who are the main ac-
tors here in this big drama? The
main actors, in my estimation,
are four. There is Dave Greenglass; there is Ruth Greenglass—
that is one team, on this side;
and in the other corner of the
ring there is Julius Rosenberg
and there is Ethel Rosenberg.

* * *

I want you to judge these
four, each of these four, as human beings, as certain kinds of
people, and in the last analysis,
what you have to determine for
yourself is whether or not the
Greenglasses were telling the
truth or whether the Rosenbergs
were telling the truth.

Now, let us take Dave
Greenglass. This didn't come out
of my mouth. This came out of
his mouth. Is he a self-confessed
spy? Is there any doubt in any of
your minds that Dave Greenglass
is a self-confessed espionage
agent? He characterized himself
that way. What did this man do?
He took an oath when he entered the Army of the United
States. He didn't even remember
what the oath was. That is how
seriously he took it. But in substance, he swore to support our
country. Is there any doubt in
your mind that he violated that
oath? Is there any doubt in your

mind that he disgraced the uniform of every soldier in the United States by his actions?

Do you know what that man did? He was assigned to one of the most important secret projects in this country, and by his own statements, by his own admissions, he told you that he stole information out there and gave it to strangers, and that it was going to the Soviet Government. Now, that is undisputed. I would like Mr. Saypol, or anybody who is going to sum up on the part of the Government to refute that. Is there any doubt in your mind about that?

* * *

But one thing I think you do know, that any man who will testify against his own blood and flesh, his own sister, is repulsive, is revolting, who violates every code that any civilization has ever lived by. He is the lowest of the lowest animals that I have ever seen, and if you are honest with yourself you will admit that he is lower than the lowest animal that you have ever seen.

* * *

Tell me, is this the kind of a man you are going to believe? God Almighty, if ever a witness discredited himself on a stand, he did. What kind of a man can we disbelieve if we are going to believe Dave Greenglass? What is the sense of having witness chairs? What is the sense of having juries subject witnesses' testimony to scrutiny and analysis? Is that the kind of a man that you would believe in your own life or

(Argumentative Content)
Moreover, in presenting the refutation argument, counsel fails to utilize the technique of factual persuasion—articulating and strategically sequencing specific facts or reasons before the general proposition they support.

(Style)
Defense uses the linguistic strategy of rhetorical question, posing the question and leaving it to the jurors to answer the question themselves. In this way, the thought becomes one that each juror believes to be his or her own.

157

would you punch him in the nose and throw him out and have nothing to do with him because he is a low rebel? Come on, be honest with yourselves, ladies and gentlemen, is that the kind of testimony that you are going to accept?

* * *

(Argumentative Content) Defense's second major argument attacks prosecution witness Ruth Greenglass.

Ruth Greenglass admitted here that she was in this conspiracy. Is there any doubt about that? Is there any doubt that in the middle of November she came out to Albuquerque and tried to induce her husband to sell secrets? Is there any doubt that she grabbed Gold's money and deposited it in the bank? Is there any doubt that she gained by the illegal fruits of her husband's venture? Is there any doubt that she knew all about it?

* * *

(Argumentative Content) The order of presentation of this portion of the argument is more clearly a two-sided approach. Specifically, the defense puts forth a probable explanation for David Greenglass' actions—to save his wife.

You try to explain to yourselves how Ruth Greenglass got out of this. She is a free woman. She is taking care of her kids. Maybe I was a little too harsh on Dave Greenglass. Because if the human race can produce a Dave Greenglass I am afraid we would all get terribly pessimistic about the future, but there is always something good in every human being, some trait of warmth, of love. Dave Greenglass loved his wife. He loved her more than he loved himself. I asked him that question. There was a reason for asking that question. And, ladies and gentlemen, this explains why Dave Greenglass was willing to bury his sister and his brother-in-law

158

to save his wife. Yes, there were other factors of course. He had a grudge against Rosenberg because he felt that Rosenberg had gypped him out of a thousand dollars, but that would not have been enough to explain Greenglass' act.

* * *

Now, ladies and gentlemen, I say finally before I leave the Greenglasses, that this case hinges on their testimony. If you don't believe the Greenglasses or if you have a reasonable doubt as to whether or not they are telling the truth, I say you should unhesitatingly acquit these defendants. . . .

* * *

Now, look, ladies and gentlemen, you saw Julius Rosenberg and Ethel Rosenberg on this stand. You judge them. You saw them. You had an opportunity to study them. I want you to compare them and the type of people they are with the Greenglasses. I want you to ask yourselves, "Are these the type of people who are spies? Are these the type of people who will lie? Does their past life indicate that they are the type of people who will lie"?

* * *

I don't care, ladies and gentlemen, I don't care whether or not you disagree or whether you all agree at one time or another, one thing alone I ask you, I am entitled to ask that of you under the law, I am entitled to ask—these defendants are entitled to ask that of you as human

(Argumentative Content) *Defense reiterates the premise of their argument—the jurors must believe either the Greenglasses or the Rosenbergs.*

(Argumentative Form) *The third major argument put forth is a plea to judge the defendants by their character. Again, no factual persuasion is advanced to support this premise. Counsel does not give any specific suggestions regarding the witnesses' credibility, inferences to be drawn, or reasoning options.*

(Argumentative Content) *Defense ends with a final plea to the jurors' sense of justice and fairness, thus invoking anchoring strategy. That is, counsel seeks to link the jurors' determination of the issues to their perceived commitment to producing a fair trial.*

159

beings: Please take the evidence and sift it, analyze it, take what I said, take what Mr. Saypol is going to tell you, take what Mr. Kuntz is going to tell you when he sums up for Sobell—take these things, weigh them, weigh them carefully, because in your hands human lives are at stake.

That's all I ask you to do, and I say that if you do that, you can come to no other conclusion than that these defendants are innocent and you are going to show to the world that in America a man can get a fair trial.

The Prosecution's Closing Argument

The prosecution's interpretation of the events that transpired in the Rosenberg case included portraying the defendants as conspiring to commit espionage for the advantage of the Soviet Union. In elaborating on this conspiracy theme, the prosecution stated that the object of the parties was to dispatch information vital to America's national defense, to the Soviet Union (Transcript of Record, p. 1508).

Closing Argument for the Prosecution. [Transcript of Record, pp. 1508–36]

(Narrative Content)
The prosecution begins its closing argument with ingratiation, expressing appreciation to the jurors for having fulfilled their function.

Mr. Saypol: May it please the Court, Mr. Foreman, ladies and gentlemen of the jury, throughout the three weeks we have been together in this courtroom, I have observed that each of you has displayed great interest and close attention as the evidence was unfolded here. For your courtesy, for your consideration my colleagues and I acknowledge our appreciation.

* * *

(Narrative Form)
Prosecution's closing begins in

The grand jury in this Court has charged that these three de-

160

the narrative form. This approach functions to provide a basic, logically organized review of the facts and evidence using a narrative, story form.

(Narrative Content)
The content of this portion of the narrative functions to review the charges in the indictment, parties, issues, and basis of guilt in a narrative fashion.

fendants on trial before and several others, who were named with them but who are not on trial before you, were members of a conspiracy to commit espionage for the advantage of the Soviet Union. The grand jury has charged that these three defendants and others agreed to communicate, deliver and transmit to the Soviet Union, documents, writings and sketches relating to various aspects of the national defense of the United States. I told you in my opening, and as you have seen and heard this case is one of the most important that has ever been submitted to a jury in this country. I feel most inadequate to express to you in words the enormity of the thing, but its seriousness and implications for all of us does not make it a complicated case. The issue here is a simple one. You must determine whether or not these defendants were parties to this conspiracy to transmit information to the Soviet Union. A conspiracy, of course, is merely an agreement between two or more persons to violate some law of this country—in this case the Espionage law. The law actually need not be broken, as it was here. The agreement alone to break the law would be enough. Every person whom you should find entered into this agreement becomes guilty of the crime of conspiracy. If any one of the members of the conspiracy commits any overt acts, any physical act to further the objects of the conspiracy, all are guilty.

161

(Narrative Content)
This narrative portion of closing argument also serves to reiterate the prosecution theme of defendants' conspiring to commit espionage for the advantage of the Soviet Union. Thus, prosecution is setting up the argumentative portion of the closing argument by injecting a rationale by which the jury can assess all the evidence of the case.

In this case if you find that the three defendants had become members of this conspiracy to commit espionage, they all become guilty as charged in the indictment.

If any one of them, Rosenberg, Mrs. Rosenberg or any one of the co-conspirators who are not on trial, commits any one act in furtherance of this conspiracy, such as meetings and conferences between any of the conspirators in furtherance of the conspiracy, such as trips made by any of the conspirators in furtherance of the conspiracy, like Harry Gold's trip to Albuquerque or Sobell's drive with Max Elitcher to Catherine Slip—any one such act by any conspirator supplies the requirements of the law as to all those who were members of this conspiracy.

* * *

(Style)
Prosecution uses the linguistic technique of analogy. By likening a conspiracy to a business enterprise, prosecution enables the jurors to better understand the nature of the conspiracy charge.

A conspiracy in operation, such as the conspiracy we have here, is in many ways familiar to the structure of a business enterprise, with a number of partners. All of the partners and employees of the firm do not do the same thing at the same time. While one partner talks to a customer, another may be negotiating with another prospect. While one employee is traveling, selling merchandise, so another employee may be in another city, buying merchandise, but the act of each partner and each employee is not an individual, isolated act performed only for the benefit of the actor. Each act by each party, by each employer in

162

the course of business is an act performed for the benefit of the firm and for the benefit of his fellows.

Imagine a wheel. In the center of the wheel, Rosenberg, reaching out like the tentacles of an octopus. Rosenberg to David Greenglass. Ethel Rosenberg, Ruth Greenglass; Rosenberg to Harry Gold; Rosenberg, Yakovlev. Information obtained, supplied. Rosenberg, Sobell, Elitcher—always the objective in the center coming from all the legs, all the tentacles going to the one center, solely for the one object: The benefit of Soviet Russia. The sources, Government sources, Los Alamos, atomic information. Sobell, Elitcher, information from the Navy, relation particularly to gunfire control; always secret, always classified, always of advantage to a foreign government.

* * *

(Style)
Here, prosecution uses imagery to invoke audience participation. Moreover, by describing the nature of the conspiracy in language that calls up mental images, the characterization is more easily understood and remembered.

(Narrative Form)
This portion of the narrative is effective in bringing the case back together into a logical relationship, a cohesive story. This portion of the discourse functions to lay a foundation for the subsequent argument.

Let us now review the evidence in the case. It will be brief because you saw the witnesses, you heard them, you examined the exhibits. Your recollection is the standard which will prevail. The association of Rosenberg and Sobell began at City College, and it continues until today. They have been held together by one common bond: Their mutual devotion to Communism and the Soviet Union, and their membership in this conspiracy to commit espionage for that Soviet Union. That is why their classmate, Max Elitcher, was asked to join the Young Communist League when

163

they were at college. That is why Sobell recruited Elitcher into the Communist Party. That is why Sobell and Rosenberg joined in the concerted action to recruit Elitcher into their Soviet espionage ring.

While Sobell was chairman of his Communist Party unit in Washington, delivering to its members weekly directives concerning worship of the Soviet Union, Rosenberg was working his way up in the Communist Party underground. The significance of the relations of the membership in this Party, of their membership, the defendants' membership, conspirators' membership, their incidental allegiance to the Communist Party of the United States of America and the Communist National, is revealed in the testimony of Elizabeth Bentley.

* * *

(Narrative Form)
Prosecution demonstrates the effective narrative form by weaving the testimony revealed in the evidentiary portion of the trial into the cohesive story.

You saw her and heard her on the witness stand here. You are in a position to judge in the whole setting the substance of her narrative. She revealed the significance of membership in the Party, open membership and underground membership; the nature of its activities, including espionage in behalf of Soviet Russia; how it operated; how its contacts were established and maintained, always secret, always furtive, always to avoid detection.

* * *

(Argumentative Form)
Counsel now moves into the argumentative portion of the dis-

These defendants were not dealing in public information or magazine articles. The testimony

164

course. The purpose of this
portion of the closing argument
is to argue the important evidence to support the prosecution's theory of conspiracy.

(Argumentative Form)
Counsel here questions the contentions of the defense and refutes the opposition using the
stylistic device of rhetorical question.

(Style)
Prosecution selects vivid adjectives in this portion of the argument. These vivid words are
dramatic and persuasive by invoking visual participation.

of the highly secret nature of the
atom bomb material, of the classified nature of the work being
done by Sobell at General Elec-
tric and at Reeves is established
and uncontradicted.

There has been some argu-
ment here in the course of the
defendants' summation with respect to those exhibits in evidence, the sketches of the lens
mold, for instance, the sketch of
the bomb, and a demand has
been voiced, I take it, hardly serious, although highly vocal:
where are those exhibits? Why
aren't they produced here? Well,
isn't it obvious having been delivered by Greenglass to Rosenberg, aren't the originals now in
the place which Rosenberg or
which the defendants intended,
some place far away on the other
side of the ocean behind the Iron
Curtain? How could they possi-
bly be here?

* * *

We know of these other
henchmen of Rosenberg in this
plot by him, by Sobell, by the
Soviet Union and its representatives and by other traitorous
Americans to deliver the safe-
guards to our security into the
hands of a power that would
wipe us off the face of the earth
and destroy its peace. We don't
know all the details, because the
only living people who can supply the details are the defendants. Rosenberg and his wife
have added the supreme touch to
their betrayal of this country by
taking the stand before you, by
taking advantage of every legal

165

opportunity that is afforded defendants, and then, by lying and lying and lying here, brazenly in an attempt to deceive you, to lie their way out of what they did.

(Argumentative Content) Prosecution uses the strategy of factual persuasion. Factual persuasion involves articulating and strategically sequencing specific facts or reasons before the general points they support. This portion of the argument provides the factual details, inferences, and counsel's view of the evidence in a manner that then allows the jurors to draw their own conclusions.

I have said that there is much about this that we have not disclosed or that we do not know, but there is one part of the scheme that we do know about. You know about it because it was disclosed right before you. We know that these conspirators stole the most important scientific secrets ever known to mankind from this country and delivered them to the Soviet Union. We know that Julius Rosenberg and Ethel Rosenberg infected Ruth and David Greenglass with the poison of Communist ideology. We know that Julius Rosenberg and Ethel Rosenberg were engaged in a continuing campaign to enlist recruits for the Soviet cause through the Communist Party. And we know that in 1944 Julius and Ethel Rosenberg carried their campaign one step further and persuaded David Greenglass to steal atomic bomb secrets for the Rosenbergs to be turned over to the Soviet Union.

(Argumentative Content) The argument presented is a two-sided communication. Here, prosecution acknowledges that Greenglass is a self-confessed spy but goes on to develop this point to the prosecution's advantage. In this way, prosecution presents and refutes the opposition's counterargument.

There is no condonation for the activities of the Greenglasses in 1944 and 1945. David Greenglass is a confessed member of the Rosenberg espionage ring. You heard his testimony and you observed him. You heard him confess his guilt. You heard him describe in detail his participation in this conspiracy. By his own plea of guilty, by his own

166

voluntary act, without weaving a web of lies in an attempt to deceive you, he has made himself liable to the death penalty, too. The spurious defense that Greenglass, or the Greenglasses, in order to satisfy a business grudge, a business dispute against the Rosenbergs has concocted a story about espionage, making himself liable to the capital penalty by his plea of guilty because of the business disagreement, is as much of a concoction as the story of the defendants that Greenglass went to his worst enemy, Julius Rosenberg, for help when he wanted to flee the country.

* * *

The issue in this case, we are all agreed, transcends any family consideration; but clearly the breach of family loyalty is that of an older sister and brother-in-law dragging an American soldier into the sordid business of betraying his country for the benefit of the Soviet Union. The difference between the Greenglasses and the Rosenbergs? The Greenglasses have told the truth. They have tried to make amends for the hurt which has been done to our nation and to the world. The Rosenbergs, on the other hand, have magnified their sins by their lying.

* * *

These defendants seek to escape the consequences of their own acts by hiding behind straw men like that. Greenglass is a confessed spy and Elitcher has admitted that some years ago he

(Style)
Prosecution describes Greenglass as an American soldier who was dragged into espionage. This technique of imagery is persuasive by provoking visual participation. Counsel also uses the linguistic device of rhetorical question to invoke audience participation.

(Argumentative Content)
Counsel uses anchoring strategy here, linking perceived juror values of honesty and patriotism to the arguments presented.

(Argumentative Form)
This portion of prosecution's argument seeks to corroborate the testimony and exhibits favorable to the conspiracy theory being promoted.

167

did not disclose his Communist Party membership in an application; but these men under the greatest stress have stood up here and disclosed the truth about their past activities—the truth established beyond any doubt by independent, uncontradicted and corroborated evidence. Unlike the defendants on trial, these witnesses have come forward and told the truth. They have not compounded their sins by trying to lie to you here in this courtroom. The question here is not the fate, present or future, of other people. The question here is the guilt of these three defendants named by the grand jury here on trial before you in this courtroom. That is the single issue and the evidence on that issue is overwhelming.

(Argumentative Form) Prosecution goes on to question the testimony of the opposition.

In the face of the testimony of the Greenglasses, of Gold, of Elitcher, and the documentary proof and testimony of disinterested witnesses, all corroborated, all that the defense has offered is the testimony of Ethel and Julius Rosenberg, who plainly have the greatest motive in the world for lying, and just as plainly lied throughout before you.

* * *

(Argumentative Content) Prosecution ends the closing argument with the anchoring tactic, in an effort to induce resistance to counterpersuasion. Prosecution emphasizes perceived juror values of loyalty, justice, and the American jury system.

These three defendants stand before you in the face of overwhelming proof of this terrible disloyalty, proof which transcends any emotional consideration which must eliminate any consideration of sympathy.

No defendants ever stood before the bar of American justice less deserving of sympathy than these three.

I am a firm believer in the American jury system. I have confidence in the perception of a jury of 12 intelligent American citizens.

I am confident that you will render the only verdict possible on the evidence presented before you in this courtroom—that of guilty as charged by the grand jury as to each of these three defendants.

Evaluation of the Closing Arguments

The arguments of advocates in closing may be assessed by whether the advocate achieves the purpose of closing argument. To achieve their purpose, advocates must develop a narrative that provides an organized review of the facts and evidence, weaving the testimony, documents, and other evidence into the cohesive story presented originally in opening statements. Additionally, counsel must advance an argument that corroborates the testimony and exhibits favorable to the theory being promoted, questions the testimony and exhibits of the opposing theory, refutes the contentions of the opposition, summarizes the key jury instructions, and argues damages or a verdict.

Moreover, closing arguments must be persuasive. Strategies that involve the audience are the most effective because they engage the audience in the argumentive process; listener participation is the goal. Accordingly, communicating in ways that promote listener involvement through mental and sensory activity is the primary technique of participatory persuasion. Specifically, invoking such devices as reviewing the story, ingratiation, reiteration of theme, factual persuasion, order of presentation, and tactics to induce resistance to persuasion are methods of invoking participatory persuasion through message content. Additionally, linguistic devices such as use of analogy, visualizing techniques, language choice, and rhetorical question are methods of achieving listener involvement by way of message style.

The closing arguments of the defense and prosecution reveal some contrasts in form, content, and style. The strategy of the defense is to refute the prosecution's interpretation of events and vilify the Government's witnesses, rather than to promote an alternative narrative to explain the events that transpired from the defendants' perspective. A refutation defense such as that promoted by counsel in this case is, of course, a legitimate trial strategy from a technical, legal perspective. From a communication perspective, however, such an approach is much less persuasive than one that fully develops both functions of the closing speech—narration and argumentation. As a consequence of the defense's strategic choices in the Rosenberg case, the closing argument does not fully develop the narrative function of the speech and is, therefore, less effective than the prosecution's counterpart.

Significantly, the narrative techniques that were employed by the defense were not employed effectively. Ingratiation strategy, for example, was too profuse and overused, resulting in what has been termed "ingratiator's dilemma"—the strategy backfires because the ingratiation is obvious. Additionally, in contrast to the persuasive narrative form of weaving the testimony, documents, and other evidence into a cohesive story, the defense in this case merely lists the evidence and dismisses each exhibit without explanation. Again, no probable alternative explanation is advanced and thus the defense's argument is less persuasive.

In the argumentative portion of the closing argument, the defense refutes the story of the prosecution by attacking the credibility of the witnesses and questioning the testimony given. The defense does not, however, develop more sophisticated argument techniques such as factual persuasion. Finally, the defense utilizes few linguistic strategies in the development of the closing argument. Rhetorical questions are effectively posed by counsel; other participatory persuasion techniques, however, such as analogy, imagery, or vivid word choice, are not developed by the defense in closing argument.

In contrast, the prosecution skillfully develops both narrative and argumentative speech functions in the closing argument. By developing the narrative form in the beginning of the argument, counsel provides jurors with an organized review of the facts and evidence that serves to bring the case back together into a logical relationship and weaves the testimony and other evidence into a cohesive story. Counsel reviews the charges in the indictment, parties, issues, and basis of guilt in a narrative fashion. Additionally, the narration of events serves to reiterate the theme of the prosecution—communists conspiring to commit espionage.

Thus, the overview of the story establishes the foundation for the argumentative form of the speech that selectively argues the evidence deemed most persuasive to the prosecution's theory. The content of the argumentative form develops sophisticated persuasive strategies such as factual persuasion, two-sided communication, and tactics to induce resistance to persuasion.

Significantly, the prosecution develops both the narrative and the argumentative speech forms in a way that demonstrates the persuasiveness of participatory stylistic strategies. Counsel effectively utilizes the analogy, and throughout the argument are found selective word choices and rhetorical questions. These strategies serve to enhance audience participation, which in turn results in communication that is more persuasive and more easily remembered.

Implications for Trial Practice

The advocate's purpose in closing argument is twofold: first, to make sense out of the disjunctive and often confusing evidentiary portion of the trial and, second, to persuade jurors toward a particular view of the events in question. These functions of closing argument are properly conceived as distinct, albeit related. Conceptualized in this way, the need for two separate but entwined closing speeches becomes clearer. Effective closing arguments thoroughly develop two speech functions: narration and argumentation.

The narration and argumentation functions are separate in that each speech has its own unique form, content, and purpose. The form of the narrative speech essentially parallels the opening statement. The narrative discourse functions to provide a basic, logically organized review of the facts and evidence using a narrative, story form. The purpose of the narrative discourse is to bring the case back together into a logical relationship, weaving the testimony, documents, and other evidence into the cohesive story presented originally in the opening statement. This portion of the closing argument provides the foundation upon which counsel subsequently will argue the case for the jury. The content of the narrative speech is consistent with its function; it generally reviews the story of the case and the theme, as introduced in the opening statement and developed in the evidentiary portion of the trial.

It is axiomatic, therefore, that if counsel does not develop a probable story in opening statement and direct examination, an effective closing argument is foreclosed. This principle is exemplified in the closing argument given on behalf of the Rosenbergs—yet this appears to be the exception and not the rule. The closing arguments of the other trials considered in this volume fit the model more consistently; a more probable story was developed in earlier portions of the trial and therefore the narrative speech was reconstructed more easily in closing argument.

The form of the argumentative speech, in contrast, is traditional, linear argument. It functions to argue those witnesses, exhibits, and inferences that will persuade the jurors to support the particular position taken on the issues at the trial. In this portion of the discourse, counsel's purpose is to corroborate the testimony and exhibits favorable to the theory being promoted, question the testimony and exhibits of the opposing theory, refute the contentions of the opposition, summarize key legal concepts and relate them to the evidence, and argue damages or verdict. Consistent with its argumentative function, the content of the argumentative discourse includes such techniques as factual persuasion, order of presentation, and tactics to induce resistance to persuasion such as commitment and anchoring strategies.

Yet the narrative and argumentative functions of closing argument are also related; the overriding purpose of both speeches is to persuade the particular audience of jurors. Persuasive speeches in closing argument are those that involve the jurors as participants in the reasoning process. The goal is to arm those jurors favorably disposed with logic, facts, explanations, and arguments so they may in turn convince doubtful jurors, during deliberations in the jury room, to adopt a favorable view of the case. To achieve this goal, the advocate must invoke particular participatory strategies of persuasion.

Participatory persuasion techniques include, in addition to the elements of message content already outlined, specific linguistic devices that enhance listener involvement. Strategies such as use of analogies, visualizing techniques, language choices, and rhetorical questions are methods of achieving listener involvement and therefore enhancing persuasion.

Thus, to be effective, advocates in closing argument must develop both narrative and argumentative speeches in a manner that utilizes participatory strategies of persuasion. Such persuasive strategies may be developed not only through message content but also through the linguistic development of that content. Such communication strategies will enhance persuasion and therefore are critical to achieving effective closing argument skills.

A Trial Lawyer's and Trial Practice Professor's Reaction

J. Alexander Tanford

Good trial lawyers need more than intuition, experience, and stage presence in order to make effective closing arguments. They also must have a rudimentary knowledge of social psychology and communication theory. At the time of the Rosenberg trial, however, most attorneys were unaware of the basic principles of participatory persuasion, and they rarely used such concepts when preparing closing arguments. This resulted too often in wholly ineffective arguments such as the one given by the Rosenbergs' defense attorney. Luckily, most trial lawyers today have been exposed to the literature on effective communication, and are able to give better arguments as a result. It is in our interests, as lawyers, that this dialogue between the legal profession and the communications field continue.

As part of that dialogue, I have been graciously allotted a few paragraphs to react to this chapter from my perspective as a trial lawyer and trial practice professor. I can only give my personal reaction; space does not permit a detailed discussion of the range of reactions likely to be found among trial lawyers. I approach the subject as a modern trial lawyer who is aware of the underlying theory and accepts it (albeit with some skepticism), although I am apt to vary from it somewhat according to my own experiences. This should not be read as a disagreement with any of the points made in this chapter; indeed, I teach these very concepts to my own trial practice students.

J. Alexander Tanford is an Associate Professor of Law at Indiana University-Bloomington. He has an A.B. degree from Princeton Univerity, and J.D. and LL.M. degrees from Duke University. Before coming to Indiana, he was a trial attorney in the New York County District Attorney's Office and a John S. Bradway Fellow at Duke. He has taught trial practice for ten years at Duke, Indiana, and Washington universities. Professor Tanford is the author of *The Trial Process: Law Tactics and Ethics,* and several articles on trial procedure.

However, I differ slightly with the authors on the importance of the narrative form to closing argument. I do not doubt that a persuasive *presentation* must contain both narration and argumentation, but I question whether any substantial part of a *closing argument* should be in narrative form. Closing argument is only one phase of the overall trial, and it does not have to persuade the jury by itself. This old-fashioned notion that closing argument is sufficiently self-contained and independent of the rest of the case that it can "rescue a lost cause" has been replaced by the conception of closing argument as one small part of an integrated whole trial. Within that trial, the opening statements and witness examinations supply the necessary narrative, so closing argument can be limited to argumentation. Thus, I think the chapter overemphasizes the importance of narration to the modern idea of closing argument.

But just because I think the narrative *form* inappropriate during closing argument (a point on which some trial lawyers would disagree), does not mean that the concept of narrative *content* is also unimportant. To the contrary, the elements of story-development and the reiteration of themes, which are critical to the creation of a successful narrative, are vital to the construction of an effective closing argument also. Of the three content elements of narration discussed in this chapter, only ingratiation strategy is losing favor with trial lawyers (for reasons made obvious by the authors' comments). The other two are recognized as essential elements of a successful trial strategy. The first requirement of an effective closing argument is that the lawyer develop a complete, plausible theory (story) of the case. Another high priority is the development of one or more unifying themes, to which the lawyer can return throughout the trial. A good closing argument must summarize the complete theory of the case, explaining who did what to whom and why they did it, and reiterate the basic themes. However, the lawyer need not (and should not) do this in too much detail—he or she should be able to summarize the theory in a paragraph or two—since a good lawyer will have been making the theory clear to the jury at every stage of the trial. Indeed, it may be more effective participatory persuasion for the lawyer to leave some details of the story implicit, to be filled in by the jurors.

From this perspective, the main problem with the defense argument is that it lacked a theory of the case. The defense has no explanation for the events consistent with the Rosenbergs' innocence, no alternative explanation for the incriminating evidence, and no satisfactory explanation for why the prosecution witnesses were trying falsely to implicate the defendants. All he had was a theme—that the Rosenbergs were victims of anticommunist hysteria. Even that theme was not very appropriate, since the major witnesses against the Rosenbergs were admitted communists, and therefore unlikely to be suffering from anticommunist hysteria. In addition, the theme attacked the integrity of the jurors by suggesting they would vote guilty based on emotions rather than evidence—hardly the most ingratiating theme to select.

By contrast, the prosecuting attorney had a clear theory, which he articulated fairly well in his closing argument. The prosecutor offered a plausible story that explained what happened, why it happened, what motivated the Rosenbergs to do such a thing, why the witnesses against them came forward, and why the contrary evidence should be rejected. To top it all off, the prosecutor anchored his argument with themes of patriotism and the Soviet threat. It is a much better argument than the one given by the defense.

Several specific comparisons illustrate why the prosecuting attorney gave the better argument:

(1) Choice of theme. The prosecutor's major themes were patriotism and the Soviet threat. These were undoubtedly easy for the jury to accept. The defense theme was that anticommunist hysteria was responsible for the situation. This theme suggests that the jurors may themselves be biased, an accusation they are likely to reject.

(2) Ingratiation strategy. The defense attorney tried an ingratiation strategy that was destined to fail. He was representing admitted communists with whom the jurors were unlikely to sympathize. The prosecutor made a better choice and did not attempt to ingratiate his coconspirator witnesses with the jury, but instead characterized them in the same kinds of negative terms as the jurors probably were doing (e.g., henchmen, traitorous Americans).

(3) Two-sided communication. The prosecutor used two-sided communication in which he admitted weaknesses. One example was his recognition that his witnesses were spies and traitors who were cooperating out of self-interest, but then using that to his advantage by comparing their apparent repentence and attempt to "make amends for the hurt which has been done to our nation," to the Rosenbergs' compounding of their betrayal with lies and deception. The defense used only one-sided communication, never admitting any weaknesses and addressing only the favorable evidence.

(4) Rhetorical questions. Both sides asked similar rhetorical questions concerning why certain crucial documents were not pro-

duced in court. For the defense attorney it was a bad choice, because he wanted the jury to draw an improbable conclusion that they were not produced because they never existed. For the prosecutor, it was a good decision, because he wanted the jury to draw the obvious answer, that the documents could not be produced because they had been delivered to the Soviet Union.

(5) Primacy and recency effects. The defense attorney had an opportunity to take advantage of a strong primacy effect since he argued first, but failed to take advantage of it. The prosecutor, arguing second, derived the greatest benefit from the recency effect because he got the last word. He made better use of his opportunity, by ending on a vivid reiteration of his patriotism theme.

There are however several weaknesses in the prosecutor's argument. The prosecuting attorney wastes the opportunity to take advantage of the primacy effect when he does not begin his argument on a dramatic point he wants the jury to remember. He apparently failed to use any visual techniques, although several suggest themselves: he could have reinforced his marvelous image of a wheel by drawing one on the chalkboard, he could have emphasized the seriousness and size of the conspiracy by holding up all the exhibits at once, or he could have listed on the board the acts committed by the conspirators instead of just referring to them orally. In addition, the prosecutor committed two legal errors that might have required the conviction to be reversed if the defense had objected: he attempted to arouse anticommunist emotions in the jury and he suggested that there was some significance in the fact that the grand jury named the Rosenbergs as defendants.

In summary, if my trial practice students had given these closing arguments, I would give the prosecutor a grade of "B" and the defense attorney a "D". The prosecutor's argument was good, but the lawyer did not take advantage of the primacy effect, failed to use any visual aids, and committed several legal errors. The defense argument was not very good, but the attorney was saved from a failing grade by his occasionally successful use of rhetorical questions, by the one good argument concerning David Greenglass' credibility and motivations, and because he reminded the jury of its commitments.

The contribution of communication theory to trial practice in the last thirty years has been great. I would expect any trial lawyer today to display a better grasp of its principles when making closing arguments than did the attorneys in the Rosenberg case.

6

Advocate Argumentation in the Appellate Process: The Sam Sheppard Trial

Appellate arguments demonstrate how the stories of the case met or failed to meet the legal dictates for the litigation. Using a communication model grounded in legal assumptions as a framework for examining how advocates communicate legal arguments, this chapter investigates how the elements of appellate argumentation are successfully crafted in the advocates' briefs and how these elements influence the court's reasoning as explained in the judicial opinion. The chapter identifies the persuasive strategies underlying effective brief writing, strategies that are then generalizable to the appellate brief of the contemporary practitioner.

The landmark decision rendered in the Sam Sheppard appeal in 1966 was the first decision by the United States Supreme Court recognizing that "massive, pervasive, and prejudicial publicity" of a trial may prevent a defendant from receiving a fair trial consistent with the Due Process Clause of the Fourteenth Amendment. Prior to the Supreme Court decision in the Sheppard case, many cases received intensive and often prejudicial media coverage. The Haymarket case was a *cause célèbre* in the Chicago papers and the anarchist press; the Sacco-Vanzetti defense raised thousands of dollars through the international press for its defense fund; Hauptmann's wife gave exclusive rights to the Hearst papers if they agreed to pay for her husband's defense; the anticommunist feelings of the public were aired before, during, and after the Rosenberg case in national and international papers. Because Sam Sheppard was a well-known doctor residing in an upper-class neighborhood and because the murder of Sheppard's wife was so heinous, his case grabbed the attention of the Cleveland press. From the day after the crime until Sheppard's sentencing, the press participated actively in the drama not only as recorders of history, but often as investigators and jurors. In the Sam Sheppard case, the arguments advanced in the briefs on appeal had been developed and refined over a long period of time and, accordingly, provide an excellent opportunity to review effective argumentation strategies in the appellate process.

The Trial

On June 6, 1966, in an eight to one decision, the United States Supreme Court ruled that Samuel H. Sheppard, convicted in 1954 of murdering his wife, had received an unfair trial. The Court decreed that Sheppard was entitled to a new trial "within a reasonable time" (*Sheppard v. Maxwell*, 384 U.S. 333, 363 [1966]) or to be set free by the State of Ohio. The events leading up to this historic reversal (the Sheppard conviction was the first ever to be overruled by the United States Supreme Court on grounds of prejudicial publicity resulting in an unfair trial [Pollack, 1972, p. 169]), unfolded over a twelve-year period, beginning on July 4, 1954, in Bay Village, Ohio.

Sam Sheppard awakened in the early morning hours on July 4, to his wife's cries for help. Dr. Sheppard entered his wife's bedroom, saw a "form" standing next to his wife's bed, and struggled with this "form" until being struck on the back of the neck and rendered unconscious. On regaining consciousness, he saw a "form" running out the door and followed it to the shores of the lake on which the Sheppard home was located; he there again struggled with the "form" until being knocked unconscious. Upon his recovery, he returned to his home, checked his wife's pulse, and determined she was dead. Subsequently, he called his neighbor, Mayor Houk of Bay Village, who in turn notified the police and the coroner.

Following a brief investigation into the murder, the authorities concluded that Dr. Sheppard had killed his wife, despite the absence of any concrete evidence (Pollack, 1972, p. 14). Just as quickly, the press determined Sheppard's guilt and demanded that the doctor be brought to "justice." The resulting news coverage of the Sheppard investigation and trial was unlike any that had occurred in recent years—perhaps since the coverage of the Lindbergh kidnapping. In reporting the Sheppard case, not only did the media release information that was inadmissible at trial but, equally disturbing, the slanted and emotional newspaper coverage of the case fanned public opinion to a near frenzy.

The publicity grew in intensity until the indictment of Sheppard on August 17. Typical of the news coverage that occurred are the following headlines, announcing that: "Doctor Evidence Is Ready for Jury," "Corrigan Tactics Stall Quizzing," "Sheppard 'Gay Set' Is Revealed By Houk," "Blood Is Found In Garage," "New Murder Evidence Is Found, Police Claim," "Dr. Sam Faces Quiz At Jail On Marilyn's Fear Of Him" (*Sheppard v. Maxwell*, 384 U.S. at 342). Additionally, mounting public pressure resulted in a coroner's examination of Sheppard, without counsel, in a televised three-day inquest, conducted in a gymnasium before an audience of several hundred spectators (*Sheppard v. Maxwell*, 384 U.S. at 339–40).

With the case finally set for trial, seventy-five potential jurors were called; all three Cleveland newspapers published the names and addresses of the veniremen. Consequently, anonymous letters and phone calls regarding the pending prosecution were received by all of the prospective jurors (384 U.S. at 342). Moreover, the courtroom in which the trial was held was largely taken over by newsmen, as special procedures were initiated to accommodate the press coverage of the trial. For example, the majority of the seats in the court were assigned to newsmen, rather than left vacant for the public; private telephone lines and telegraphic equipment were installed in separate rooms so that news reports from the trial could be delivered quickly to the papers; broadcasting facilities were set up on the third floor of the courthouse next door to the jury room (*Sheppard v. Maxwell*, 384 U.S. at 343).

All of these arrangements with the media and their massive coverage of the proceedings continued during the entire nine weeks of the trial (*Sheppard v. Maxwell*, 384 U.S. at 344). The trial itself came to an end in December 1954, when the jury returned a verdict convicting Sheppard of the second-degree murder of his wife and sentencing him to life imprisonment. Subsequently, the decision was appealed four times through the Ohio state court system, with a fifth appeal to the United States Supreme Court ending in a denial of application for *certiorari* in 1956 (*Sheppard v. Ohio*, 352 U.S. 910 [1956]).

A second round of appeals was instigated in the United States District Court on a *habeas corpus* petition (*Sheppard v. Maxwell*, 231 F. Supp. 37 [S.D. Ohio 1964]), where the District Court for the Southern District of Ohio, Chief Judge Weinman, found five separate violations of the petitioner's constitutional rights and concluded that the judgment and sentence holding Sheppard in custody was void (*Sheppard v. Maxwell*, 231 F. Supp. at 72). An appeal of this decision was taken to the United States Court of Appeals for the Sixth Circuit, where Circuit Judge O'Sullivan reversed the District Court's finding and held the petitioner had failed to sustain the burden of demonstrating the unconstitutionality of his trial (*Sheppard v. Maxwell*, 346 F.2d 707, 737 [6th Cir. 1965]). The petitioner again applied for *certiorari* to the United States Supreme Court; on November 15, 1965, *certiorari* was granted.

The Supreme Court that finally heard the arguments on February 28, 1966, was comprised of Chief Justice Earl Warren, and Associate Justices Hugo L. Black, William O. Douglas, Tom C. Clark, John Marshall Harlan, William J. Brennan, Jr., Potter Stewart, Abe Fortas, and Byron R. White (Pollack, 1972, p. 162). The petitioner, Sheppard, was represented by F. Lee Bailey, who was arguing his first case before the Supreme Court. Bailey had taken over the defense of Sheppard after William J. Corrigan, who represented Sheppard in the initial trial and appeals process, died at the age of seventy-five in August 1961 (Pollack, 1972, p. 105). The respondent, formally listed as E. L. Maxwell, warden of the Ohio State Penitentiary, was represented by William B. Saxbe, attorney general of Ohio.

The United States Supreme Court, in a landmark eight to one decision, held that the "massive, pervasive, and prejudicial publicity attending petitioner's prosecution prevented him from receiving a fair trial consistent with the Due Process Clause of the Fourteenth Amendment" (*Sheppard v. Maxwell*, 384 U.S. at 334, 349–63). Further, the Court remanded the case to the District Court with instructions "to issue the writ and order that Sheppard be released from custody unless the State puts him to its charges again within a reasonable time" (*Sheppard v. Maxwell*, 384 U.S. at 363). The lone dissenter, Justice Black, dissented without opinion. The State of Ohio retried their case against Dr. Sheppard and, on November 16, 1966, the defendant Sam Sheppard was found not guilty— acquitted of all charges, twelve years after the initial event.

The final appeal to the U.S. Supreme Court in 1966 was the culmination of a twelve-year journey through the judicial system in the United States. The arguments advanced in the briefs on appeal were arguments that had been developed and refined over a long period of time. Because the appellate arguments of the Sheppard trial were so thoroughly developed by the time of this final appeal, they provide an excellent opportunity to review effective argumentation strategies in the appellate process.

The purpose of this chapter is to explore components of effective argumentation in the appellate process. The essay posits that effective argumentation is persuasive and, therefore, likely to be adopted by the court in the subsequent judicial decision as the explanation for the reasoning in the court opinion. Utilizing a communication model grounded in legal theory as a framework for examining how advocates communicate legal arguments, the investigation seeks to understand how the elements of appellate argumentation are successfully manipulated in the advocates' briefs and, further, how these components may influence the court's reasoning as explained in the judicial opinion. The Sam Sheppard trial provides the vehicle for examining the effective appellate argument.

To achieve this end, the essay (1) examines the appellate review process in the United States; (2) considers the appellate advocate's contribution to this appellate review process; (3) identifies argumentation theory that provides a useful method for judging effective arguments; (4) analyzes the arguments contained in the appellate briefs according to this theory; (5) evaluates the effectiveness of these arguments; and (6) suggests the implications of the investigation for appellate practice.

The Function of Appellate Review
and the Advocates' Contribution to the Appellate Process

Legal Procedure and Norms

The appellate review process in the United States seeks to provide: (1) a prompt review by a panel of judges; (2) a determination of the correctness of a final judgment of the trial court after a submission by the parties of their views on the issues; (3) a consideration by the judges as the complexity of the appeal dictates; and (4) a statement of reasons by the appellate court (Carrington, Meador, & Rosenberg, 1976, pp. 8–12; Martineau, 1985, p. 11). The basic justification for this review process is the desire for uniformity of decisions among the trial courts. Judge John Parker (1950) explains that in order for the rules and standards of society to be accepted, they must be objectively and uniformly applied. This requires that trial court decisions be submitted to review by a panel of judges who are "removed from the heat engendered by the trial and are consequently in a position to take a more objective view of the questions there raised to maintain uniformity of decisions" (Parker, 1950, p. 1). Specifically, appellate courts function to correct errors in the trial court's judgment and to review the impact of the lower court's decision upon the further development of the law (Joiner, 1957, p. 503; Carrington et al., 1976, pp. 2–4; Martineau, 1985, pp. 20–23).

Error Correction. Error correction is concerned primarily with the effect of the judicial process in the trial court upon the individual litigant; it not only protects that person from arbitrariness in the administration of justice but also provides a release for dissatisfaction with the system resulting from the decision of the lower court (Martineau, 1985, p. 20). In most cases, error correction will be exercised only when the law is clear and the action of the trial court is inconsistent with the law.

When exercising its error correction function, appellate courts are concerned with the impact of the lower court's decision on the specific parties to the action. Typically, evidence considered sufficient to legitimize a claim that the lower court erred in its judgment includes a showing that the trial court was incorrect in its procedural or evidentiary ruling, or applied an incorrect legal principle, or misapplied a correct legal principle (Martineau, 1985, p. 21).

Law Development. The second function of appellate review is that of law development. This type of review is concerned with the effect of the lower court's decision on the law and the legal process as a whole as opposed to focusing on the individual litigant (Martineau, 1985, p. 21). Also known as "institutional review," its purpose is twofold. One is to provide for the development of the common law, that is, to accommodate the demands of the individuals and institutions as the fact situations change from those in prior cases. The second function is to enforce the law as previously interpreted or declared by judicial or legislative bodies. (Carrington et al. 1976, p. 2; Martineau, 1985, p. 21).

As suggested by the purposes of law development review, persuasive evidence in support of a claim that the law needs to change or be reinterpreted will vary from case to case. If the court is exercising its law development function, types of issues typically reviewed include: a constitutional or statutory provision in need of interpretation or reinterpretation; an existing case precedent that needs to be overturned or expanded as it is no longer in keeping with societal changes; or a law, while correctly interpreted, in need of specific enforcement (Martineau, 1985; Houts & Rogosheske, 1986). When focusing on the appropriate development of the law, the appellate court balances a recognition that the law must evolve and adapt with a realization that if the court changes the rules too sharply or unpredictably, it will disturb the general feeling of the law's stability.

"Doing Justice." In addition to the specific functions of error correction and law development, the appellate court is concerned with the overall function of "doing justice" (Martineau, 1985, p. 22). Appellate judges are, or should be, constantly aware that their decisions are not rendered in the abstract but, rather, directly and immmediately affect the parties before the court. This concern must be balanced against the realization that the decision in one case will also be precedent in future cases. Known as *stare decisis*, this concept is one of the essential features of a common law legal system—the result that seems just for the present case must be a principled one that will afford just results in similar conflicts arising at future times with different parties (Martineau, 1985, p. 22). Moreover, if the decision is a controversial one, the opinion must also gain acceptance for the court's holding; that is, it must convince the court's various audiences, including the public, that the decision is sound (Toulmin, Rieke, & Janik, 1979, p. 217; Prentice, 1983, pp. 87, 92).

Additionally, this function of seeking justice is necessarily influenced by the individual constraints that each judge brings to the case; that is, the differing beliefs, attitudes, traditions, interests, and motives that influence each judge's notion of justice. Indeed, judges themselves admit that an important part of the decision-making process is best categorized as the exercise of "trained intuition" (Pound, 1923, p. 951), or a judicial "hunch" (Hutcheson, 1929, p. 274). Thus, all legal decisions, whether arrived at by hunch or otherwise, involve value judgments. (See, generally, Cardozo, 1921; Wechsler, 1959, p. 15; Wechsler, 1964, pp. 290–93; Greenawalt, 1978, pp. 991–92.)

The appellate advocates contribute to this review process by supplying the court with alternative approaches to the issue under review. These arguments are advanced by the advocates in their briefs on appeal (Houts & Rogosheske, 1986). Ideally, the attorneys present the appellate court with every possible theory and rationale relevant to the decision (Prentice, 1983, p. 91). While occasionally the judges will themselves contribute a new theory or perspective

183

for deciding the case, the choices presented on appeal have been developed and refined in the lower court proceedings and, therefore, are usually exhaustively explored (Prentice, 1983, p. 91). Theoretically, when the court makes its decision the judges weigh the alternatives presented by the attorneys to determine which choice is supported by the more persuasive reasons (Crable, 1976, p. 117).

Thus, the various elements of the appellate process are interrelated and complex. The appellate court functions in the process to correct erroneous rulings of the lower courts and oversee the continual development of the common law, while at the same time providing specific litigants with the sense that justice has been served, that the parties have been fairly and uniformly treated. Specifically, there are several factors that influence appellate judges, either directly or indirectly, in reaching a decision in any given case, including constitutional and/or statutory interpretations, case law precedent, and the differing predispositions of the judges. These factors may vary according to the function the court conceives itself as undertaking at the time, thus, the kind of argument found persuasive will fluctuate from case to case. Usually, though, one or more of these factors will influence the final judicial opinion.

Moreover, the appellate advocate contributes to this process of review by providing well-reasoned legal arguments for the court to consider in reaching its decision. Although the appellate court may look beyond the arguments submitted in the briefs, ideally the court adopts one position or the other, in whole or in part, as the explanation of the court's reasoning for the decision reached. Thus, the strength and persuasiveness of an argument in the advocate's brief is a crucial link in the appellate process. For this reason, appellate advocates consider the brief the single most important aspect of appellate review, stating, for example, that in a close case the brief is the factor on which the "entire case will be won or lost" (Wiener, 1950, p. 49). Identifying the communicative strategies underlying persuasive brief writing is, therefore, of central importance to effective appellate advocacy.

Analysis focusing on the appellate brief as the critical link in the appellate process, however, is not found either in the literature of law or in the literature of communication. Although scholars have examined the rhetorical strategies underlying court opinions (Prentice, 1983) and have speculated on the philosophical processes in reaching those decisions (Cardozo, 1921; Wechsler, 1950, 1964), none have undertaken a systematic analysis of the advocate brief as the critical link in the appellate process. Thus, analysis of the effectiveness of the argumentation contained in appellate briefs is both necessary and appropriate.

Communicative Features of Appellate Argument

An appellate argument, to be effective, must address all of the legal norms and individual values that appellate judges consider in reaching their decisions. That is, all relevant issues, whether constitutional or statutory provisions, case law precedent, or values, must be dealt with in the successful advocate's brief. Furthermore, each of these factors must be argued effectively.

Stephen Toulmin's work in argumentation theory provides a useful method for judging effective arguments (Toulmin, 1969; Toulmin et al., 1979). Toulmin's model is particularly appropriate for this analysis, as his theory is based on legal argument; that is, grounded in legal analogy and practical reasoning rather than formal logic (Foss, Foss, & Trapp, 1985, p. 90). Specifically, Toulmin's work is useful to rhetorical and legal scholars because it provides "an appropriate structural model by means of which rhetorical arguments may be laid out for analysis and criticism" (Brockriede & Ehninger, 1960, pp. 44–53).

Toulmin's layout of argument involves six interrelated components: claim, grounds, warrant, backing, modal qualifier, rebuttal. The first three components, claim, grounds, and warrant, are the primary elements of an argument and may be the only components in simple arguments (Foss et al., 1985, p. 87). Theoretically, the most sophisticated, complex and, therefore, more effective arguments will contain all six components.

The first component of Toulmin's layout of argument is the "claim." The claim is the conclusion of the argument, the merits of which the arguer is seeking to establish or justify (Toulmin, 1969, p. 97). The second component is "grounds," that is, the underlying foundation of facts or other information that is required if the claim is to be accepted (Toulmin, 1969, pp. 97–98). In complex arguments, a series of grounds may be necessary before the claim will be believed or accepted. Third, is the element of "warrant." The warrant is the portion of the argument that provides the necessary bridge between the claim and the grounds; it provides the rules, principles, or inferences necessary to make the step (Toulmin, 1969, p. 98). These three elements comprise the primary argument, which, as noted, may be all that is necessary to persuade in simple arguments. Graphically, this primary argument may be depicted as shown in Figure 1. To use a simplistic example from the Sheppard case, see Figure 2.

Three additional elements complete the layout of a complex argument. The fourth component is called "backing" and provides additional support for the argument. Backings consist of other assurances without which the warrants would not be authorized (Toulmin, 1969, p. 103). In the legal field, for example, backings consist of rules of law or statutory provisions that have been validated either judicially or legislatively. Fifth is the notion of "modal qualifiers." Toulmin recognizes that not all claims are supported with the same degree of certainty. Thus, the argument may vary in the degree and kind of strength with which one may argue. That is, some conclusions may be characterized as merely "probable" while others may be characterized as "presumptive" or "possible." Qualifiers, then, allow the arguer to make the step from grounds to claim either tentatively, or subject to conditions, exceptions, or qualifications (Toulmin, 1969, p. 100). The final element of an argument is "rebuttal," which refers to situations where the move from grounds to claim is not seen as legitimate and, therefore, is set aside (Toulmin, 1969, p. 101). The complete depiction of Toulmin's layout of argument is shown in Figure 3. To complete the example from the Sheppard case, see Figure 4.

Thus, claims as arguments are well founded only if sufficient

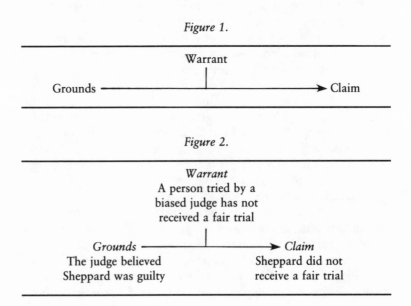

Figure 1.

Warrant

Grounds ────────────── ⟶ Claim

Figure 2.

Warrant
A person tried by a
biased judge has not
received a fair trial

Grounds ────────── ⟶ *Claim*
The judge believed   Sheppard did not
Sheppard was guilty   receive a fair trial

Figure 3.

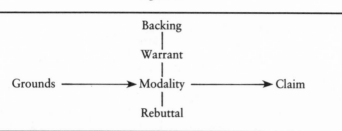

and relevant grounds are offered in their support. These grounds, if effective, are connected to the claims by reliable warrants, which in turn are justified by appeal to sufficient backing of a relevant nature. This entire structure of argument may be qualified as having a certain degree of reliability and, further, may be subject to a rebuttal argument.

Analysis of Appellate Argument

In analyzing the appellate argument, several factors must be considered. It is first necessary to determine the function in which the court is acting. Once the court's function is determined, then the types of arguments that are considered legitimate according to legal norms or traditions may be determined. These legitimate arguments must then be considered in terms of the arguers' ability to set forth the various claims, grounds, warrants, backings, modal qualifiers, and rebuttals.

Petitioner's Argument

The introductory note to the petitioner's argument focuses the court on performing its law development function, specifically noting that:

Certainly the primary issue in this case, and the issue of greatest general concern to our courts, lawyers and society is that of publicity tainting the trial. Although this Court has in earlier decisions dealt with the general question of invasive news media vitiating by their conduct a state criminal judgment, [citations omitted], we believe that this case presents new and important questions somewhat different than those heretofore considered. [Brief for Petitioner at 15]

187

Figure 4.

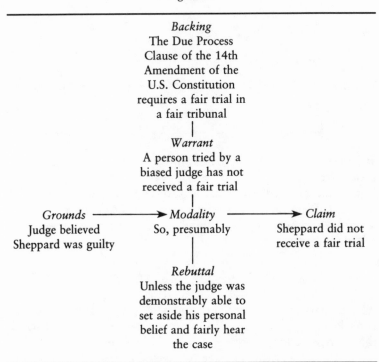

Backing
The Due Process
Clause of the 14th
Amendment of the
U.S. Constitution
requires a fair trial in
a fair tribunal
|
Warrant
A person tried by a
biased judge has not
received a fair trial
|
Grounds ————→ *Modality* ————→ *Claim*
Judge believed   So, presumably   Sheppard did not
Sheppard was guilty   receive a fair trial
|
Rebuttal
Unless the judge was
demonstrably able to
set aside his personal
belief and fairly hear
the case

In this way, the petitioner clearly sets the stage for the court regarding its expected function.

By setting forth the petitioner's expectations of the court, the framework for the subsequent argument is also implictly laid out for the court. According to legal norms and tradition, the types of evidence the court anticipates hearing, when functioning in a law development capacity, include that a constitutional or statutory provision is in need of reinterpretation, that an earlier ruling is in need of specific enforcement, or that the existing case precedent needs to be expanded in order to keep current with the societal changes. The degree to which the petitioner effectively argued these norms is next considered.

The petitioner advanced several claims in the brief on appeal. The dispositive issue, however, and that for which the case is now a landmark, was the claim that due to prejudicial publicity Sheppard had not received a fair trial. It is on this claim and its supporting arguments, therefore, that this analysis will focus. This issue was the most complex, the most thoroughly developed in the brief, and thus most completely and clearly demonstrates the characteristics of effective argumentation in the appellate process.

The first component of Toulmin's argumentation theory is the claim. In the Sam Sheppard appeal, the petitioner expressly states his claim as follows: "The petitioner was so thoroughly tried and convicted by news media that a fair trial in the courtroom could not and in fact did not occur" (Brief for Petitioner at 14). This statement is the end result—the specific conclusion—that the petitioner is seeking to establish.

Having clearly stated the claim, the petitioner next seeks to supply the underlying foundation or information to support the claim in such a way as to cause the court to adhere to that claim. In this case, due to the complexity of the issue, a series of grounds were advanced. Specifically, the petitioner contended: first, the pretrial publicity precluded the assembly of an impartial jury; second, the publicity during the trial prevented the maintenance of an impartial jury, assuming one had been impaneled in the first place; third, the conduct of the press in the courtroom deprived the petitioner of due process of law. Each of these grounds and their accompanying warrants, backings, qualifiers, and rebuttal arguments will be considered in turn.

Ground I: Publicity Before Trial. The first foundation set forth to establish the claim that the petitioner did not receive a fair trial was that of pretrial publicity. The evidence marshaled to establish that pretrial publicity had occurred was of several types. First, the petitioner reproduced conclusions of the lower courts that had considered the issue, including in his brief eighteen citations from the lower court opinions. In this way, the petitioner authenticated his view of the pretrial issue by providing support from state and federal judges who had previously passed upon the nature and extent of the publicity in this case. For example, the Ohio Supreme Court described the pretrial publicity in the following representative statement:

> Murder and mystery, society, sex and suspense were combined in this case in such a manner as to intrigue and captivate the public fancy to a degree perhaps unparalleled in recent annals. Throughout the preindictment investigation, the subsequent legal skirmishes and the nine-week trial, circulation-conscious editors catered to the insatiable inter-

est of the American public in the bizarre. Special seating facilities for reporters and columnists representing local papers and all major news services were installed in the courtroom. Special rooms in the Criminal Courts Building were equipped for broadcasters and telecasters. In this atmosphere of a "Roman holiday" for the news media, Sam Sheppard stood trial for his life. [Brief for Petitioner at 17–18]

The primary components of the petitioner's subargument are completed by the petitioner's warrant that proceedings of this kind "[are] directly out of phase with the serious and ordered decorum which is supposed to be the controlling environment of our American criminal trials" (Brief for Petitioner at 22). This statement provides the inference, the link, the connection between the ground of the pretrial publicity and the claim of the defendant that he did not receive a fair trial.

Additionally, the petitioner backs this warrant stating that many of the lower court judges acknowledged explicitly the pretrial publicity was not in keeping with notions of a fair and impartial hearing. This backing thus validated the petitioner's assertion.

The fifth element of Toulmin's model is also present in this subargument—the modal qualifier. While the petitioner sets out this limitation in the context of this subargument of the pretrial publicity issue, the limitation qualifies the entire pretrial argument and not just this particular subissue. Because the petitioner asserts the limitation in the context of this subargument, however, it will be delineated at this time. The petitioner expressly

pause[s] . . . to define the limits of our argument . . . [and to] concede that in appropriate instances news media may, and indeed ought to, cast their single or collective harsh light upon shady official conduct. . . . Surely there can be found some limitations within whose perimeter news media can be required to function without materially diminishing that power necessary to their ability to attack and expose when the public is being duped by irresponsible official conduct. [Brief for Petitioner at 22–23]

Apparently, the petitioner is well aware of the need to balance delicately the First Amendment right of free press and the Sixth Amendment right to a fair trial and, therefore, sets a boundary or limitation to his argument.

Finally, the petitioner anticipates and deals with the rebuttal component—the counterargument that suggests that the petitioner's claim is not legitimate in an attempt to set it aside. Specifically, the petitioner acknowledges that the facts of the Sheppard trial are not exactly the same as those in other cases involving pretrial publicity and recognizes this might lead some to conclude there was no prejudice. The petitioner goes on to "respectfully disagree" with this analysis, however, arguing that Dr. Sheppard's position, while different in fact from the earlier cases, was in the same position in effect (Brief for Petitioner at 27). Thus, the petitioner acknowledges the potential rebuttal argument and, at the same time, by way of analogy, turns the "distinguishing fact" into "similar effects" demanding the same kind of treatment. This first subargument to the pretrial publicity ground asserted in the petitioner's brief may be depicted as shown in Figure 5.

The second piece of evidence offered to support the petitioner's pretrial publicity argument concerned the inquest in the case by Cuyahoga County Coroner Samuel Gerber. Specifically, the peti-

Figure 5. Ground I: Pretrial Publicity

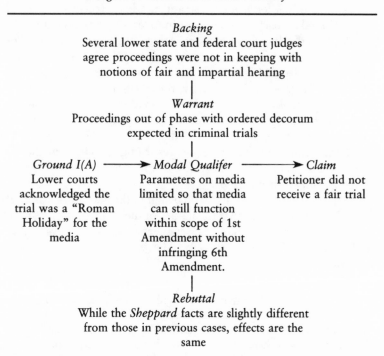

Backing
Several lower state and federal court judges
agree proceedings were not in keeping with
notions of fair and impartial hearing

Warrant
Proceedings out of phase with ordered decorum
expected in criminal trials

Ground I(A)	⟶ *Modal Qualifer*	⟶ *Claim*
Lower courts acknowledged the trial was a "Roman Holiday" for the media	Parameters on media limited so that media can still function within scope of 1st Amendment without infringing 6th Amendment.	Petitioner did not receive a fair trial

Rebuttal
While the *Sheppard* facts are slightly different
from those in previous cases, effects are the
same

tioner argued the inquest was improperly conducted; the purpose of an inquest is to determine the cause of death and whether homicide is involved, facts about which there was no question in this case. Further, the inquest was conducted in a school gymnasium, rather than the morgue where such inquests are typically held, and before an audience, also extraordinary. Finally, Sheppard was called to testify following the forcible ejection of his counsel from the proceedings; thus, he was unrepresented during the inquest proceedings (Brief for Petitioner at 28–29).

The primary components of the petitioner's subargument are completed by the warrant made by the petitioner that the inquest proceedings "served to drive deep the roots of prejudice in the Cleveland community" (Brief for Petitioner at 29). This warrant provides the connection or link between the ground that the inquest was improper and the claim that it contributed to the prejudicial environment with the end result that the petitioner did not receive a fair trial.

The petitioner provides additional support for this argument, noting that this inference or warrant had been recently validated by the United States Supreme Court in *Estes v. Texas*, 381 U.S. 532 (1965). Specifically, the petitioner stated: "[T]hat a pre-trial proceeding may be relevant to a determination of the eventual trial has already been decided by this Court, *Estes v. Texas*, 381 U.S. 532" (Brief for Petitioner at 29). Finally, the strength of the petitioner's argument is qualified in the following manner: "We mention the *outrageous* nature of this unnecessary sham proceeding. . . ." (Brief for Petitioner at 29, emphasis added).

Graphically, this subargument regarding the effect of the inquest on the prejudicial atmosphere in the community may be depicted as shown in Figure 6.

The final support advanced on behalf of the petitioner's pretrial publicity argument was that the names of the veniremen were published in all three Cleveland newspapers twenty-five days before trial (Brief for Petitioner at 29). The warrant offered for this subground was that:

The moment one learns that one's neighbor is about to be a candidate for jury duty in a case which has provoked the community, the temptation to discuss the matter is irresistible. Such discussions cannot help but promote a concentration of information of every type and source being foisted off upon the talesman, *until by the time he is finally im-*

192

Figure 6. Ground I: Pretrial Publicity

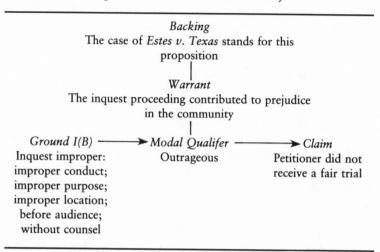

Backing
The case of *Estes v. Texas* stands for this
proposition
|
Warrant
The inquest proceeding contributed to prejudice
in the community
|
Ground I(B) ⟶ *Modal Qualifer* ⟶ *Claim*
Inquest improper: Outrageous   Petitioner did not
improper conduct;   receive a fair trial
improper purpose;
improper location;
before audience;
without counsel

Figure 7. Ground I: Pretrial Publicity

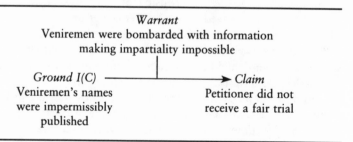

Warrant
Veniremen were bombarded with information
making impartiality impossible
|
Ground I(C) ⟶ *Claim*
Veniremen's names   Petitioner did not
were impermissibly   receive a fair trial
published

*panelled he is so infused with extraneous information that impartiality
is impossible.* [Brief for Petitioner at 30, emphasis added]

Thus, the petitioner argued, these circumstances contributed to the
unconstitutional nature of the petitioner's trial. Graphically, this
subargument may be depicted as shown in Figure 7.

In summary, the petitioner's first ground offered in support of
the claim that the proceedings below were not fair and impartial
was that of pretrial publicity. Specifically, the petitioner contended
the proceeding was so unorderly as to amount to improper decorum
for a criminal trial proceeding, the inquest was improperly con-

ducted, and the potential jurors' names were impermissibly published. All of these grounds, the petitioner argued, supported the petitioner's position on appeal that Sam Sheppard had not received a fair and impartial hearing in the trial proceedings.

Ground II: Publicity During Trial. The second foundation set forth to establish the claim that the petitioner did not receive a fair trial was that of prejudicial publicity during the trial. The petitioner offered two subgrounds in support of this contention.

First, the petitioner contended that members of the jury had been exposed to numerous newspaper articles prior to and during the trial proceeding, which articles not only suggested that Dr. Sheppard was guilty, but also printed testimony of witnesses held inadmissible at trial (Brief for Petitioner at 31–34). The warrant offered to provide the necessary bridge between the prejudicial newspaper articles and the petitioner's unfair trial was that the jurors exposed to the articles would not be impartial (Brief for Petitioner at 33–34). This subground regarding the publicity during trial can be depicted as shown in Figure 8.

Second, the petitioner argued that the failure of the trial judge to control this exposure to extrinsic material shows beyond a doubt that the jury was biased (Brief for Petitioner at 39). The warrant offered to connect the grounds of exposure to the impartial jury and unfair trial was that the "failure to take the jury into the custody of the court and shield it absolutely from extrinsic influence, was under the circumstances, a federal constitutional violation" (Brief for Petitioner at 34). Clearly, the backing for this warrant was found in the Sixth Amendment to the United States Constitution establishing a defendant's right to a trial by an impartial jury. This

Figure 8. Ground II: Publicity During Trial

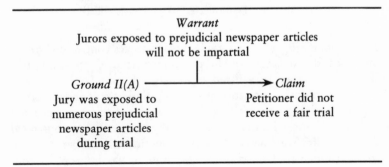

Warrant
Jurors exposed to prejudicial newspaper articles
will not be impartial

Ground II(A) ⟶ *Claim*
Jury was exposed to Petitioner did not
numerous prejudicial receive a fair trial
newspaper articles
during trial

subground regarding the publicity during trial can be depicted as shown in Figure 9.

Thus, the second ground advanced in support of the petitioner's claim that Sheppard did not receive a fair and impartial hearing was that of prejudicial publicity during the trial. Specifically, the petitioner alleged that the trial was unfair because the jury was exposed to extrinisic, prejudicial material and, furthermore, that the judge himself failed to secure adequately the petitioner's right to an impartial jury. Accordingly, the petitioner urged the court to find the trial proceedings below could not have been impartial and, therefore, Sheppard's constitutional rights had been violated.

Ground III: Disruption of the Trial by Newsmen. The third foundation set forth to establish the claim that the petitioner did not receive a fair trial was that the conduct of the press disrupted the trial and, consequently, deprived the petitioner of due process of law.

The evidence offered to support this third ground included: all but a few seats in the courtroom were assigned to newsmen by the trial judge; a special room was set up adjacent to the courtroom for teletypes and other equipment; the presence and activities of the newsmen was disruptive and disorderly; the trial judge did not adequately correct the situation.

Figure 9. Ground II: Publicity During Trial

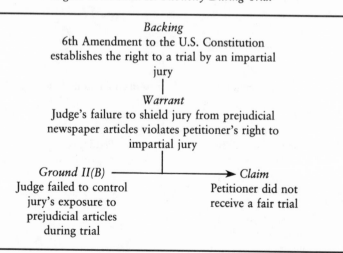

Backing
6th Amendment to the U.S. Constitution
establishes the right to a trial by an impartial
jury
|
Warrant
Judge's failure to shield jury from prejudicial
newspaper articles violates petitioner's right to
impartial jury
|

Ground II(B)	Claim
Judge failed to control jury's exposure to prejudicial articles during trial	Petitioner did not receive a fair trial

The inference provided by the petitioner to connect the disruption at trial with denial of a fair and impartial trial was that "intrusion upon a trial by newsmen which materially disrupts the somber decorum of the proceedings does not comport with minimum standards of due process" (Brief for Petitioner at 39). The backing for this warrant was provided by the Supreme Court ruling in *Estes v. Texas*, 381 U.S. 532 (1965), which expressly held in support of this proposition. This third argument may be depicted as shown in Figure 10.

Thus, the third foundation set forth to establish the claim that the petitioner did not receive a fair and impartial hearing and, further, was deprived of due process of law was based on evidence of disruptive and disorderly activities of the press while covering the trial in the courtroom. The petitioner's conclusion of the effect of these activities on the trial process was that "such tolerated and uncontrolled interference by newsmen is repugnant to our whole concept of a criminal trial" (Brief for Petitioner at 41).

In summary, the petitioner's argument consisted of one major claim: The petitioner was so thoroughly tried and convicted by the media that he did not receive a fair and impartial hearing as required by the United States Constitution. Several relevant grounds were offered in support of this claim. Specifically, the petitioner offered evidence of pretrial publicity adversely affecting the petitioner as

Figure 10. Ground III: Disruption of Trial By Newsmen

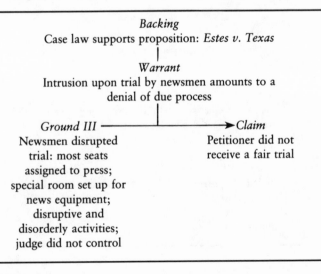

Backing
Case law supports proposition: *Estes v. Texas*
|
Warrant
Intrusion upon trial by newsmen amounts to a
denial of due process
|
Ground III ——————————————➤*Claim*
Newsmen disrupted   Petitioner did not
trial: most seats   receive a fair trial
assigned to press;
special room set up for
news equipment;
disruptive and
disorderly activities;
judge did not control

demonstrated by lower court opinions, evidence of an improper inquest, and publication of the jurors' names prior to the trial. The petitioner went further in supporting this claim, by offering evidence of prejudicial publicity during the trial, citing the judge's failure to control the jurors' exposure to various inflammatory articles. Finally, the petitioner contended the newsmen were so disruptive during the trial itself as to amount to a denial of due process.

But the petitioner did more than merely offer sufficient foundational grounds in support of the unfair trial claim; the petitioner went on to provide reliable warrants, which were in turn justified by a sufficient backing of a relevant nature. Moreover, where appropriate, the petitioner qualified the claim and grounds set forth and anticipated rebuttal arguments. Thus, the petitioner demonstrated not only an ability to set forth several layers of complex argumentation in support of his claim but, further, connected these grounds to the claim by reliable warrants that in turn were justified by relevant backings.

Respondent's Argument

In contrast to the petitioner's argument focusing the court on performing its law development function, the respondent urges the court to function only in its error correction capacity. When functioning in this error correction role, the court anticipates reviewing the impact of the lower court's decision on the specific individuals. Specifically, the court reviews evidence of the lower court's action to determine whether the lower court erred in a procedural or evidentiary ruling, or applied an incorrect legal principle, or misapplied a correct legal principle. From this focal point, the respondent in the Sheppard appeal argues the lower court's action was consistent with the law and, therefore, there is no error for the court to correct. The persuasiveness of the respondent in setting forth the claims in support of this argument is next considered.

The respondent sets forth two major claims in his error correction argument. First, the respondent claims the evidence presented at trial was sufficient for the jury to conclude that Sam Sheppard was guilty of murdering his wife. Second, the respondent claims the publicity relating to the trial was not so pervasively prejudicial to the petitioner as to require the presumption that the jurors were partial, nor was there any demonstrated evidence of juror partiality. Each of these claims and their accompanying grounds, warrants, backings, qualifiers, and rebuttal arguments will be considered in turn.

Claim I: The Sufficiency of the Evidence. The respondent first claims there was sufficient evidence presented at trial for the jury to have concluded that the petitioner was guilty of murdering his wife (Brief for Respondent at 8–9). This claim is the ultimate conclusion that the respondent is seeking to establish. To support this claim, the respondent reviewed for the court the evidence that was presented to the jury at trial—the underlying foundation of facts— in an effort to demonstrate there were sufficient grounds to support a determination of guilt.

Specifically, the grounds offered by the respondent in support of his sufficiency of evidence claim amounted to a listing of the evidence presented to the jury at trial. This evidence tended to show: first, that Sheppard's story was inconsistent and thus the jury could have determined it to be untrue (Brief for Respondent at 12–26); second, that the evidence adduced from the state's witnesses, that is, the state's version of the story, was sufficiently plausible for a jury to have concluded the petitioner was guilty (Brief for Respondent at 26–41); and third, that the defense's story told to the jury was ineffective in terms of persuading the jurors as it did not materially add to the defense but, rather, merely placed Sheppard's character in evidence—that is, witnesses testified that Sheppard was a nice individual, but did not explain facts surrounding the crime (Brief for Respondent at 41–48).

The warrant offered by the respondent to provide the necessary bridge between the claim of sufficient evidence and the grounds of specific evidence presented to the jurors was that, contrary to the petitioner's argument that Sheppard's conviction was brought about *not* by evidence at trial but by "evidence" in newspapers (Brief for Respondent at 9), there was indeed sufficient evidence presented at the trial for a jury to have reasonably concluded the petitioner was guilty (Brief for Respondent at 48–52). Thus, the respondent urged the court that

> there was but one conclusion that the jury could reach as a result of all evidence adduced during the trial of Sheppard, that being, there was no burglar or intruder in the Sheppard home during the early morning hours of July 4, 1954, that the scene of the Sheppard home was "faked" to appear that a burglary had been committed and that Dr. Sheppard was in the murder room at the time of the murder and that he had a reason and temperament to commit murder. The ultimate

conclusion beyond any reasonable doubt being that Dr. Samuel H. Sheppard murdered his wife, Marilyn, by brutally beating her to death with 35 crushing blows to the head. [Brief for Respondent at 52]

The respondent's argument also contains Toulmin's component of rebuttal, in that it anticipates and refutes the petitioner's claim that Sheppard's conviction was brought about only by the "evidence" presented in the newspapers "with the effect that newspaper publicity took the place of a fair trial" (Brief for Respondent at 9). Specifically, the respondent claims that the petitioner's argument is not legitimate and attempts to set it aside, urging the court to believe instead that the jury's decision was based on the evidence presented at trial.

The respondent's first claim that there was sufficient evidence presented at trial for the jury to have concluded the petitioner was guilty of murdering his wife may be depicted visually as shown in Figure 11.

Claim II: Publicity. The respondent's second claim is that the publicity surrounding the trial was not so pervasively prejudicial against the petitioner to presume the jurors were partial, nor was

Figure 11. Claim I: Sufficiency of Evidence

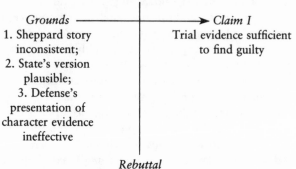

Warrant
Petitioner's argument that Sheppard was
convicted on extrinsic evidence must fail
because evidence heard at trial was sufficient to
sustain verdict

Grounds ⟶ *Claim I*
1. Sheppard story   Trial evidence sufficient
   inconsistent;   to find guilty
2. State's version
   plausible;
3. Defense's
presentation of
character evidence
ineffective

Rebuttal
Petitioner's claim that Sheppard convicted on
"evidence" presented in newspapers is not
legitimate

there any demonstrated evidence of such partiality. The respondent expressly stated: "The facts of this case do not warrant a presumption of community prejudice inherent in the nature of the pretrial publicity nor do they justify a finding of actual juror prejudice against the petitioner" (Brief for Respondent at 61–62). The underlying foundation of fact—the grounds—offered in support of this second claim was that there was a lack of evidence of actual community prejudice generally, or juror prejudice specifically.

Specifically, the respondent contended that when the evidence of newspaper publicity was considered as a whole, the coverage of the Sheppard case was not slanted for or against the petitioner but, rather, was a fair presentation of both sides. The respondent noted:

> The difficulty in characterizing the sum total of newspaper publicity is greatly compounded when, as here, there are parts highly favorable to the accused as well as unfavorable; when, as here, insinuation, surmise, and conjecture fill every unfavorable and some favorable articles; when, as here, the parts contain no direct evidence of guilt, no confession, or even unequivocal accusations of guilt; when, as here, the reputation of the accused is not marred by any past record of conviction; when, as here, there is no significant publication of any evidence not offered at trial. Each article has its meaning and each meaning has its effect upon the sum total nature of pre-trial and trial newspaper publicity. [Brief for Respondent at 55–56]

Thus, the respondent argued, the court could not reasonably presume there was actual community prejudice based on the newspaper articles alone as they fairly treated both sides of the issue.

Additionally, the respondent urged the court that, in order to determine the specific amount of actual juror prejudice, the "best initial method of determining the existence or absence of actual community and/or juror prejudice in a highly newspaper-publicized trial is . . . an independent review of the *voir dire* record" (Brief for Respondent at 61). This is so, the respondent urged, because the record of the *voir dire* proceeding presents the "most accurate opportunity for a view of the *effect* of publicity upon a cross-section of the community[;] [b]ut more important, it is the *effect* of publicity upon the *jurors* with which we are ultimately concerned" (Brief for Respondent at 61, emphasis in the original). The respondent then asserted that when the *voir dire* record is considered, there is no evidence of actual prejudice on the part of the jurors impaneled (Brief for Respondent at 74–81) and that, absent such a nexus, prejudice on the part of the jurors cannot be presumed.

The respondent's warrant connecting the claim the jurors were not partial with the ground of lack of evidence of actual community or juror prejudice is: a conclusion that community prejudice resulted in the impaneling of a partial jury must be based on demonstrated evidence of prejudice. The respondent, however, offers no backing to provide additional support for this assertion. Finally, the respondent anticipates the petitioner's counterargument that some types of publicity are so pervasive as to be inherently prejudicial, noting that "the ultimate factor of deciding importance is not the inherent nature of the publicity but its probable effect on the community from which the jurors are to be selected" (Brief for Respondent at 56). The respondent's second claim, that the trial publicity did not result in juror partiality, may be shown as depicted in Figure 12.

In summary, the respondent's argument consisted of two claims. First, the respondent claimed the evidence presented at trial was sufficient to support the jury's verdict of guilty. The respondent offered several grounds as evidence of this claim, and connected the grounds to the claim with a reasonable inference or warrant. Notably, however, the warrant offered in connection with this first claim was not justified by a sufficient backing; that is, the respondent did not offer a rule of law or statutory provision that had been validated either judicially or legislatively in support of the inference that the respondent was drawing.

The second claim made by the respondent was the publicity of

Figure 12. Claim II: Publicity

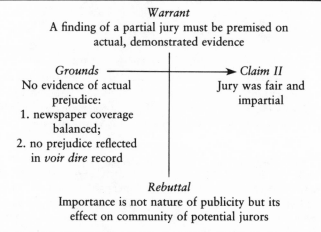

Warrant
A finding of a partial jury must be premised on actual, demonstrated evidence

Grounds ————————————→ *Claim II*
No evidence of actual   Jury was fair and
prejudice: impartial
1. newspaper coverage
balanced;
2. no prejudice reflected
in *voir dire* record

Rebuttal
Importance is not nature of publicity but its effect on community of potential jurors

the trial was not so pervasively prejudicial against the petitioner to presume the jurors were partial and there was no demonstrated evidence of juror partiality. The respondent offered two grounds in support of this argument and drew a reasonable inference in connecting the grounds and the claim. Again, however, the respondent did not have a relevant, authoritative backing to support the warrant.

Finally, while neither of the respondent's claims were qualified in any way, the respondent did anticipate and refute the expected counterarguments. Thus, the respondent's arguments were relatively simple, consisting of the three primary elements plus the element of rebuttal. The respondent demonstrated less of an ability to justify the claims alleged in the brief, leaving the inferences of the warrants reasonable, yet unsupported.

Supreme Court Opinion

The modes of reasoning and argumentation characteristic of the advocates' arguments contained in their briefs—the claim, grounds, warrants, backing, qualifiers, and rebuttal—are similarly characteristic of the communication used in an appellate court opinion to explain the decision the court has reached.

The claim set forth by the Supreme Court opinion in the Sheppard case was that "[t]he massive, pervasive, and prejudicial publicity attending petitioner's prosecution prevented him from receiving a fair trial consistent with the Due Process Clause of the Fourteenth Amendment" (384 U.S. at 334). The grounds relied on by the Supreme Court in supporting this claim were twofold: first, the evidence adduced from the record of the trial; and second, case law precedent.

Ground I: Record of the Trial. The first ground on which the Court relied was the record of the original trial. The Court's opinion cites specific examples as evidence of the prejudicial publicity (*Sheppard v. Maxwell*, 384 U.S. at 337–49). The following brief excerpt noting the extent of the pretrial publicity is representative:

> For months the virulent publicity about Sheppard and the murder had made the case notorious. Charges and countercharges were aired in the news media besides those for which Sheppard was called to trial. In addition, only three months before trial, Sheppard was examined for more than five hours without counsel during a three-day inquest which ended in a public brawl. The inquest was televised live from a

high school gymnasium seating hundreds of people. [*Sheppard v. Maxwell*, 384 U.S. at 354]

Additionally, the Court considered evidence of the publicity during the trial to support its claim of pervasive prejudicial publicity. The Court cited specific instances of journalistic conduct that the Court considered the most "flagrant episodes" (*Sheppard v. Maxwell*, 384 U.S. at 345). For example, the Court's opinion refers to the various newspaper articles and editorials published while the jury was being selected, the live debates broadcast over radio during the *voir dire* examination, and newspaper stories reporting "evidence" that was inadmissible at trial (*Sheppard v. Maxwell*, 384 U.S. at 345–49).

The Court also looked to evidence of the conduct of the press during the trial itself, noting:

> The fact is that bedlam reigned at the courthouse during the trial and newsmen took over practically the entire courtroom, hounding most of the participants in the trial, especially Sheppard. . . . Having assigned almost all of the available seats in the courtroom to the news media the judge lost his ability to supervise that environment. . . . And the record reveals constant commotion within the bar. Moreover, the judge gave the throng of newsmen gathered in the corridors of the courthouse absolute free reign. [*Sheppard v. Maxwell*, 384 U.S. at 355]

The rule or principle the Court relied on as the warrant or link between the Court's claim that the prejudicial publicity attending the petitioner's prosecution prevented him from receiving a fair trial and the evidentiary foundation of facts or grounds supporting the claim was:

> The theory of our system is that the conclusions to be reached in a case will be induced only by evidence and argument in open court, and not by any outside influence, whether of private talk or public print. [*Sheppard v. Maxwell*, 384 U.S. at 351 (citations omitted)]

Additionally, throughout the argument the Court was relying on the text of the appropriate constitutional provision, the Due Process Clause, as further support or backing for the argument. The Due Process Clause, embodied in the Fourteenth Amendment, simply states that no state shall "deprive any person of life, liberty, or property, without due process of law." This notion of due process

provides additional support for the Court's warrant, particularly in that, as a constitutional provision it clearly has been validated both judicially, legislatively, and popularly.

Finally, the modalities in this particular appellate reasoning are clearly expressed in the Court's written opinion. The Supreme Court states the scope and force of application intended for the rule of law embodied in the decision, for the Court knows that future courts will use the opinion in deciding still other cases. In the Sheppard opinion, the Court expressly acknowledges the tension operating within the facts of the Sheppard case; specifically, between the First Amendment right to free speech and the Sixth Amendment right to a fair trial (*Sheppard v. Maxwell*, 384 U.S. at 350). In an effort to give guidance to future courts and litigants, the Sheppard Court notes:

> Freedom of discussion should be given the widest ranges compatible with the essential requirement of the fair and orderly administration of justice. [citations omitted] But it must not be allowed to divert the trial from the "very purpose of a court system . . . to adjudicate controversies, both criminal and civil, in the calmness and solemnity of the courtroom according to legal procedures." [citations omitted] Among these "legal procedures" is the requirement that the jury's verdict be based on evidence received in open court, not from outside sources. [*Sheppard v.Maxwell*, 384 U.S. at 350–51]

Graphically, the Court's first ground in support of the claim that the petitioner did not receive a fair trial may be depicted as shown in Figure 13.

Ground II: Case Law Precedent. Further support for the Court's claim that the publicity surrounding the prosecution of Sheppard prevented him from receiving a fair trial was found by looking to case law precedent, that is, the content of past decisions dealing with the same or an analogous issue.

Specifically, the Sheppard Court relied on the then-recent decision of *Estes v. Texas*, 381 U.S. 532 (1965), wherein a conviction was set aside despite the absence of any showing of prejudice. The Estes Court stated:

> It is true that in most cases involving claims of due process deprivations we require a showing of identifiable prejudice to the accused. Nevertheless, at times a procedure employed by the State involves such a probability that prejudice will result that it is deemed inher-

Figure 13. Ground I: Record of the Trial

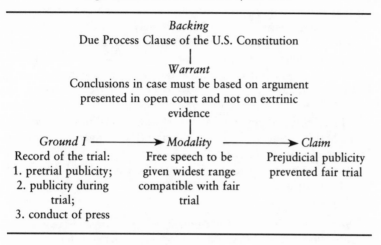

Backing
Due Process Clause of the U.S. Constitution
|
Warrant
Conclusions in case must be based on argument
presented in open court and not on extrinic
evidence
|

Ground I ————————➤	Modality ————————➤	Claim
Record of the trial:	Free speech to be	Prejudicial publicity
1. pretrial publicity;	given widest range	prevented fair trial
2. publicity during	compatible with fair	
trial;	trial	
3. conduct of press		

ently lacking in due process. [*Sheppard v. Maxwell*, 384 U.S. at 352, citing *Estes v. Texas*, 381 U.S. at 542–43]

The Sheppard Court then noted that "[i]t is clear that the totality of circumstances in this case also warrants such an approach" (384 U.S. at 352), and went further to explain how the Sheppard circumstances were similar to, or more serious than, the circumstances present in Estes. For example, the Court noted that:

Unlike Estes, Sheppard was not granted a change of venue to a locale away from where the publicity originated; nor was the jury sequestered. The Estes jury saw none of the television broadcasts from the courtroom. On the contrary, the Sheppard jurors were subjected to newspaper, radio and television coverage of the trial while not taking part in the proceedings. They were allowed to go their separate ways outside of the courtroom, without adequate directions not to read or listen to anything concerning the case. . . . The press coverage of the Estes trial was not nearly as massive and pervasive as the attention given by the Cleveland newspapers and broadcasting stations to Sheppard's prosecution. [*Sheppard v. Maxwell*, 384 U.S. at 352–54]

Against this background, the Sheppard Court determined "the arrangements made by the judge with the news media caused Sheppard to be deprived of that 'judicial serenity and calm to which [he] was entitled' and which the Estes holding mandates" (*Sheppard v. Maxwell*, 384 U.S. at 355).

205

Thus, the Court's warrant in the Sheppard case for this second ground is the common law notion of *stare decisis*, which provides that, while no two cases will be absolutely identical, cases having relevant similarities must be treated alike. Further backing for this warrant is found in that this notion of *stare decisis* is the hallmark of common law jurisdictions such as the United States; this approach has been validated again and again over hundreds of years and is central to the common law approach to justice.

Finally, the Sheppard Court provided modalities to limit the scope of the argument and provide certainty and guidance for future litigants and courts. Specifically, the Court suggested the following guidelines to avoid repeating the "carnival atmosphere" present in the Sheppard trial:

> The trial court failed to invoke procedures which would have guaranteed petitioner a fair trial, such as adopting stricter rules for use of the courtroom by newsmen as petitioner's counsel requested, limiting their number, and more closely supervising their courtroom conduct. The court should also have insulated the witnesses; controlled the release of leads, information, and gossip to the press by police officers, witnesses, and counsel; proscribed extrajudicial statements by any lawyer, witness, party, or court official divulging prejudicial matters; and requested the appropriate city and county officials to regulate release of information by their employees. [*Sheppard v. Maxwell*, 384 U.S. at 334, 358–62]

This second ground set forth by the Court in support of the claim that the petitioner did not receive a fair trial may be depicted graphically as shown in Figure 14.

In summary, the opinion of the Supreme Court set forth as its claim the petitioner did not receive a fair and impartial hearing due to the prejudicial publicity that attended the petitioner's case. The Court offered two grounds in support of this claim: first, evidence contained in the trial record regarding the amount of publicity, and second, facts in the trial record analogous to the Estes case. The Court then connected both of these grounds to the major claim by reasonable and reliable warrants, which in turn were justified by very authoritative backings—the Constitution of the United States and the common law notion of *stare decisis*. Moreover, the Court utilized the modality qualifier in an effort to give scope and force of application to the rule of law resulting from the decision.

Figure 14. Ground II: Case Law Precedent

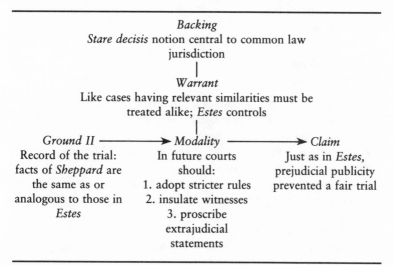

Backing
Stare decisis notion central to common law
jurisdiction
|
Warrant
Like cases having relevant similarities must be
treated alike; Estes controls
|

Ground II	⟶	Modality	⟶	Claim
Record of the trial: facts of *Sheppard* are the same as or analogous to those in *Estes*		In future courts should: 1. adopt stricter rules 2. insulate witnesses 3. proscribe extrajudicial statements		Just as in *Estes,* prejudicial publicity prevented a fair trial

Evaluation of Arguments
Presented in the Sheppard Appellate Case

In evaluating the effectiveness of appellate arguments, several factors must be analyzed. It is first necessary to determine the function in which the court was directed to act and whether the types of arguments set forth in the briefs were legitimate in terms of the court's perceived function. These legitimate arguments must then be analyzed for their effectiveness, as demonstrated by the arguers' ability to set forth the various claims, grounds, warrants, backings, modal qualifiers, and rebuttals.

Finally, in appellate argument, the ultimate determination of a brief's persuasiveness is the degree to which the court opinion adopts the reasoning set forth in the brief to explain its own reasons for deciding a case a certain way. In reaching a decision, appellate judges consider the arguments detailed in the briefs from each attorney and consider the reasoning set forth by each side; they consider opposing interpretations of relevant statutes, codes, and precedents, and they accept arguments from competent authorities as to what the proper interpretation should be. Ultimately, it is the task of the appellate court to show the reasons why one or the other party's position is more consistent with the court's particular function in the case as well as with the overall demands of justice. Thus, the "fit" between the court's opinion and the advocate's argument must be considered.

Petitioner's Argument

At the outset, the petitioner's brief very clearly states that the issue before the court, prejudicial publicity resulting in an unfair trial, raised questions going beyond those previously addressed by the courts. The petitioner was, of course, suggesting that the then current state of media technology was such that the existing laws were no longer adequate to meet societal needs. In this way, the petitioner focused the court on the need to expand or reinterpret existing law, rather than merely determine if the trial court had acted impermissibly. Thus, the court was already anticipating the subsequent argument; the framework had been set. Subsequently, the petitioner did marshal arguments appropriate to a law development functioning court. Specifically, the petitioner set forth examples of both pretrial and trial proceedings that were not in keeping with notions of fair and impartial hearings, such as slanted news articles, improper inquest procedures, publication of jurors' names, and a trial disrupted by press coverage.

Significantly, the petitioner's law development argument, while focusing on the effect of the lower court's decision on the trial process generally, also interspersed the argument with notions of doing justice for Sheppard individually. That is, while making the law development argument, the petitioner did not lose sight of the individual litigant and the effect this prejudicial environment had on the immediate parties to the action. In this way, the petitioner appealed to the "doing justice" function of the court, which is present anytime the individual judges or justices are involved. The petitioner, therefore, did not allow the court to lose sight of the values, beliefs, and traditions on which our system of justice depends.

The petitioner next set forth several layers of well-defined complex arguments in support of the claim that the petitioner did not receive a fair trial. The arguments regarding prejudicial pretrial publicity, prejudicial publicity during the trial, and the effects of a disruptive press were sufficiently grounded, connected by reliable warrants and relevant backings. Further, where appropriate, the arguments were qualified and rebuttal arguments anticipated. The petitioner thus demonstrated an ability to manipulate successfully the components of effective argumentation.

Finally, the petitioner's argument was endorsed almost entirely by the Supreme Court opinion; the "fit" between the petitioner's reasoning and that of the Court's was almost exact. The claim advanced by both the petitioner and the Court was the same. Moreover, although framed somewhat differently, the grounds, warrants, and backings set forth by the petitioner as a foundation for the reasoning in the argument were adopted in whole by the Court.

Thus, according to both legal norms and communication theory, the petitioner's appellate brief is an example of effective argumentation. That is, the petitioner clearly set forth the court's function and the corresponding arguments, the arguer demonstrated an ability to manipulate the components essential to effective argumentation as determined by argumentation theory, and, as a result, the appellate opinion adopted the reasoning of the petitioner almost entirely.

Respondent's Argument

In contrast to the petitioner directing the Court to function in a law development capacity, the respondent directed the Court to function only to correct the error in judgment of the court below. From this focal point, the respondent then argued there was no need to modify the lower court's judgment as the procedural and evidentiary rulings were correct and the lower court had correctly applied the correct legal principle. Convincing the Court to operate only to review errors in the lower court's application of existing law was, therefore, a critical juncture for the respondent. If the Court rejected the respondent's direction and chose instead to function to develop new law, the respondent's arguments would be no longer relevant to the determination.

The subsequent arguments made by the respondent were appropriate to this error correction approach. Specifically, the respondent argued the evidence was sufficient to support the determination of the jury and the publicity did not have a demonstrably adverse effect on the jury, leading the respondent to the conclusion there was no reversible error below. Yet the grounds and warrants supporting these claims were not appropriately justified by authoritative backings; as a result the inference was less persuasive and the argument less effective. Thus, in comparison to the petitioner's abilities, the respondent was less successful in his manipulation of the components of effective argumentation.

Finally, the respondent's argument was not accepted by the Supreme Court opinion; indeed, the claims raised by the respondent were not even addressed in the Court opinion. Thus, judged by legal norms and communication theory, the respondent's argument was less effective than the petitioner's argument. Although the respondent clearly set forth the role in which the Court was to function and was aware of the arguments that corresponded to this function, the arguments themselves were less effective; the grounds were not sufficiently connected by reliable warrants, and the warrants were not justified by sufficient, relevant backings. Consequently, the opinion issued by the Court did not adopt the respondent's reasoning in explaining its decision.

Implications for Appellate Practice

The advocate brief functions in the appellate review process to provide well-reasoned legal arguments for the court's consideration in reaching its final judgment. Most often, the court adopts the reasoning advanced by one of the parties as the explanation for the subsequent judicial decision. Thus, identifying the persuasive strategies underlying effective brief writing is a crucial link in the appellate process.

To be effective, appellate argumentation must address all of the legal norms and individual values that appellate judges consider in reaching a decision. Specifically, the advocate needs to direct the court as to the function it should be performing and then develop persuasive arguments appropriate to that particular function. Thus, all relevant issues, including constitutional and statutory provisions, case law precedent, and overall values, must be dealt with in the successful advocate's appellate brief.

Moreover, each of these relevant arguments must be advanced effectively. Persuasive argumentation presents a reasonable claim, and offers sufficient and relevant grounds in support of the claim. To be effective, these grounds must be connected to the claim by reliable warrants, which in turn must be justified by appeal to sufficient backing of a relevant nature. This entire structure of argument must be qualified to the intended degree of reliability and, further, rebuttal argument must be anticipated where appropriate. The advocate's ability to articulate appropriate claims, grounds, warrants, backings, modal qualifiers, and rebuttals contributes sig-

210

nificantly to the effectiveness and persuasiveness of the argumentation.

All of the trials considered in this volume, with the exception of the Hinckley trial, were appealed. The Haymarket trial was appealed to both the Illinois and the United States supreme courts. Although these appeals technically were unsuccessful (the verdict was affirmed by the Illinois court, and the United States Supreme Court denied application for a *writ of error*), the governor of Illinois eventually pardoned three of the eight anarchists—a form of "appeal" outside the scope of the judiciary.

The New Jersey Court of Error and Appeal refused to overturn the verdict of the Hauptmann trial. Subsequently, the United States Supreme Court refused to hear the case. Eventually, the New Jersey governor, Harold Hoffman, intervened and publicly expressed his concern that the verdict was unfair. Based on this public comment, the New Jersey Court of Pardons and Clemency considered the case, but refused to pardon Hauptmann by a narrow margin.

Appeal of the Sacco-Vanzetti trial took six years to complete. Sacco and Vanzetti's arguments, however, in consideration with other influencing factors, were not enough to carry the day. The Supreme Judicial Court of Massachusetts heard the appeal and upheld the trial court's verdict; the United States Supreme Court refused to hear the case. Finally, the governor of Massachusetts refused to grant clemency to Sacco and Vanzetti.

Prior to the Rosenbergs' execution, the trial was reviewed and affirmed by a federal appellate court. The United States Supreme Court subsequently declined to review the case three times and refused to stay execution of the Rosenbergs. In contrast to the Chicago Anarchists' successful extrajudicial appeal, President Eisenhower refused to grant the Rosenbergs executive clemency.

The defense in the Chicago Eight trial was successful on appeal. The Seventh Circuit Court of Appeals reversed all long-term contempt citations and remanded the contempt proceedings for a trial before a jury; thereafter the prosecutors elected not to seek a new trial, except as against Bobby Seale. The short-term contempt sentences, imposed against Dellinger, Hoffman, Rubin, and Kunstler, were upheld. All other charges were reversed by the Seventh Circuit, based on errors committed by Judge Hoffman and the prosecutors.

Of all the trials in this volume, however, the Sheppard trial is a particularly appropriate vehicle for focusing on effective argumentation strategies in the appellate process. Considered by many to be F. Lee Bailey's finest work, the petitioner's brief is exemplary of effective communication strategies in the appellate process. As illustrated by the Sheppard appeal, effective argumentation is more persuasive and, therefore, more likely to be adopted by the court in the subsequent judicial decision as the explanation for the reasoning in the court opinion. Utilizing a communication model grounded in legal theory as a framework for examining how advocates communicate legal arguments, this chapter demonstrates how the elements of argumentation are successfully manipulated in the advocates' briefs and, further, how these components may influence the court's reasoning as explained in the judicial opinion.

A Judge's Reaction

David S. Nelson

The chapter on appellate advocacy is a significant contribution toward understanding the role of the advocate's brief in the appellate process. Yet while the authors recognize the constituent set of interrelated factors that go into crafting such an advocate's brief, the full process is probably even more complex than the authors suggest. The experienced appellate advocate may well utilize several additional devices in order to improve the chances that his or her arguments will carry the day.

For one thing, in cases where the facts and the trial record allow, it is frequently useful to hint, even if one does not directly argue, that the defendant might in fact be innocent and that a new trial, played out according to a fairer set of rules, might indeed result in a just acquittal.

In a case like Sheppard, such a tactic was especially important, since the government based much of its appellate argument upon a claim that there was more than sufficient evidence of guilt presented at the trial to justify the conviction. An appellate tribunal that senses a possibility that a factually innocent person may have been wrongfully convicted may be more likely to reverse the conviction even if the reversal were predicated on procedural grounds alone. Procedural grounds might simply be the hook upon which the court may hang its hat in reversing a verdict that appears to be a substantive miscarriage of justice.

Interestingly, in the Sheppard case, the defendant was indeed

David S. Nelson is a United States District Judge for the District of Massachusetts. He has his B.S. and J.D. degrees from Boston College. Before being appointed to the federal bench in 1979, Judge Nelson was a Justice of the Superior Court for the Commonwealth of Massachusetts and, prior to that, was a partner in the Boston law firm of Crane, Inker, and Oteri. Judge Nelson has taught trial advocacy courses at Harvard, Boston University, and Boston College law schools, and has taught the law of communications at Boston University School of Public Communications. He also has been a lecturer at the National Institute for Trial Advocacy. Judge Nelson acknowledges Harvey Silverglate, Esq., Boston, for his cogent and valuable assistance in the preparation of this response.

acquitted at his retrial, lending retrospective credence to any argument on the appeal that the evidence was weak, and that only the circus atmosphere would account for the conviction.

Another factor not discussed in the chapter is the relationship between the written brief and the oral argument. It would surely be interesting to study the Sheppard oral arguments in tandem with a study of the briefs since there is some controversy within the legal community as to the degree to which oral arguments help determine the outcome of an appeal. But students of appellate advocacy do tend to agree, however, that in a significant minority of cases the outcome likely changed as a result of oral arguments.

The brief and the oral argument should complement, not duplicate, each other. The advocate must exercise careful judgment about such things as when to omit something from the brief so as to enhance reserving the opportunity to more effectively make the point during oral argument, presumably in a context where the point can best be molded to meet the court's apparent view of the case, which view only becomes evident to the advocate once the oral argument has begun. Thus, while it may be true that "appellate advocates consider the brief the single most important aspect of appellate review," the potential extant in the oral arguments should not be ignored nor denigrated.

Furthermore, an appellate brief's force and persuasive power can be substantially enhanced if the proceedings at the lower court trial were managed with an eye toward creating an effective appellate record. A good trial lawyer will always have one eye on the appellate record and will, at each stage of the trial, balance the need to create an effective appellate record against the more immediate need to maximize the chances of a jury acquittal. To the extent that it is possible, one should lay out facts and legal arguments on the trial record in a way that would maximize the effectiveness of appellate advocacy in the event of a conviction. A good record is a kind of "insurance policy" in the event of a conviction.

One other aspect of appellate advocacy that is entitled to more weight than has been given in the chapter is the need for the advocate to craft his or her arguments in a way that would minimize the extent to which a decision in favor of the client may not have been seen by the court as damaging any broader or longer-term societal or legal interests or principles. Conversely, one method for rebutting the other side's arguments is to demonstrate that a ruling in the opponent's favor would lead to a "parade of horribles"—that is to say, it would have untoward results in future cases and situations.

The appellate advocate has a number of other tools in his or her arsenal. For example, in a case where the trial judge may have been somewhat responsible for the problems created at the trial, the advocate sometimes will want to draw attention to systemic or other factors, rather than place the blame squarely on the trial judge. This tactic assumes that appellate judges will tend to avoid direct criticism of a trial judge, when not critical to the result. The advocate should perhaps consider presenting the appellate tribunal with a ground or a method for reversing the conviction that places the least onus on the trial judge personally. Sometimes an argument that tends to be critical of the trial judge will be followed by an argument blaming the problem on some other factor, giving the appellate court the option of choosing the latter ground on which to base its reversal. In Sheppard, for example, there were arguments that blamed the trial judge for the circus atmosphere, and other arguments that blamed the news media. The Supreme Court was given the option of focusing on the role of the media.

There are yet other situations where a court may be led to decide in favor of one's client without really having to choose between two conflicting substantive arguments. Some particularly difficult cases can often be decided without the court's having to make any ultimate decisions on substantive matters. For example, in a case where each side appears to have a strong factual case, the court might decide the case by imposing on one side or the other the burden of proof. If the strength of the two sides' arguments appears to be in equipoise, the side having the burden would be declared the loser for failure to satisfy its burden.

Finally, something has to be said about the tension between making fact-bound arguments and arguing sweeping policy or constitutional grounds in an appellate brief. Sometimes the advocate argues his or her case by citing to the facts, either because the facts are particularly sympathetic or strong, or because the legal basis for the argument is weak, or because the advocate wants to offer the tribunal a basis for limiting its ruling only to a case factually similar to the case at hand. (This latter tactic helps the court avoid issuing a very broad ruling that might create that feared "parade of horribles" in its wake.) Yet in other situations, the advocate might choose to argue the case broadly, making social policy and consitutional arguments, or even arguing that prior precedent is inadequate due to new social realities.

The decision as to whether to argue a case broadly—that is, on a policy or "law development" basis; or narrowly—that is, on a "fact-bound" basis—is nowhere more difficult yet important than in the petition for *writ of certiorari*. This petition is the document by which a litigant who loses a case in the lower court seeks to obtain review by the United States Supreme Court. It is the advocate's job to persuade the Supreme Court, not that the claim of his or her client is legally correct, but rather, that the case has important legal principles that require review and decision by the court of last resort. The petitioner thus usually argues very broadly in a *certiorari* petition, while the respondent usually argues that the case below is fact-bound, is not likely to recur, and that in any event a decision in the particular case is not likely to create a useful precedent for, nor give guidance to, future parties.

In short, the respondent would argue that reviewing the case would not be worth the Supreme Court's limited and precious time. Yet once review is granted, both sides are then faced anew with the question of whether to argue narrowly or broadly in order to convince the high court to accept their positions on the merits of the issues presented for decision.

As has been demonstrated by the chapter and by this reactive commentary, the communicative and rhetorical devices that go into the construction of an appellate brief and oral argument are extremely complex, as is the process by which courts decide the many difficult issues placed before them on a daily basis. The genius of the English common law tradition, which our nation inherited in 1776 and which has continued to develop since that time, is embodied in the observation made by Justice Oliver Wendell Holmes, Jr., when he wrote in his great 1881 essay *The Common Law*: "The life of the law has not been logic; it has been experience."

7
Courtroom Drama:
The Trial of the Chicago Eight

Courtroom storytelling and story listening are part of a more complete drama with characters, plot, denouement, action, and setting. Although all of the trials in this volume present a drama, the Chicago Eight case illustrates an uncharacteristic dramatic form for the courtroom. This analysis suggests that the Chicago Eight is a burlesque drama that subverts the conventional courtroom form by unconventional subject matter. In short, the participants in the trial mocked the cherished ideals of the court by vulgar speech, manner, and appearance. This interpretation focuses first on a general description of trials as drama and second on an analysis of the situations, scripts, roles, performances, and staging of the Chicago Eight trial. The Chicago conspiracy case illustrates that all trials have a theatrical dimension, but this quality is often invisible because it is an expected and traditional dramatic form. By analyzing an eccentric drama such as burlesque, the latent and traditional dramatic form of all trials is illuminated.

Despite the evolution of legal codes and appellate guidelines for conducting a trial, the Chicago Eight case showed that the unorthodox acts by judges, advocates, spectators, and defendants can subvert the norms typical of a courtroom drama and thereby alter the judicial process. This deviation from the traditional norms of courtroom drama occurs only when exceptional legal and political factors force a test of the existing codes, as they did in this case. The disparate ingredients of the Chicago Eight case resulted from politically motivated indictments, which in turn stemmed from questionable laws that attempted to restrict dissent; a conservative law-and-order judge who based his rulings on political assumptions rather than legal grounds; a bright, cynical, and angry group of defendants, whose case was presented by skillful but politically motivated attorneys; and a zealous press eager to participate in the drama.

The Trial

After five months of name calling, personal insults, and legal challenges, the Chicago Eight trial came to an end on February 18, 1970, five months after it began. When the trial ended, *Time* (23 February 1970) characterized the case as "horrendous provocation" and "guerilla theater" (p. 38); *Newsweek* (2 March 1970) as "wild eccentricity" and "pyrotechnics" (p. 27); and the *Nation* (2 March 1970) claimed it was an "attempt to suppress dissent" and "intimidate" protest (p. 326). Arbetman and Roe (1985) referred to the case as "the most important political trial of the century" (p. 151).

The trial resulted from planned protests of a variety of groups opposing the Vietnam war including the Yippies, Students for a Democratic Society (SDS), the Black Panthers, and others who identified themselves as the New Left. Hundreds of unaffiliated antiwar protestors also joined the action prior to and during the 1968 Democratic convention in Chicago. At the time of the convention, antiwar sentiment was particularly high because President Lyndon Johnson had increased troop strength in Vietnam from 20,000 to 500,000.

The defendants, labeled the "Chicago Eight" by the media, worked with others to organize the over 10,000 demonstrators gathered at the site of the national political convention. Prior to the convention, organizers sought permits to assemble, march, and camp near the site. When the city refused permits, it anticipated confrontations from the demonstrators and therefore mobilized hundreds of city policemen and National Guardsmen. Even though they received no permits, the demonstrators marched and camped in Chicago prior to and during the convention, causing major conflicts with the law enforcement personnel, who retaliated against the demonstrators with tear gas, billy clubs, and mass arrests.

Ramsey Clark, United States attorney general, considered prosecuting the leaders of the demonstrations but changed his mind after his legal advisers told him the recent antiriot law might be unconstitutional. However, when Richard Nixon took office in 1969, he and his attorney general, John Mitchell, decided to bring charges against eight leaders of the demonstrations—Abbie Hoffman, Bobby Seale, Rennie Davis, Tom Hayden, Lee Weiner, John Froines, David

Dellinger, and Jerry Rubin. They were arrested and charged with conspiracy to riot.

The trial began in Federal District Court in Chicago with Julius J. Hoffman presiding. On the first day of the trial, Hoffman ordered the arrest of four lawyers who telegraphed him they were resigning from the case instead of appearing in person to give their resignations. That same day, Hoffman refused to delay the trial even though Charles R. Garry, attorney for defendant Bobby Seale, was entering the hospital for surgery and could not appear at the trial.

Thomas A. Foran and Richard G. Schultz served as the United States attorneys prosecuting the case. William Kunstler and Leonard Weinglass led the defense. After the trial concluded, Kunstler (1970) commented about the high level of tension and conflict in the trial. He noted that Hoffman could not understand the defendants or their motivation. And as a result, the judge "used the judicial process against them exactly as Don Quixote had flailed his spear against a windmill's rotating vanes, destroying, along the way, his own credibility and undermining the very system he thought he was saving" (p. xvi).

Not only did Judge Hoffman behave in an unconventional manner, but the defense attorneys, witnesses, spectators, and defendants acted in a contentious way opposing the traditions and decorum of the court. The combination of unorthodox behaviors produced mayhem in the courtroom. When viewed through the lens of standard trial procedure, the actions and behaviors of the Chicago Eight trial participants are incomprehensible. But the use of the dramatic categories reveals what occurred and provides reasons for the unconventional communication within the trial. This chapter (1) describes trials as dramatic persuasion, (2) presents an illustration of courtroom communication in the dramatistic mode of burlesque by examining the definitions of the legal situation, the creation of scripts, the enactment of roles, the quality of performance, and the method of staging the event; and (3) demonstrates the potential of the dramatistic metaphor for the study of communication in the courtroom.

Trials as Dramatic Persuasion

Many scholars use drama as a metaphor for understanding social action. This tradition has developed in the social science literature and has been labeled "dramatism." The development of the dramatic metaphor discloses some of the assumptions of this approach for the study of social behavior. Simmel (1968) notes that dramatic art forms resemble the structure and function of actual social interaction. Burke (1968) elaborates this definition through his analysis of society in terms of lived dramas portraying how persons participate in conflict. For Burke, the "difference between staged drama and the drama of real life is the difference between obstacles imagined by the artist and those actually experienced" by persons in their daily lives (pp. 444–50). Duncan (1968) claims that social interaction is a dramatic way whereby persons enact their roles in order to change, modify, or sustain the social order.

Participation in the trial drama permits attorneys to reconstruct the real crime, portray the conflicts of lived experience, and use witnesses to re-create the reality of their lived experiences for the courtroom audience. Much of this dramatic action of the trial is part of the prescribed process of litigation. Other theatrical behavior is contrived by participants to achieve even greater persuasiveness with the courtroom audience.

Criminal trials are the epitome of social dramas. Harbinger (1971) calls a trial "a dramatic thing put to legal use" (p. 122). Acting as a director, the effective advocate dramatizes the setting, characters, themes, and actions of the crime so the trial will capture the attention and involve the emotions of its audiences.

Trial Drama as Persuasion

Harbinger (1971) explains that courtroom drama is a complex theatrical spectacle. It is one play within another play, each of which persuades audiences differently. Greek terms from classical rhetoric, *mimesis* and *phantasia,* explain how the two dramas persuade jurors. The most obvious play is the external play, featuring advocates trying to win a verdict. The external play persuades by mimesis, that is, the advocates artistically re-present the facts to the the jurors by their second-order interpretations of the crime. The other drama is an internal play, a play within the drama created by the advocates. The internal play persuades by phantasia; the people tell the crime story directly, trying to persuade jurors by appealing to their imagination, experiences, and understanding. The internal play features the participants in the crime recollecting and reporting their first-order experiences to jurors.

The press and the public spectators often view the external play as the only trial drama. Attorneys develop their roles by their summary of the case in opening statement; ordering and directing the dialogue in direct examination; reshaping the story in cross-examination; and reconstructing, refuting, and giving jury instructions in closing argument. In this way, advocates control the dialogue and delineate the themes and actions presented in the courtroom. Advocates both direct and star in the external dramas they construct.

The external drama is mimetic because it emphasizes the attorney-actors artistically re-creating the crime in the way prescribed for them by the traditions and norms of the litigation process. Advocates artistically reconstruct the crime through the questions they ask and the answers they elicit during the examination of witnesses. Specifically, litigators achieve mimetic persuasion in several ways. First, advocates show, as well as tell, the audience about the crime. They present exhibits and ask witnesses to talk about how the visual evidence relates to the facts of the case. Second, the attorneys reconstruct the crime in their own speeches with their emotive language, vivid character descriptions, and realistic re-creations of setting. Third, the director-actors emphasize the feelings of witnesses, such as anger, sadness, pity, jealousy, or distrust. The reconstruction of the crime in the external drama demonstrates to the public spectators that advocates are upholding their responsibilities and trying to make the American system of justice work.

The internal drama differs from the external. The internal drama appeals to jurors through phantasia; it emphasizes the witnesses, particularly defendants and victims, recollecting and reporting their experiences. Achieving the effect of phantasia is more natural and subtle than mimetic persuasion. In fact, the direct communication of the witnesses' perceptions and experiences is supposed to convince jurors beyond a reasonable doubt of the innocence or guilt of the accused. Thus the internal drama stars the defendants and the victims who recount their own personal experiences. The internal drama is not a battle between advocates as the external drama is; it is instead a struggle of individual persons to recall and report the truth, even as they experience the fears and pressures resulting from intense adversarial interrogation. This reporting of the crime story leads to phantasia; it persuades by penetrating the imagination, memory, and experiences of jurors. In the crime story, the verdict is not victory or defeat for an advocate, but a decision affecting the outcomes of their lives. The internal drama emerges in the witnesses' authentic (or perhaps contrived) verbal re-creations of the crime. Often the external drama is irrelevant to witnesses because they are caught up in their own personal obligations.

221

The mimesis and the phantasia effects vary from one trial to another. In many cases, the external drama is more persuasive than the internal crime story. In other cases, the internal crime story reiterates the pretrial persuasion presented by the press. In still other cases, the external drama dominates the persuasion of the trial, but the internal play is emphasized in the postverdict persuasion. In other words, the trial drama does not always reveal an external and an internal play of equal importance. Harbinger (1971) notes that mimetic trial dramas can capture jurors' attention to such a great extent that they base their verdicts not on the facts of the case but on the performances of the advocates. In other trials, jurors pay attention to the crime story and are largely unaware of the external drama between advocates. The system of trial by jury assumes the facts of the crime stories will produce a phantasia effect on jurors and that they will decide their verdicts according to the relative merits of the crime stories.

The trials that we have analyzed in earlier chapters show the predictable differences in the function of mimesis and phantasia. In the Hinckley case, phantasia was dominant. The press re-created the crime story and appealed to the imagination of its readers in order to get them to understand the emotions, motives, and experiences of the defendant. The trial record also indicates the centrality of the crime story told by Hinckley, his parents, and the psychiatrists. The case clearly focuses on the life of John W. Hinckley, Jr., instead of on the performances of advocates, judge, jurors, and spectators.

The Haymarket and Sacco-Vanzetti cases illustrate trials where the mimesis dominates over the phantasia. These trials are strong adversarial duels on the courtroom stage, focusing more on the attorneys as actors and directors than on the crime story of victims, as would have been the case in phantasia. The courtroom drama in the Haymarket case featured competent adversaries, Black for the defense and Grinnell for the state. In the Sacco-Vanzetti case, the central drama was enacted by the respected defense attorneys, Moore and the McAnarney brothers, and an equally competent prosecutor named Katzmann. Although the crime stories were present within the external courtroom drama, the internal play surfaced more as part of the postverdict dramatizations than it did in the trial itself.

In the Hauptmann, Rosenberg, and Sheppard trials, the internal drama dominated the courtroom performances. The verdicts seemed to depend much more on the crime story and its phantasia effect.

222

In each of these cases the story of the defendants and victims dominated the trial record. The stories of Lindbergh and Hauptmann, of the Rosenbergs and Greenglasses, and of Sam Sheppard and his family and neighbors, all appealed to the imaginations and experiences of the jurors, and emphasized the facticity of their firsthand accounts of the crime. In each of these trials, the crime story was more compelling than the duel between the courtroom adversaries even though the external courtroom drama received some attention in the press.

The Chicago Eight case is exceptional because it features mimetic persuasion in an extreme form. Despite the fact the defendants were indicted on many charges, the crime story was not an important facet of this litigation process. The defendants and victims did not direct their stories about the crime to the experiences and imagination of jurors and thereby try to persuade through phantasia. The persuasive goal was instead to focus attention on their own satirical performances. The advocates and judge persuaded by eccentric performances contrived to achieve a mimetic effect. The crime story became less and less relevant as the trial progressed, and the courtroom drama became increasingly significant to the outcome of the case. The Chicago Eight case is an extreme example of how the courtroom performers can capture the attention of all audiences—jurors, judge, witnesses, and spectators. In this kind of case the courtroom becomes a spectacle dominated by the second-order interpretations and verbal re-creations of the meaning of the event rather than the factual reports of the stories of the crime.

Chicago Eight as Burlesque Drama

Courtroom interaction can be classified according to a variety of dramatic modes ranging from tragedy and melodrama to farce. In the trials we have studied thus far, the most common dramatic form is tragedy. Through its persistent violations of courtroom norms, the Chicago Eight case illustrates the burlesque mode of drama. Burlesque is a type of satirical drama in which the conventional form of a genre or activity is subverted by unconventional subject matter. Burlesque takes two forms: parody satirizes established practices by treating inconsequential subject matter with dignity; and travesty subverts recognized or standard forms by presenting a lofty or serious subject with vulgarity (Burke, 1964; Holman, 1972; Styan, 1973). Travesty is the most common form of burlesque used in the Chicago conspiracy case; this form is evident when the defense repeatedly mocks the cherished ideals of the court by vulgar speech, manner, and appearance. Parody occurs less often, but takes place when the defense raises inconsequential matters, such as requesting a birthday cake for one of the defendants. The defense demands that many inconsequential matters be treated as if they were an important part of the trial drama.

Burlesque drama features several distinct types of courtroom communication that completely alter the traditions and norms of the trial. First, the burlesque mode uses language that mocks the formality and clarity of courtroom discourse by using slang, informal address, vulgar words, and words with private meanings. Second, this mode subverts traditional legal norms by adopting demeanor that is sarcastic, disrespectful, and offensive. Third, burlesque undermines the standard legal form of drama by unorthodox dress, postures, and gestures. Fourth, the customary legal assumptions about presumption of innocence and burden of proof, witness testimony, and contested issues are transformed into a drama where the presumption of innocence, the evidence given by witnesses, and the issues are irrelevant to the indictments. Each strategy by itself is not sufficient evidence of burlesque drama, but when these strategies are so pervasive, obvious, and consistent that observers no longer recognize the traditional form, the event is burlesque.

This analysis of the Chicago Eight case relies on the work of Goffman (1959), who identifies several variables that explain the drama of real social interactions. These variables help explain the interaction within the courtroom as drama in general and as the mode of burlesque in particular. Goffman contends that persons plan their communication so that it fits with the norms and expectations of the social context. A criminal trial results from definitions of the legal situation; the character development of the judge, attorneys, defendants, witnesses, and spectators; selection of the appropriate staging for verbal and nonverbal communication; adoption of roles to manage impressions; and creation of believable performances for the jury, judge, and media.

Definitions of a Situation

Goffman (1959) indicates that when participants define a situation in a certain way, that definition predicts the behaviors that are to follow. In the litigation process, persons consciously respond to the courtroom according to the norms and rules associated with that context. The examination of witnesses relies on two definitions of the courtroom situation. The first is the implicit and mutually agreed definitions whereby the judge, attorneys, jury, witnesses, and accused agree to abide by the rules and follow the norms of the judicial system. The second is when the attorneys decide upon a theory of the case that affirms or denies the allegations of the indictment.

Most participants in the trial agree about common definitions of the judicial process; that is, criminal trials follow the standards of "reason, objectivity, fairness of purpose, diligent preparation and presentation of evidence, clear, just rules, an orderly proceeding, and, at least, modest efficiency" (Clark, 1970, p. vi). When these expectations are shared by the participants, the trial moves forth in a formal and dignified process. However, when participants choose different definitions, they may transform the court from a dignified dramatic setting into a radically different situation.

In the Chicago Eight case, the participants in the trial converted the event from a criminal case against the defendants on charges of conspiracy to cross state lines to riot into a burlesque drama featuring confrontation between the "legal order" and the "new radicalism" (Kalven, 1970, p. xi). Instead of the state assuming its burden to prove the defendants guilty of the indictment, the state defended the legal process and the tactics of the police during the demonstrations. Moreover, rather than the defense upholding the presumption of innocence for the accused, they advocated an end to the war, acceptance of unorthodox life-styles, and the rejection of authority.

These unusual definitions of the legal situation created a courtroom proceeding characterized by unreason, subjectivity, and disorderliness. For example, although it was unreasonable to refuse to delay the trial when Seale's attorney could not participate, Judge Hoffman did so. Moreover, the defense attorneys and witnesses played their part in the burlesque by presenting matters for discussion in the court inconsequential and irrelevant to the trial, such as having a birthday party for defendant Seale, gaining bathroom privileges for the defendants, and delaying the trial to attend a peace rally in Washington, D.C.

A second factor contributing to the burlesque theater of this trial occurred in the development of the theories of the case by both the prosecution and defense. Standard courtroom procedure is to present the theory of the case using a theme or detailed explanation to "create a cohesive and logical position" (Mauet, 1980, p. 9). Attorneys usually preview their theory of the case in the form of a story in opening statement, develop this theory with the testimony of witnesses, and reiterate the theory in closing argument.

At the beginning of the Chicago Eight trial, the opening statements presented defendable theories of their respective cases. Richard G. Schultz, for example, argued "the Government will prove that each of these eight men . . . united and conspired together to encourage people to riot during the convention." He explained the defendants did so in three stages: using the antiwar issue to get people to Chicago, inflaming the people against the police, and encouraging resistance to police action (Transcript of Record, p. 11). Although the theory adopted a plausible position for the prosecution, the witnesses and evidence that followed failed to prove these allegations; instead the case stressed that the city of Chicago and its law enforcement personnel justifiably took action against the demonstrators.

Similarly, the theory of the case presented by the defense seemed justifiable. Kunstler outlined the theory in his opening statement: "But we are going to show the real conspiracy is not against these defendants as individuals; the real attack was on the rights of everybody . . . to protest under the First Amendment to the Constitution; to protest against a war that was brutalizing all of us" (Transcript of Record, p. 19). The witnesses and evidence presented by the defense, however, did not develop this theory but instead explained the ideology of the various protest groups. Moreover, the defense did not develop the innocence of the defendants but instead took on a burden to prove the government engaged in malicious and violent acts during the demonstrations.

These unconventional theories of the case resulted in a number of anomalies in the trial, including the following: neither side presented undisputed facts related to the indictments; the advocates dealt with issues external to the case, such as the rights of black people, the reasons for pacifism, and the role of women in society; both sides assumed the burden of proof; and neither side related the issues they established to the indictments. The result was the case turned into a debate about the legitimacy of police action versus the rights and ideology of the New Left. Such actions accorded superior status to the moral issues of the war and traversed the legal issues inherent in the indictments.

Since participants in the Chicago trial adopted unconventional definitions of the courtroom situation, the norm to "avoid conflict and to develop a working consensus" among interactants (Goffman, 1959) never occurred. Rather the participants established the norm that the trial was to be a satire about the system of criminal justice. This definition then legitimized changes in courtroom rules so the judge did not monitor the procedure in accordance with the accepted standards for his role. Thus, the defense decided the trial was to be burlesque, and they delineated the satirical form that the prosecution, judge, and spectators would follow.

Scripts

The definitions of the courtroom situation affect how attorneys elicit the testimony from their witnesses, present the issues, and develop evidence in the trial. The dramatic scripts of the trial consist of the discourse evolving from advocates' formal speeches, the questioning of witnesses, interactions between trial participants, and the nonverbal appearance and manner of the courtroom performers. Traditionally, attorneys assist the development of the scripts of witnesses by the way they conduct direct and cross-examination.

Several guidelines, delineated in chapter 3, explain how attorneys should ask questions so that the scripts of witnesses evolve into coherent, consistent, and believable testimony. In order for witnesses to introduce necessary evidence, attorneys must "lay the proper foundation," a procedure that requires that they demonstrate the evidence exists, is pertinent to the case, and contributes to the overall reasoning of an advocate's theory of the case (Oliphant, 1978, p. 42). Moreover, in direct examination, attorneys should encourage witnesses to provide descriptive detail, ask questions in chronological sequence, repeat crucial data as facts in subsequent questions, make causal connections between the testimony of witnesses, and assist their own witnesses to tell an accurate and believable story.

The direct examination of prosecution and defense witnesses followed some of the rules of this process and violated others. The government called seventy witnesses; many were policemen, FBI undercover agents, and city officials from Chicago. The direct examination followed a routine of asking witnesses their name, occupation, their activities during the time of the demonstrations, and their observations of the speech and actions of the defendants during the convention demonstrations. Although Prosecutor Schultz tried to conduct routine direct examinations, his questioning was frequently interrupted.

The scripts created by the prosecution were an odd mixture of reports of obscene and violent language used by the defendants, interruptions and outbursts from the defendants, and frequent motions for changes in the courtroom action by the defense. Although the prosecution, for the most part, conducted examinations of witnesses according to the rules, the defense distorted the clarity and credibility of the testimony by verbal interruptions.

During the trial, the abrasive and obscene language came not only from the mouths of the defendants but also from the reports about the accused given by the prosecution witnesses. For example Police Sergeant Robert Murray recounted his observations of Jerry Rubin at the demonstration: "He says the pigs are in our park. They're—the same word I used before—mother fuckers, they're shitheads" (Transcript of Record, p. 5).

Interruptions and outbursts frequently erupted in the courtroom. These interruptions featured the ridicule of Judge Hoffman by Seale, Dellinger, A. Hoffman, and Rubin, who repeated "Good Morning" after the judge addressed the jury with that greeting. The defendants also refused to rise when the judge entered, made satirical comments about the trial action such as "ridiculous" or "unfair," and interjected sounds such as "oink, oink" when a government witness would point to one of the defendants (Clark, 1970). The prosecution's testimony was also interrupted by lengthy motions of protest by defense counsel, such as challenges against the court marshal who forbade Seale's wife and child from being spectators in the court. In combination, these actions impugned the character of the prosecution witnesses by distorting the logic of their story and ruined the continuity and believability of their scripts, characteristics fitting with burlesque drama. Schultz could not maintain the standard form of direct examination because the subject matter interjected by the witnesses, the defense, and the judge undermined the customary way of conducting the questioning.

The questioning of witnesses by the defense overtly and deliberately violated the rules of the court concerning direct examination. The defense called 113 witnesses in a random order so that the responses of one witness had little, if any, connection to the testimony of the persons who preceded and followed. The content of the testimony bore only faint resemblance to the defense's theory of the case. Furthermore the defense laid no foundation for the evidence they introduced. As a result, the prosecution made hundreds of objections and most were sustained by the judge. The examination did highlight the issues and ideology of the antiwar dissidents, clearly differentiating the character and beliefs of the defense from the

228

prosecution witnesses. Whereas the defense forcibly altered the scripts of the prosecution, Kunstler and Weinglass molded their witnesses' unconventional scripts so that the style and content mocked the orthodox law-and-order stories of prosecution witnesses. Defense witnesses included folksinger David Ochs, who sang a song; Allen Ginsberg, who responded to inquiries about Yoga and Eastern religion and chanted mantras; Abbie Hoffman, who read the demands of the Yippies; Cora Weiss, who lamented the evils committed in the My Lai massacre; and Judy Collins, who recited words to her popular war protest song, "Where Have All the Young Men Gone?"

The defense also introduced a parade of New Left leaders and radical heroes. As the trial progressed into the fourth and fifth month, the scripts of the defense witnesses became more confrontive. Kunstler encouraged contentious testimony during his examination of witnesses. For example, he asked the witness Paul Krassner to identify spectators, mocking the fact the prosecution witnesses identified defendants. Krassner also interrupted Kunstler who was questioning him, ridiculing the judge's complaint that Kunstler interrupted him (Transcript of Record, pp. 448–50). These examples illustrate that the defense mocked the customary form of introducing logical evidence relevant to the indictments by introducing philosophical and artistic evidence pertaining to their ideology. In this way, the defense developed a burlesque script for the courtroom drama.

Whereas direct examination creates the script, cross-examination seeks to alter the script. As explained in chapter 4, script-altering tactics typically used by counsel during cross-examination include the following: forcing "Yes" and "No" answers, previewing questions with contradictory testimony, pointing out omissions and oversights in the testimony, and using questions that elicit "I don't know" responses (Kuvin, 1965; Heglund, 1978; Mauet, 1980).

The defense's cross-examination of prosecution witnesses did not challenge their scripts in the manner prescribed for legal procedure. Two maneuvers fitting the burlesque mode characterized Kunstler and Weinglass' questions. First, the defense tried to force every prosecution witness to admit the police harassed and beat up demonstrators. Kunstler's interrogation of Chicago policeman Kenneth Carcerano illustrates this strategy:

K: Did you see the police using nightsticks on demonstrators?
C: Yes, I did. . . .
K: Did you see any other type of wound on the demonstrators outside of the head injuries?

229

C: I saw demonstrators limping, holding parts of their bodies.
        [Transcript of Record, p. 117]

Second, although forbidden to do so by court rules, the defendants made verbal comments and nonverbal gestures while their attorneys conducted cross-examination of witnesses by raising their middle finger, pointing, remarking "that's a lie," holding up radical newspapers, and calling the rulings of the judge "pathetic" (Transcript of Record, pp. 125–33). These maneuvers showed the disdain of the defense for the police and judicial system, distracted the jury and judge from the content of the testimony of prosecution witnesses, and thereby focused attention on the ideology of the political left.

The prosecution's cross-examination was particularly difficult because the scripts presented by defense witnesses lacked relevance to the indictment. Both Schultz and Foran tried to elicit omissions and oversights and to preview their questions with contradictory testimony. Since defense witnesses often resisted giving serious answers and belittled the questioner, cross-examination was difficult. The following excerpts from the interrogation of Abbie Hoffman illustrate how a witness responded satirically to the questions he was asked:

S: Did you see some **people urinate** on the Pentagon? . . .
H: I didn't get that close. **Pee on the** walls of the Pentagon? You are getting to be out of **sight**, actually. You think there is a law against it? [Transcript of Record, p. 368]

Later in the examination, Schultz tried to establish Hoffman's whereabouts on August 22nd:

S: Do you recall having coffee with some police officers?
H: With the policemen that were tailing me from the Chicago Red Squad? Yes. They bought me breakfast every morning and drove me around.
S: Do you recall while having coffee with—
H: I don't drink coffee. . . . It is one of the drugs I refrain from using. [Transcript of Record, p. 370]

In ways similar to A. Hoffman, other defense witnesses refused to act as if the questioning process was a serious way of gathering facts pertaining to the indictments. Thus, one of Schultz' obligations in cross-examination, according to legal norms, to impugn the credibility of witnesses, was unnecessary; most of the witnesses volunteered information for the jury that damaged their own credibility.

Thus the cross-examination of witnesses did not produce evidence pertinent to the indictments; rather the subject matter of the testimony transformed potentially serious responses into a travesty. In this case, the interrogation contributed to the satirical reversal of form through the irrelevant, ill-conceived, and trivial subject matter of the questions and responses.

Roles

Roles constitute a third element of the trial drama. Whereas the definition of the situation predicts the content and issues, and scripts create the discourse, roles refer to the way persons participate in the courtroom action. More simply, roles are the slots people occupy in a social order. The testimony of witnesses usually begins with questions that reveal to the jury the witnesses' roles. Jeans (1975), Heglund (1978), and Mauet (1980) recommend that each trial participant perform his or her role so the trial can accomplish its goals. In conventional criminal trials, judges decide legal issues; attorneys advocate the best possible case for their clients; witnesses tell the truth as they see it; and juries decide the case. The roles of all courtroom participants affect all others. The proper behavior for a role is prescribed by professional codes and courtroom rules and norms.

The rules of the court accord a high degree of respect to the judge. Jacob (1978) notes that the architecture of the courtroom is built to "focus on the judge who sits on a pedestal above other participants"; the court operates below the judge and is subject to his or her power; the role of judge is accentuated by special costumes; all members of the court are expected to rise when the judge enters or leaves the court; and participants address the judge as "Your Honor" (pp. 10–11). Additionally, the American Bar Association Code specifies that a judge should be "courteous" to counsel, "studious to avoid controversies" that are apt to obscure "the merits of the case," and "avoid interruptions of counsel" in arguments (Karlen, 1971, pp. 1025–26).

In the Chicago Eight trial, the judge did not gain the respect usually associated with the role of judge. Macdonald (1970) characterized the role of Judge Hoffman as "arrogant without dignity, wisecracking without wit, a combination of Torquemada and

Borscht-circuit tummeler" (p. xi). Kunstler (1970) reflected on Hoffman's behavior in this way: "One of his favorite techniques in seeking to attain this goal was that of discreditation . . . no insult was too gross, no humiliation too excessive, no degradation too cruel" (p. xiii).

Judges should facilitate reasoned legal decisions and decorous personal behavior. As an umpire in the court, the judge should moderate disputes rather than create conflict and controversy among courtroom adversaries. Because Hoffman violated the rules of legal fairness and interjected his personal values and feelings, he contributed to the burlesque mode of the trial.

The following legal decisions called into question Judge Hoffman's competency: he failed to grant a change of venue despite massive trial publicity in Chicago; refused a motion to delay the trial so that Seale's attorney could be present; conducted a cursory *voir dire* that failed to eliminate prejudiced jurors; did not sequester the jury until four days after the start of the trial; arrested pretrial lawyers; removed black spectators from the courtroom; sustained over 90 percent of the objections of the prosecution and only about 2 percent of the defense; and gave unreasonable sentences for contempt to defense attorneys and defendants. Prior to and during the trial, these actions impaired his credibility.

A second role violation occurred when Judge Hoffman engaged in petty and unnecessary interpersonal conversations with defense attorneys and defendants in the form of personal quibbles and linguistic ploys. Throughout the trial, Hoffman quibbled with defense attorneys; that is, he insisted on making irrelevant distinctions not suited for the courtroom. For example, Kunstler reminded Hoffman that it was 12:30, the time for noon recess. Instead of finishing up and recessing the trial, the judge quibbled: "I know I am watching the clock. You leave the time-watching to me, Mr. Kunstler. I will watch the clock for you . . . I will determine the time we recess. I don't need your help" (Transcript of Record, p. 42).

Many times during the trial Hoffman used linguistic ploys, such as intentionally mispronouncing Defense Counsel Weinglass' name, calling defendant Dellinger "Derringer," and inserting word plays into his responses to defense objections. An example of Hoffman's word plays occurred when Weinglass objected to a tape recorded speech of one of the defendants on the grounds that it produced "a chilling effect" on free speech. Hoffman retorted: "Through this trial you have almost frozen the Court up here by

232

repeating the word 'chilling' so often" (Transcript of Record, p. 233). These linguistic ploys elevated petty matters to a level of importance they should not have had in the courtroom. In combination the subject matter of Hoffman's satirical responses helped to transform the standard role of a judge into a role suited for a burlesque character.

In addition to the judge, the advocates also trivialized their roles. Courtroom advocates, by legal tradition, should advance "a legal cause in a legal setting, restrained by rules of procedure, confined to theories of discovery and defense, and gentled by the awareness of conscience" (Jeans, 1975, p. 3). The Code of Professional Responsibility of the American Bar Association elaborates the role of advocates, noting they "should represent their clients zealously, preserve the secrets of their client . . . prevent interference with the administration of justice," refrain from engaging in "undignified or discourteous conduct," refuse to use perjured testimony knowingly, or assist clients in giving fraudulent testimony (Jacob, 1978, p. 55). Moreover, advocates must demonstrate "an attitude of professional respect toward the judge, opposing counsel, witnesses, defendants, jurors, and others in the courtroom" (Karlen, 1971, p. 1024).

In the Chicago Eight trial, both the prosecution and defense attorneys undermined their roles as advocates by engaging in disputes and interjecting extraneous issues, making them appear central to the case when, in fact, they lacked legal relevance. Extraneous disputations refer to verbal controversies or quarrels about nonlegal matters. For example, Kunstler made a motion indicating he believed the government was involved in sending threatening letters to the jury. Foran responded: "The Government objects to the totally frivolous, idiotic proposal that you have hearings to determine inferences of possibilities of circumstantial evidence . . . of a totally ridiculous charge. . . . I wish the show boat tactics would stop" (Transcript of Record, p. 38).

Additionally, the advocates engaged in disputations with Judge Hoffman. This illustration occurred when Kunstler made a motion to suspend the court session to observe "Vietnam Moratorium Day," a motion irrelevant to the case indictments. Hoffman responded by saying the motion was cynical and that the defendants were trying to gain publicity. Kunstler then accused Foran of giving a political speech. Hoffman countered saying Kunstler's speech was also political. Kunstler attacked Foran saying his comments were abrasive to all American citizens. Judge Hoffman responded: "You just include yourself [rather than including everyone in the category of American citizens]. Don't join me with you. Goodness!" (Transcript of Record, p. 88).

Finally, the advocates engaged in quarrels with the defendants. Schultz' examination of Chicago Deputy Police Chief Riordan produced the following dispute involving defendant Dellinger:

S: Did Dellinger say anything when this announcement was made?
R: I did not hear him say anything.
S: Did you see where he went?
R: He left with the head of the group that was carrying the flags.
D: Oh bullshit. That is an absolute lie. . . .
Kunstler: Sometimes the human spirit can stand only so much. I think Mr. Dellinger reached the end of his. . . .
S: No further questions.
D: You're a snake. We have to try to put you in jail for ten years for telling lies about us. [Transcript of Record, pp. 529–30]

These quarrels occurred in the presence of the jury rather than in the judge's chambers so the advocates compromised the standard practice associated with their roles, engaged in undignified and discourteous conduct, and contributed to the ridicule of the serious and respectful atmosphere of the court.

The final set of roles are the ones enacted by witnesses. Jeans (1975) notes that most witnesses "consider themselves to be unbiased reporters of the truth." They do not think of themselves as partial either to the prosecution or the defense, they "are in court to tell what they know" (p. 300). Jurors expect witnesses to be informed and accurate reporters of the truth, and most report the facts to the best of their ability. In most trials, advocates select, coach, and arrange their witnesses so that their testimony offers evidence essential to their respective theories of the case.

In this case, the non-normative behavior of the witnesses contributed significantly to the burlesque mode of the trial. At first glance, the roles of the prosecution witnesses seemed conventional. These witnesses reported incidents as they remembered them. But their roles were altered by the defendants and spectators who yelled phrases such as "right on," "liar," and "shut up."

The witness' testimony failed to relate directly to the legal issues of the case; it did, however, enhance the burlesque quality of the courtroom drama in several ways. First, a number of radical witnesses testified about their ideology and beliefs, a satire of the responses of government witnesses who gave testimony about their values of law and order. Second, since Judge Hoffman did not permit several of the early defense witnesses to explain their testimony, the defense called other witnesses who gave evidence completely irrelevant to the legal issues, satirizing the process of giving evidence. Finally, the wide spectrum of witnesses ranging from the Reverend Jesse Jackson to singer Judy Collins, offered a broad range of support for the antiwar movement. In this way, the defense showed the jury that the antiwar demonstrations at the convention were not the result of a conspiracy to riot on the part of the defendants but resulted from a moral consensus and commitment to change by a large segment of society. Thus, the defense succeeded in making issues external to the legal process central to this trial. The unorthodox roles of the witnesses show how the burlesque mode is able to turn the standard legal procedure upside down; that is, the defense charges the state with a crime rather than the state charging the defendants.

Performance

The situational definitions, scripts, and rules contribute to the content of the drama, and the quality of the performance enhances the persuasive effect. Goffman (1959) describes performance as the means for fostering favorable or unfavorable impressions. Sincere performances incorporate the accredited values of the American court system through conveying respect, tactfulness, and decorum. Cynical performances show impropriety and disrespect, evince lack of concern for other participants, and discredit the norms of the court.

Courtroom performance consists of nonverbal stimuli—manner and appearance. Manner is the attitude and tone of interaction, such as acting apologetic, anxious, or haughty. In addition to manner, theories of nonverbal communication emphasize the importance of performers' appearance—dress, posture, eye contact, gesture—for making favorable impressions on audiences (Knapp, 1972). Manner works interdependently with appearance to convey favorable impressions to the jury. Colley (1981) reports that although jurors forget much of the content of the trial discourse, they recall general impressions and attitudes that then enter into their decisions. Moreover, Kuvin (1965) stresses that subtle changes in appearance and manner are adopted by skilled advocates to create doubt or belief in the testimony they elicit from witnesses.

Goffman (1959) distinguishes performances according to the teams of actors staging the drama. Performance teams are "any sort of individuals who cooperate in staging an event" (p. 79). In the courtroom, the prosecution and defense teams act as protagonists and antagonists. The attorneys and witnesses of the prosecution act as one team, and the attorneys and witnesses of the defense act as another team. Each of these sets of courtroom performers work together as teammates striving to foster a common impression, that is, a belief in and commitment to their theory of the case. To do this, the teammates act according to similar definitions, respond with compatible scripts, and adopt collaborative appearances and manner.

Audience teams differ from performance teams since they react rather than create the drama. Audience teams in the courtroom consist of judge, jurors, spectators, and the press. Conventional audience teams evaluate the facticity, credibility, and relevance of scripts, roles, and impressions of the performance team. The judge is expected to set standards for the behavior of the other members of the audience team.

In the Chicago conspiracy case, the prosecution team appeared with short hair and formal attire, and some dressed in their law enforcement uniforms. For the most part, the witnesses acted in a respectful manner, observing the rules of the court. Although the prosecutors acted with civility and respect during much of the questioning of witnesses, they occasionally adopted an attitude of arrogance and vilification in reaction to the defendants and their attorneys.

An example of their manner of vilification surfaced when the defendants continued laughing during Schultz' examination of witness Irwin Bock. Schultz requested: "I would ask the Court again if he would direct the marshal to direct the defendants and their lawyers to stop laughing out loud as they just did. Mr. Kunstler was probably more guilty of it than any of the defendants." Judge Hoffman acted on the request by ordering the marshal to quiet the defense team and stated emphatically: "This is a trial in the United States District Court. It is not vaudeville theater." Kunstler defended the defense's disrespectful manner saying: "Your honor, we are human beings too. You can't make automatons out of us, or robots; we are human beings and we laugh. . . . I don't really see how that really becomes a court matter." Schultz recognized the burlesque mode of the defense when he responded: "Mr. Kunstler is laughing so he can influence the jury with the impression that this is absurd" (Transcript of Record, pp. 208–9).

Given the burlesque mode of this trial drama, the prosecutors faced a double bind concerning their performances. If they ignored the behavior of the defense team, they might give the impression of not caring or not respecting courtroom norms. On the other hand, by challenging the defense team's behavior, they presented themselves in a disparaging and belittling attitude that spoiled the impression of respect and formality toward the court. Goffman (1959) explains that when the behaviors of one part of the performance team lack consistency with other members of the team, the entire group risks having their performance misinterpreted.

The defense team intentionally conveyed ridicule and satire, and this impression was consistent among all members of the team. As a result, the defense team succeeded in conveying a unified, negative impression of the court and its participants. They turned the court into burlesque by converting the respectful into a disrespectful setting, by elevating the inconsequential and vulgar to places of importance, and by jointly adapting an irreverent and discourteous manner and appearance.

Appearance was important to the performance of the defense team. They accentuated the trappings associated with radicals and dissenters, such as drugs, peace symbols, beads, black arm bands, long hair, and unshaved faces. Additionally, they brought guitars, poems, and pacifist literature with them to the courtroom as artifactual evidence of their connection to antiwar and counterculture groups. Body postures also contributed to the mockery of the court. The defendants sat on the floor, the witnesses slouched in their chairs, or they sauntered to the witness stand. Members of the defense team used exaggerated and sometimes obscene gestures to indicate their disgust with the prosecution team. Such gestures as the middle finger, plugging their ears with their fingers, and brushing one finger across another to indicate shame disparaged the prosecution team and thereby contributed to the impression of the burlesque drama of the courtroom.

The defense conveyed an impression of contempt for the court in various ways. They used diminutive first names rather than formal titles and last names, slang and poor grammar, obscenities, name calling, acronyms, and vulgar words rather than euphemisms. Moreover, their manner expressed contempt through interruptions of the court's procedures, insertions of malicious and derogatory comments, ignoring sustained objections and giving different answers, and failing to answer questions in a serious way.

In the contempt proceedings, Judge Hoffman explained the extent of the ridicule conveyed by the defense: "No record can adequately portray the venom, the sarcasm and tone of voice by a speaker. No record . . . can adequately reflect the applause, the guffaws, and other subtle tactics employed by these contemnors in an attempt to break up the trial" (Clark, 1970, p. 43). Appearance and manner were the grounds for some of the contempt of court charges as well as a major source of the burlesque behavior in the trial.

These excerpts from Weinglass' direct examination of Abbie Hoffman demonstrate how the witness created a burlesque performance for the spectators of the trial:

> H: My name is Abbie. I am an orphan of America. . . .
> W: Abbie, what is your last name? . . .
> H: My slave name is Hoffman. My real name is Shaboysnak-off. . . .
> W: Where do you reside?
> H: I live in Woodstock nation. . . .
> W: Between the date of your birth November 30, 1936 and May 1, 1960, what if anything occurred in your life?
> H: Nothing. I believe it is called American education. [Transcript of Record, p. 344]

Adopting an obvious theatrical appearance and manner, Abbie Hoffman's three days of testimony was the most well-executed performance for the defense team. He dressed in a radical garb and satirized the courtroom procedure in many different ways.

Kunstler and Weinglass contributed to the performance by making ridiculous motions in a manner suggesting they were completely serious, such as moving to have a Viet Cong flag placed beside the American flag in the courtroom. Moreover, the attorneys directed with skill the burlesque performances of other members of the defense team, producing a consistent and thorough portrait of radical beliefs by consistently adopting the speech, appearance, and manner of the New Left.

The audience team also affected the burlesque quality of the drama. Judge Hoffman, although relegated by rules of procedure to membership on the audience team, acted as though he were a member of the performance team by trying to upstage the litigants and their witnesses rather than perform his designated role as stage manager.

To integrate himself into a performer-team role, Judge Hoffman portrayed himself as an omniscient and omnipotent director of the court. He created his character by inserting details about his part into the rulings he made about objections and motions of advocates, and he also described himself as powerful, experienced, efficient, and fair. He presented the omnipotent quality of his role in the following response to a defense motion to have the pretrial lawyers dismissed from the case. He asserted: "I will determine the disposition of this case. . . . They are now held in contempt. . . . I will impose a sentence. I am not going to let these men play horse with the court as some of these men have done with me" (Transcript of Record, p. 25). At another time, Hoffman informed the court about his superlative record "with Negroes," a record resulting in a "discrimination free" court. Using the trappings of his judicial office— garb, gavel, and seat of importance in the court, he moved from audience to performer team. As performer he mimicked the insults, name calling, and emotional displays typical of the defense performers. Introducing this kind of judicial performance into the respectful form of the court contributed to the burlesque quality of the case.

Courtroom spectators also aspired to roles as performers although court rules restricted the participation of the audience team. Because the press was prohibited by the court from observing the trial in the courtroom, the spectators consisted of sympathetic antiwar dissenters, the police, city officials, and members of the defendants' families. Despite the court rules, spectators clapped, laughed, commented on testimony, and jeered public officials. The court attempted to control the crowd by having as many as fourteen court marshals to maintain the decorum of the proceeding, but their presence seemed to encourage rather than quiet the crowds who insisted on being performers. This unorthodox spectator behavior also mocked the rules and enhanced the burlesque action of the trial.

The only members acting in accordance with their prescribed roles as the audience team were the jurors. Despite the courtroom confusion, the length of the trial, and the unconventional scripts, the jurors managed to uphold their audience roles as adjudicators abiding by the rules of the court.

Although excluded from the courtroom, members of the press made known to the public their reactions through newspapers, magazines, and television broadcasts. Dee (1985) concludes that the conservative press lauded the performance of the prosecution and Judge Hoffman, whereas the liberal press applauded the satirical performances of the radicals and condemned the actions of Judge Hoffman.

Critics can appraise the impressions made by the courtroom performers in two ways—by context and audience. The context of the trial was both legal and political. According to legal ideals, the trial was both a parody and a travesty, satirizing the ideals of the litigation process. According to political standards of the New Left, the trial succeeded in demonstrating to the public and the judge the truth of defendant Dellinger's words, "Justice is more important than decorum" (Kalven, 1970, p. xiii). For the most part, radical audiences enjoyed the burlesque drama because it furthered their political cause, but the government abhorred the satirical content, conceiving it as an attack on the American system of justice.

Staging

A final element of the dramatistic analysis identifies the areas in which trial performances are staged. Front stages are regions where the performances intended for the audience teams are staged (Goffman, 1959, p. 107). Participants in the court perform front stage behavior in and outside of the courtroom through their statements in the official trial record and their public responses for the media. Back stages are regions where trial participants can be themselves, where the impression designed for the consumption of the audience team is "knowingly contradicted" (Goffman, 1959, p. 112).

Goffman (1959) warns that participants may spoil the favorable impressions they have earned by acting with sincerity when they present back stage behavior in the front region. In a typical trial, audience teams glimpse back stage behavior when participants, outside of the courtroom, say and do things contrary to the scripts, roles, and performances presented during the trial.

In the Chicago Eight case, the performers repeatedly and willfully transposed back stage behavior on to the front region so they could accomplish their goal of subverting the norms and rules of the trial process. The satirical responses of the defense team so degraded and belittled other participants that they were unable to perform according to the appropriate region of the courtroom. This burlesque drama turned expectations upside down, converting one set of norms into another by ridiculing conventions associated with courtroom manners and overtly violating the rules of procedure. Adopting this dramatic mode requires that back stage behaviors enter into the front region so they can be observed by the audience teams.

Many of the back stage behaviors of the defense became grounds for the contempt charges after the trial such as Dellinger's calling the court "fascist"; Davis' accusation that the marshals were "torturing" him; Hayden's refusal to sit at the defendants' table; Rubin's charging the judge with interrupting his attorney; Weiner's calling the judge an "executioner"; and Froines' calling attorney Schultz a "tattletale" (Clark, 1970). These back stage behaviors are among the 175 contempt citations issued against the defendants and their attorneys, and most all of the citations identified instances where the defense team placed back stage behavior on the front region of the courtroom.

A second instance of publicly designed back stage behavior resulted from the out-of-court appearances during the trial of Kunstler, Weinglass, and the defendants. They attended news conferences, gave speeches, and offered their opinions to the press about the trial. These exposés of the drama inside of the courtroom functioned as a theatrical interlude, that is, intervening episodes performed between the acts of the main drama for the audience team. This interlude permitted the media a firsthand accounting of the trial and served as an important outlet for the defense to re-present their case to the media. Judge Hoffman joined in the interlude by giving an interview to *Time*. In all cases, the participants transferred behavior from the back to the front region.

A striking example of this type of back stage behavior occurred during the trial when Jerry Rubin interrupted the examination of a witness to protest that a marshal was removing his wife from the courtroom:

R (Rubin):   Bill (Kunstler), they are taking out my wife . . .

K (Kunstler):   Your Honor, must we always have this force and power of government? . . .

R: They are dragging my wife out—will you please—

K: They like to strike women, your Honor, we've seen that constantly here. [Clark, 1970, p. 191]

Back stage performances, such as this one, when heard and seen by the jury, gave the impression that the court was not a respectful arena. In the same way, Judge Hoffman's constant removal of the

241

jury to prohibit them from observing back stage performances conveyed a negative impression, what Kalven (1970) calls "a sense of crisis after crisis" (p. xxiii).

Third, the back stage behavior entered on to the front region when spectators functioned as a "studio audience" giving verbal feedback to the trial performers. A number of episodes within the courtroom drama exemplified the intrusion of spectators into the front stage process. For example, defendant Dellinger interrupted the testimony of defense witness Riordan and called Judge Hoffman "a liar" for revoking the defendant's bail. Dellinger went on to present a short speech claiming the defendants were fighting for "all the rest of the people in this country who are oppressed." Spectators added their comments: "Damn right, assert yourselves," "Right on," and "I agree" (Clark, 1970, p. 66).

Judge Hoffman's remarks offer a fourth example of how back stage behaviors enter into the front region. During the trial, on the way to the courtroom, observers overheard the judge say: "Now we are going to hear this wild man Weinglass." The defense entered this statement into the record as one of the grounds for a mistrial. Another time, Hoffman confronted Kunstler about the frequent laughter from the defendants saying: "I will not sit here and you must know it by now, certainly—and have defendants laugh at my rulings, sir. And I will not hear you on that" (Clark, 1970, p. 184). Hoffman also frequently directed marshals to remove spectators, quiet and restrain witnesses, and seize objects from the defendants and spectators. These punitive measures caused frequent intrusions into the litigation process. However, the most extreme measure of the judge was to bind, gag, and tie the defendant Bobby Seale to a chair in the courtroom. By these actions, Judge Hoffman showed that he was placing the actions reserved for the back stage onto the front region of the courtroom.

On many occasions, the advocates showed out-of-character behavior not meant for the audience team. Jeans (1975) notes that trial lawyers should be combative about legal issues while they maintain a genuine commitment to the welfare of their clients. In this conspiracy trial, the confrontations between the attorneys and the judge transformed courtroom combativeness into unprofessional back stage behavior. For example, in several instances, Kunstler rose when Weinglass was examining witnesses. Hoffman demanded that Kunstler remain seated and Kunstler refused. A typical dispute followed:

H: Sit down.

K: I am not going to sit down unless I am directed.

H: I direct you to sit down.

K: Am I to be thrown in the chair by the marshal if I don't sit down? [Clark, 1970, p. 187]

Several disputes occurred directly between the attorneys over ethical matters. Kunstler charged that Schultz and Foran made derogatory personal references by saying the defense resembled television actors and engaged in theatrics (Transcript of Record, p. 54). These back stage disputes came to the attention of jurors in the form of motions for a mistrial. Regardless of who initiated the action, much of this type of behavior should have been presented out of view of the jury. The strategic placement of this behavior in front of the jury helped emphasize the burlesque quality of the trial.

An analysis of the definition of the situation, scripts, roles, performance, and staging demonstrates that the communication of trials resembles drama. The Chicago Eight case created unconventional drama, rarely observed in a court. Nonetheless the trial shows that the communication of the case closely parallels the definitions and assumptions of burlesque and that an understanding of this mode of drama makes sense out of the trial interaction as a whole.

Drama, Communication, and The Courts

After the case concluded, *Newsweek* (2 March 1970) appraised the Chicago Eight trial, referring to it as a case that tested the judicial process and proved the value of the American jury system. The magazine claimed that the trial went astray because the "American judicial process is a form of unscripted drama that works on the tacit agreement of everyone concerned to play by the rules and trust the outcome to be just" (p. 25). In this case, the external drama overshadowed the internal crime story. The participants artistically presented their case to audiences and tried to achieve a mimetic effect through a burlesque approach to the trial.

In this mimetic drama, the participants did not follow the tacit rules for defining the situation, creating scripts, taking roles, performing, and staging the case. Other trial participants allowed (and sometimes encouraged) the defense to change the orthodox legal form of drama into burlesque words and actions. The trial was historically and legally significant because the dramatic portrayals of the trial participants took an unorthodox form that satirized the norms of the litigation process.

This case illustrated two types of burlesque drama—parody and travesty. Parody appeared only a few times in the trial. For example, the preoccupation of Judge Hoffman with the defense's use of diminutive names, such as Billy, Abbie, and Rennie, raised that trivial issue to a level of extreme importance. Kunstler also used parody when he made several motions about the trivial issue of securing bathroom privileges for the defendants. But the predominant type of burlesque in the trial was travesty. The use of this mode of drama was pervasive, repetitive, and directed to a singular purpose. Travesty occurred in the definition of the trial situation, the development of the scripts, the enactment of roles, the performances, and the staging of the trial. This mode subverted the traditional decorous and respectful form of the court by treating almost all matters of importance with vulgarity.

Analyzing trials as drama has several advantages for persons interested in the role of communication in criminal trials. First, this approach accounts for the interaction and relationships among attorneys, judge, jurors, spectators, and witnesses; it demonstrates that the verbal and nonverbal action of one participant affects and is affected by all others. Second, this approach identifies the patterns of verbal communication created by the scripts of witnesses showing that these messages are jointly created by prosecution and defense attorneys as the trial develops. Third, investigating trials as drama emphasizes the nonverbal qualities of appearance and manner that impress witnesses and thereby affect the way jurors interpret the evidence presented in the trial. In sum, the dramatistic perspective permits others to observe the internal working of the trial with all the mistakes, bad performances, errors in staging, mistaken roles, and negative impressions created during the litigation process.

Effective trial performers seem to recognize that trials are drama and that good performances produce mimetic persuasion for the spectators. At one point during the trial, defendant Jerry Rubin quipped: "I like being here. It is interesting. . . . It is good theater, your honor" (Macdonald, 1970, p. xxiii). At another place in the record, Prosecutor Foran lamented: "I feel like one of the characters in Alice and Wonderland [sic] that just went through the looking glass. I have never, your honor, in twenty years of practice, heard attorneys like Mr. Kunstler and Mr. Weinglass refuse to direct their clients with decency and courtesy in the courtroom" (Transcript of

Record, p. 161). At still another point, Judge Hoffman warned the defendants: "This is not guerrilla theater" (Transcript of Record, p. 207). Additionally, many of the witnesses presented mini-performances, establishing their credentials, elaborating their roles, and promoting their point of view. Clearly, the trial participants knew that the trial resembled theater and that they were expected to follow the script as directed by the attorneys and edited by the judge.

The success or failure of a legal drama is typically evaluated by the binding legal decisions of the adjudicators. The trial decision was based on seven defendants because Seale was removed from the court halfway through the case and given a separate trial. On February 18, 1970, the jury returned a verdict of guilty of crossing state lines with intent to riot for Dellinger, Davis, Hayden, Hoffman, and Rubin; acquitted Froines and Weiner on all counts; and exonerated all the defendants on charges of conspiracy. On the same day the jury returned the verdict, Judge Hoffman sentenced the defendants and their attorneys for 175 charges of contempt. Both decisions were appealed and decided by the Seventh Circuit Court of Appeals. This court reversed the conviction on intent to riot and upheld the contempt charges against Dellinger, Hoffman, Rubin, and Kunstler. The metaphor of trial as drama gives a more complete evaluation of what occurred in the case than the legal decision does. The burlesque drama worked as a positive strategy for the defense in that it demonstrated through satire that the charge of conspiracy was not legitimate, used the trial as a platform for presenting the ideological beliefs of the political left, and showed the fallibility of the courtroom procedures when they are subjected to pervasive satirical attacks by the participants in the court.

Even though the burlesque drama partially worked, it also harmed the credibility of the New Left as a responsible and orthodox movement of dissent because the public viewed the performances as too bizarre and offensive. By failing to play their designated roles, produce legitimate legal scripts, give believable performances, and stage their behavior in an appropriate region, the judge and advocates tainted their credibility as legitimate performers on the stage of the judicial system (Karlen, 1971).

In an artistic sense, the defense achieved its purpose by satirizing the legal proceeding; burlesque succeeds when it persuades audiences of a higher truth. In this case, the defense demonstrated that justice was more important than decorum, a conclusion largely accepted by the appellate court that ruled on the case. This satirical mode of theater gains a dramatic reversal when it changes the traditional way of thinking by introducing subject matter that subverts the rules and norms of the court.

By analyzing the eccentric burlesque drama of the Chicago Eight case, the latent and traditional form of all trials is illuminated. The drama of most trials proceeds according to the standards of the court—emphasizing formality, orderliness, respectfulness, and reasonableness. The external drama should feature traditional roles and performances: the attorneys present the best case possible for their clients; the judge acts as umpire, making sure the performers do not transgress the rules of the court; the spectators act as passive observers; the witnesses report their recollections as they remember them; the defendants allow their advocates to speak on their behalf; impartial jurors decide the verdict according to the merits of the case; and all participants adopt a manner and appearance befitting a situation of dignity.

For the most part, the cases analyzed in this volume have followed the norms of the court. A few transgressions occurred. For example, in the Haymarket case, the jurors failed to keep confidentiality and showed their partiality in the deliberation process. In the Sacco-Vanzetti case, Judge Thayer abridged his role by telling the press during the trial about his opinions of the case. Defense Attorney Reilly did not represent Hauptmann as well as he could have, and the Blochs did not prepare an adequate case for the Rosenbergs. Hinckley tried to gain publicity for himself during his incarceration, a role traditionally considered unfit for a defendant. In each of these trials, one or more participants abridged one or more of the norms of the court, but did not, in the opinion of the appellate courts, violate significantly the legal standards so that the defendants failed to receive due process. The greatest aberrations of the trial drama occurred in the Sheppard case where the press assumed the role of prosecutor and jury and in the Chicago Eight case where all participants ridiculed the norms of the courtroom decorum and order. The appellate courts, however, recognized the major transgressions and overturned the verdicts in these trials.

Critics more clearly understand the importance of the rules associated with courtroom drama when they observe the negative consequences of inappropriate definitions, scripts, roles, performances, and staging. When participants ignore the dramaturgical expectations of the external drama, they call attention to their own performance and divert jurors' attention away from the facts of the crime story.

A Trial Participant's Reaction

William M. Kunstler

After reading the chapter, Mr. Kunstler requested this excerpt be reprinted from his book, Trials and Tribulations, *(New York, Grove Press, 1985), pp. 27–31.*

The Trial of the Chicago Eight, as it has come to be known, involved federal charges accusing eight carefully selected political dissidents—David Dellinger, the "aging pacifist"; Abbie Hoffman and Jerry Rubin, "two Yippie chieftains"; John Froines, "a teacher"; Lee Weiner, "a student"; Bobby Seale, "the Panther chair"; and Tom Hayden and Rennie Davis, "the SDS (Students for a Democratic Society) . . . likely pair"—of conspiring to disrupt the 1968 Democratic National Convention. After Seale was severed from the case in midtrial because of his insistence that he be represented by counsel of choice, the jury acquitted his codefendants of conspiracy, and found only five of them—Davis, Hayden, Rubin, Hoffman and Dellinger—guilty of relatively minor charges.

Judge Julius Jennings Hoffman, a tiny martinet with a voice very reminiscent of that of Jim Backus in the Mr. Magoo film cartoon series, was specially selected to preside at the trial, which began on September 23, 1969, and went on until late February of the following year. From opening day until the day of the verdicts, he did everything in his power, including pointed insults, adverse rulings,

William M. Kunstler practices law in New York City. A graduate of Yale University (B.A.) and Columbia University Law School (LL.B.), Mr. Kunstler has had a most distinguished legal career. He has been trial counsel of such notorious cases as *U.S. v. Dellinger* (1969–70 Chicago Eight conspiracy case), *Powell v. McCormack* (1966 reinstatement to Congress case), *Carmichael v. Allen* (1967 invalidation of Georgia insurrection statute case), *U.S. v. Sinclair* (1971 invalidation of government's claim of unrestricted wiretapping powers case), *U.S. v. Berrigan* (1968 defense of Catholic antiwar activists accused of destroying draft records at Catonsville, Md.), to name a few. Mr. Kunstler is also the author of several books and numerous articles that have appeared in such legal and lay publications as *Columbia Law Review, Yale Law Journal, Nation, Atlantic Monthly, New York Times, National Law Journal, Chicago Tribune, Philadelphia Inquirer, Life, Rolling Stone, Saturday Review, Juris Doctor, University Review,* and many others.

and constant denigration of the defense attorneys, to see to it that the defendants were soundly convicted. In addition, he ordered that Bobby Seale, the only black defendant, be bound and gagged when the latter persisted in vociferously demanding to be permitted to be represented by Charles R. Garry, his longtime attorney, who was recovering from a gall bladder operation.

As soon as the jury had retired to consider its verdicts, Hoffman found all of the defendants and their two attorneys guilty of contempt of court and sentenced them to varying terms of imprisonment. As one of those lawyers, I received the longest sentence—four years and thirteen days—but an appellate court eventually reversed all of the convictions, primarily because of the egregious conduct of the judge and the two federal prosecutors. The highly publicized case did much to mobilize student opposition to U.S. military involvement in Southeast Asia and sparked antiwar demonstrations on many university and college campuses.

It was not until long after the trial that it was revealed, through the Freedom of Information Act, that federal agents had spent hours with the judge before the trial began, predisposing him against the defendants, and inciting him to take strong action against them at the earliest possible moment. When I discovered that this Iago-like tactic had taken place, my attitude toward the judge changed radically, and I ultimately came to regard him as much a victim of governmental misconduct as my clients had been. Although he and I shared the same birthday—July 7—we were more than a generation apart, and I must confess that I felt a certain sadness to learn of his death, just weeks before he would have reached his ninety-first year.

The Chicago Eight

Director Hoover thought the time was due
　　To put the New Left on the thorny path,
So he invoked the aid of Nixon's crew
　　In directing the Presidential wrath.
From SDS he picked a likely pair,
　　And then two Yippie chieftains swelled the list
Filled by a teacher and the Panther chair.
　　A student and an aging pacifist.
The trial went on for almost half a year,
　　While witness after witness took the stand
To try to justify J. Edgar's fear
　　That those accused were perils to the land.

But, at the end, the jury found them free
    of any traces of conspiracy.

Judge Julius J. Hoffman No. 1

A tiny man who could have won the part,
    In some revised production of Snow White.
Of Grumpy, who is angry from the start
    At everyone who comes within his sight,
His voice as adenoidal as Magoo,
    He read the charges in such scathing tones
That all who heard him somehow deeply knew
    The eight defendants merited the stones.
Throughout the trial, he adhered to his plan
    To miss no chance to let the thought sink in
That, long before the evidence began
    They all were guilty of a mortal sin
Just like the Queen in Carroll's *Wonderland*,
    Decapitation was his first command.

Judge Julius J. Hoffman No. 2

At last the old curmudgeon closed his eyes
    And drifted off into the scheme of things,
A victim of what he considered lies
    Set loose by those for whom the truth had wings.
For months he felt that he had held the line
    Against the onslaught of the rebel eight
Who, he had been informed by word or sign,
    Had worked together to destroy the state.
We saw in him the demon's ruddy leer,
    The architect of evil from the bench,
We did not know an artful puppeteer
    Had given every string a hidden wrench.
Perhaps we should have recognized the fact
    That old men seldom see their world intact.

Bobby Seale

Throughout the paneled courtroom's mammoth
        size,
    The only black defendant's strident voice
Insisted that the system recognize
    His right to have the lawyer of his choice.

249

The judge was adamant and cried, "Sit down!"
Whenever he repeated his request,
And let the audience see, by word or frown,
The court alone, of all the world, knew
best.
At last the order from the bench was clear—
"Take Mr. Seale inside and with him deal
According to the law, then bring him here
So that this criminal trial does not congeal."
The marshals rushed him back, high in the air,
His mouth taped shut, his arms chained to
his chair.

These two founders [Jerry Rubin and Abbie Hoffman] of the Youth International Party (the Yippies) were experts in creating media events that were invaluable in giving the counter-culture of the sixties worldwide publicity. Among other things they dropped dollar bills from the visitors gallery of the New York Stock Exchange, led many thousands of antiwar demonstrations to the Pentagon for an attempted "levitation" of that mammoth building, orchestrated a "be-in" in New York's Central Park, which was attended by countless waves of young people, and ran a pig for President. Prolific writers and energetic protestors against war, racism, and contemporary mores, they personified the aspirations and accomplishments of the Woodstock generation. I represented them during the Chicago Conspiracy Trial, and at one time or another on a number of lesser charges, as well as before the late unlamented House Un-American Activities Committee (HUAC), where Jerry once appeared dressed in the uniform of a private in George Washington's revolutionary army, and Abbie in a flag shirt.

Today they have gone their separate ways. Jerry has cut his hair and opted for conservative three-piece suits and a business career. The first public sign of his metamorphosis from political activist to mainstream advocate was his employment some years ago by a stock brokerage firm. Now he operates a sort of hiring hall at New York's fabled Studio 54 for young executives on the make. Looking at his clean-cut appearance, and listening to his pitch, it is hard to believe that he was once the idol of millions of young people protesting the excesses of the system.

On the other hand, Abbie has remained steadfastly on the firing line. While he was underground because of cocaine charges pending against him, he became one of the leading figures in the fight to prevent industrial pollution of the St. Lawrence River. Since his reemergence, he has interested himself in many of the protests of the day, including those against the CIA's covert war in Nicaragua, and has even visited that beleaguered country. Last June I was arrested with him when we, along with hundred of others, blockaded the CIA office in Manhattan, as a demonstration against its Latin American tactics.

In one sense, however, they are still together. Recently they have been touring the country, billed as representatives of the Yippies (Abbie) and Yuppies (Jerry). In their debates, often before large audiences, Jerry emphasizes standard establishment values while Abbie preaches the importance of opposition to what he believes to be the evils of contemporary America. Both men used to proclaim that they could trust no one over thirty; now Abbie, conscious of the high percentage of young people who voted for Ronald Reagan in the past election, has changed that slogan to read, "I don't trust anyone under thirty."

It would be very easy to criticize Jerry for what many regard as nothing short of outright treachery and opportunism, but I cannot bring myself to do so. While I am disappointed by the change in his life style, I am also conscious of the enormous contributions he made to the ending of the Vietnamese conflict. Unfortunately, the system's apologists point to the Jerry Rubins of our time as living proof that the era of the sixties was nothing more than a temporary aberration in our national life and that the return of some of its best-known proponents to the fold amply demonstrates the bedrock value of establishment policies and practices. Because of this unfortunate interpretation, Jerry's defection has been, and will continue to be, a misleading symbol of national retrenchment.

References

Index

References

Abbey, M. R., & O'Barr, W. M. 1981. Law and language. *Trial Diplomacy Journal, 4* , 26–29.

Alix, E. K. 1978. *Ransom kidnapping in America: 1877–1974.* Carbondale: Southern Illinois Univ. Press.

Alleged Reagan assailant transferred to Quantico marine base. 19 Aug. 1981. *Washington Post,* p. B1.

Arbetman, L., & Roe, R. L. (Eds.). 1985. Chicago Eight. In *Great trials in American history,* pp. 145–61. St. Paul, MN: West Publishing Co.

Aristotle. 1960. *Rhetoric.* Lane Cooper (Ed. & Trans.). New York: Appleton-Century-Crofts.

Asch, S. E. 1946. Forming impressions of personality. *Journal of Abnormal and Social Psychology, 41,* 285–90.

Assassination attempt. 4 Apr. 1981. *Washington Post,* p. A12.

Avrick, P. 1984. *The Haymarket tragedy.* Princeton, NJ: Princeton Univ. Press.

Bailey, F. L., & Rothblatt, H. B. 1971. *Successful techniques for criminal lawyers.* Rochester, NY: Lawyers Co-Operative Publishing Co.

Barkan, S. E. 1985. *Protesters on trial.* New Brunswick, NJ: Rutgers Univ. Press.

Belknap, M. R. 1977. *Cold war and political justice.* Westport, CT: Greenwood Press.

Bennett, W. L. 1978. Storytelling in criminal trials: A model of social judgment. *Quarterly Journal of Speech, 64,* 1–22.

———. 1979. Rhetorical transformations of evidence in criminal trials: Creating grounds for legal judgment. *Quarterly Journal of Speech, 65,* 311–23.

———. 1983. *News: The politics of illusion.* New York: Longmans.

Bennett, W. L., & Feldman, M. S. 1981. *Reconstructing reality in the courtroom.* New Brunswick, NJ: Rutgers Univ. Press.

Brief for Petitioner, *Sheppard v. Maxwell,* 384 U.S. 333 (1966).

Brief for Respondent, *Sheppard v. Maxwell,* 384 U.S. 333 (1966).

Brockriede, W., & Ehninger, D. 1960. Toulmin on argument: An interpretation and application. *Quarterly Journal of Speech, 46,* 44.

Broder, D. 31 Mar. 1981. Reagan wounded by assailant's bullet. *Washington Post,* p. A1.

Brosnahan, J. J. 1979. Basic principles of advocacy: One trial lawyer's view. *American Journal of Trial Advocacy, 3,* 250.

Burke, K. 1941; rpt., 1973. *The philosophy of literary form.* Berkeley: Univ. of California Press.

———. 1950. *A rhetoric of motives.* New York: Prentice-Hall.

255

———. 1961. *The rhetoric of religion*. Boston: Beacon Press.

———. 1964. From poetic categories. In S. E. Hyman (Ed.). *Terms for order*, pp. 92–94. Bloomington: Indiana Univ. Press.

———. 1966. *Language as symbolic action*. Berkeley: Univ. of California Press.

———. 1968. *Dramatism*. In D. Sills (Ed.). *International encyclopedia of social sciences*, pp. 445–50. New York: Macmillan.

Busch, F. 1963. *Law and tactics in jury trials*. Indianapolis, IN: Bobbs-Merrill.

Campbell, K. K., & Jamieson, K. H. 1976. *Form and genre: Shaping rhetorical action*. Annandale, VA: Speech Communication Association of America.

Cannon, L. 31 Mar. 1981. The shooting. *Washington Post*, p. A1.

———. 1 Apr. 1981. Reagan staff plan for interim rule. *Washington Post*, p. A1.

———. 5 Apr. 1981. The day of the jackal in Washington. *Washington Post*, pp. A1, A12.

Caplan, L. 1984. *The insanity defense and the trial of John W. Hinckley, Jr*. Boston: David R. Godine.

Cardozo, B. 1921. *The nature of the judicial process*. New Haven, CT: Yale Univ. Press.

Carrington, P., Meador, D., & Rosenberg, M. 1976. *Justice on appeal*. St Paul, MN: West Publishing Co.

Chaffee, Z. 1969. *Free speech in the United States*. New York: Antheneum Publishers.

Chatman, S. 1978. *Story and discourse*. Ithaca, NY: Cornell Univ. Press.

Chicago trial: A loss for all. 23 Feb. 1970. *Time*, pp. 38–39.

Clark, R. (Ed.). 1970. *Contempt: Transcripts of contempt citations, sentences, and responses*, pp. v–viii. Chicago: Swallow Press.

Clavir, J., & Spitzer, J. (Eds.). 1970. *The conspiracy trial*. New York: Bobbs-Merrill.

Cohen, R. 2 Apr. 1981. The new assassins achieve instant fame without political motives or sense. *Washington Post*, p. B1.

Colley, M. F. 1981. Friendly persuasion, comprehension, and acceptance in court. *Trial, 17 (1)*, 43.

Collins, D. 30 Sept. 1981. Jodie Foster confirms that she and Hinckley talked by phone. *Washington Post*, p. A7.

Condon, J. F. 1936. *Jafsie tells all*. New York: Jonathan Lee.

Cooke, J., & Robinson, E. 3 Apr. 1981. Yale students close ranks behind Foster. *Washington Post*, p. A2.

Cooper, L. (Ed. & Trans.). 1960. Aristotle, *Rhetoric*. New York: Appleton-Century-Crofts.

Costopoulos, W. C. 1972. Persuasion in the courtroom. *Duquesne Law Review, 10*, 384.

Crable, R. 1976. Models of argumentation and judicial judgment. *Journal of the American Forensic Association, 12,* 113.

Craig v. Harney, 331 U.S. 368 (1974).

Crane, J. R. 1982. Graphic testimony and presentations. *Trial Diplomacy Journal, 5,* 18.

David, H. 1936. *The history of the Haymarket affair.* New York: Russell & Russell.

Davis, K. S. 1959. *The hero: Charles A. Lindbergh and the American dream.* Garden City, NY: Doubleday & Co.

Dee, J. Nov. 1985. Selective perception in a non-vacuum: Thoughts on the Chicago Seven trial. Symposium on popularized trials, presented at the Speech Communication Association. Denver, CO.

Defense attorneys seek transfer of Hinckley to St. Elizabeth's. 25 Nov. 1981. *Washington Post,* p. A2.

Delays in bringing case to trial. 15 Mar. 1982. *Washington Post,* p. A14.

Denniston, L. W. 1980. *The reporter and the law.* New York: Hastings House.

Denton, R. E. 1982. *The symbolic dimensions of the American presidency.* Prospect Heights, IL: Waveland Press.

Devastator bullets. 4 Apr. 1981. *Washington Post,* p. A12.

Dicks, V. 1981. Courtroom rhetorical strategies: Forensic and deliberative perspectives. *Quarterly Journal of Speech, 67,* 178.

Dipboye, R. L. 1977. The effectiveness of one-sided and two-sided appeals as a function of familiarization and context. *The Journal of Social Psychology, 120,* 125.

Douglas, W. O. 1969. The Sacco-Vanzetti case: Forty years later. *Trial Record: The Sacco-Vanzetti case,* vol. 1, pp. xv–xlix. New York: Paul A. Appel.

Dreschel, R. E. 1983. *Newsmaking in the trial courts.* New York: Longmans.

Duncan, H. D. 1968. *Communication and social order.* London: Oxford Univ. Press.

Dunston, R. 1980. Context for coercion: Analyzing properties of courtroom questions. *British Journal of Law and Social Psychology, 7,* 61–77.

Early, P. 31 Mar. 1981. The gun: A saturday night special from Miami. *Washington Post,* p. A9.

Early, P., & Babcock, C. 4 Apr. 1981. The exploding bullets. *Washington Post,* pp. A3, A4.

Ehninger, D., Monroe, A. H., & Gronbeck, B. E. 1978. *Principles and types of speech communication.* Glenview, IL: Scott, Foresman & Co.

Ehrlich, J. W. 1970. *The lost art of cross-examination.* New York: G. P. Putnam's Sons.

Ehrmann, H. B. 1969. *The case that will not die: The commonwealth vs. Sacco and Vanzetti.* Boston: Little, Brown & Co.

Epstein, E. J. 1973. *News from nowhere: Television and the news.* New York: Knopf, Vintage.

Estes v. Texas, 381 U.S. 532 (1965).

F.B.I. inquiry finds no proof Hinckley was in conspiracy. 27 June 1981. *Washington Post,* pp. A1, A19.

Feiffer, J. 1970. *Pictures at a prosecution.* New York: Grove.

Felsher, H., & Rosen, M. 1966. *The press and the jury box.* New York: Macmillan.

Feuerlicht, R. S. 1977. *Justice crucified.* New York: McGraw-Hill.

Fisher, W. R. 1984. Narration as human communication paradigm: The case of public moral argument. *Communication Monographs, 51,* 1–33.

Foss, S. K., Foss, K. A., & Trapp, R. 1985. *Contemporary perspectives on rhetoric.* Prospect Heights, IL: Waveland Press.

Fraenkel, O. K. 1931. *The Sacco-Vanzetti case.* New York: Alfred A. Knopf.

Frankfurter, F. 1960. *The case of Sacco and Vanzetti.* Boston: Atlantic Monthly Press.

Frankfurter, M. D., & Jackson, G. 1960. *The letters of Sacco and Vanzetti.* New York: Vanguard Press.

Friendly, A., & Goldfarb, R. L. 1967. *Crime and publicity.* New York: Twentieth Century Fund.

Frontes, N. E., & Bunden, R. W. 1980. Persuasion during the trial process. In M. E. Roloff and G. R. Miller, (Eds.). *Persuasion: New directions in research,* pp. 249–66. Beverly Hills, CA: Sage Publications.

Gans, H. 1979. *Deciding what's news.* New York: Pantheon.

Givens, R. A. 1980. *The art of pleading a case.* New York: McGraw-Hill.

Goffman, E. 1959. *The presentation of self in everyday life.* New York: Doubleday.

Goldberg, S. H. 1982. *The first trial: Where do I sit? What do I say?* St. Paul, MN: West Publishing Co.

Goldstein, A. H. 1975. *The unquiet death of Julius & Ethel Rosenberg.* NY: Lawrence Hill & Co.

Goodman, E. 2 Apr. 1981. How routine the unspeakable. *Washington Post,* p. A23.

Greenawalt, K. 1978. The enduring significance of neutral principles. *Columbia Law Review, 78,* 982.

Harbinger, R. 1971. Trial by drama. *Judicature, 55,* 122–28.

Haring, J. V. 1937. *The hand of Hauptmann.* Plainfield, N.J.: Hamer.

Harper, T. 1984. When your case hits the front page. *American Bar Association Journal, 70,* 78–82.

Harrell J., & Linkugel, W. A. 1980. On rhetorical genre: An organizing perspective. In B. Brock, & R. L. Scott (Eds.). *Methods of rhetorical criticism,* pp. 404–19. Detroit: Wayne State Univ. Press.

Hays, A. G. 1933. *Trial by prejudice.* New York: Covice-Friede.

Head, H. G. 1980. Arguing damages to the jury. *Trial, 16,* 28.

Heglund, K. F. 1978. *Trial and practice skills*. St. Paul, MN: West Publishing Co.

Henry, N., & Brown, C. 5 Apr. 1981. An aimless road to a place in history. *Washington Post*, p. A1.

Hinckley, J., & Hinckley, J. A. (With Elizabeth Sherrill). 1985. *Breaking Points*. New York: Berkeley Books.

Hinckley formally charged with assassination. 25 Aug. 1981. *Washington Post*, p. A8.

Hinckley given right to tape Foster. 27 Mar. 1982. *Washington Post*, p. A10.

Hinckley pleads not guilty to Reagan assassination attempt. 29 Aug. 1981. *Washington Post*, p. A1.

Hinckley prosecutor loses review bid. 6 Apr. 1982. *Washington Post*, p. A10.

Hinckley trial re-scheduled. 16 Nov. 1981. *Washington Post*, p. B2.

Hinckley trial to see film *Taxi Driver*. 14 Apr. 1982. *Washington Post*, p. C8.

Hinckley views self as love-sick assassin. 5 Oct. 1981. *Washington Post*, p. B2.

Hinckley's lawyers lose plea for records. 22 Sept. 1981. *Washington Post*, p. C5.

Hinckley's lawyers seek psychiatrists' records. 16 Sept. 1981. *Washington Post*, p. A1.

Hinckley's prosecutors oppose disclosing psychiatrists' notes. 17 Sept. 1981. *Washington Post*, p. B4.

Holman, C. 1972. *A handbook of literature*. 3rd Ed. New York: Odyssey Press.

Houts, M., & Rogosheske, W. 1986. *The art of advocacy: Appeals*. New York: Matthew Bender.

Hovland, C. I., Janis, I. L., & Kelley, H. H. 1953. *Communication and persuasion*. New Haven, CT: Yale Univ. Press.

Hughes, R. E., & Duhamel, P. A. 1962. *Rhetoric: Principles and uses*. Englewood Cliffs, NJ: Prentice-Hall.

Hutchens, R. M. 1927. Cross-examination to impeach. *Yale Law Review*, 36, 384–90.

Hutcheson, J. 1929. The judgment intuitive: The function of the "hunch" in judicial decision. *Cornell Law Quarterly*, 14, 274.

Jacob, H. 1978. *Justice in America*. Boston: Little, Brown & Co.

James Brady sues Hinckley for 46 million. 27 Feb. 1982. *Washington Post*, p. A10.

Jeans, J. W. 1975. *Trial advocacy*. St. Paul, MN: West Publishing Co.

Jensen, J. V. 1981. *Argumentation: Reasoning in communication*. New York: D. Van Nostrand.

John Hinckley responds to questions from *Newsweek*. 4 Oct. 1981. *Washington Post*, p. A10.

John Hinckley returned to army stockade at Ft. Meade. 23 Nov. 1981. *Washington Post,* p. A15.

Johnson, H. 31 March 1981. The morbid echo. *Washington Post,* pp. A1, A12.

Joiner, C. 1957. *Trials and appeals.* Englewood Cliffs, NJ: Prentice-Hall.

Jones, E. E., & Wortman, C. 1973. *Ingratiation: An attributional approach.* Morristown, PA: General Learning Press.

Jones, R. A., & Brehm, J. W. 1970. Persuasiveness of one- and two-sided communications as a function of awareness there are two sides. *Journal of Experimental Social Psychology, 6,* 47.

Joughin, G. L., & Morgan, E. M. 1948. *The legacy of Sacco and Vanzetti.* New York: Harcourt, Brace & Co.

Judge sets Apr. 27 for Hinckley trial. 8 Apr. 1982. *Washington Post,* p. A1.

Judgment in Chicago. 2 Mar. 1979. *Newsweek,* p. 224.

Julien, A. S. 1980. *Opening statements.* Wilmette, IL: Gallighan & Co.

Kalven, H. 1970. Introduction: Confrontation and contempt. In *Contempt: Transcript of contempt citations, sentences, and responses,* pp. ix–xxiv. Chicago, IL: Swallow Press.

Kalven, H., & Zeisel, H. 1966. *The American jury.* Boston: Little, Brown & Co.

Kamen, A. 8 Dec. 1981. Examinations find Hinckley competent to face trial Jan. 4. *Washington Post,* p. B2.

———. 12 Jan. 1982. Court asked to overturn rule on Hinckley papers. *Washington Post,* p. A10.

———. 30 Jan. 1982. Delahanty files suit against Hinckley. *Washington Post,* p. A14.

———. 26 Mar. 1982. Actress' testimony on videotape sought. *Washington Post,* p. A19.

Karlen, D. 1971. Disorder in the courtroom. *Southern California Law Review, 44,* 996–1035.

Keeton, R. E. 1973. *Trial tactics and methods.* Boston: Little, Brown & Co.

Kelner, J., & McGovern, F. E. 1981. *Successful litigation techniques.* New York: Mathew Bender & Co.

Kennedy, L. 1985. *The airman and the carpenter.* New York: Viking Press.

Kiernan, L. 23 June 1981. Psychologist, 3 psychiatrists end examination of Hinckley. *Washington Post,* pp. B2, B7.

———. 22 Aug. 1981. Hinckley's lawyers act on searches. *Washington Post,* p. C2.

———. 20 Sept. 1981. Hinckley letter affirms interest in Jodie Foster. *Washington Post,* p. A1.

———. 29 Sept. 1981. Hinckley will claim insanity in shooting of president. *Washington Post,* p. A1.

————. 20 Oct. 1981. Paper seized in Hinckley cell debated. *Washington Post,* p. A2.

————. 21 Oct. 1981. Hinckley reportedly wrote he was in conspiracy with others. *Washington Post,* p. C8.

————. 17 Nov. 1981. John Hinckley rests after suicide attempt. *Washington Post,* p. A1.

————. 18 Nov. 1981. U.S. judge rules Hinckley's rights violated by FBI during questioning. *Washington Post,* p. A12.

————. 26 Nov. 1981. Judge to review Hinckley's competency. *Washington Post,* p. B8.

————. 24 Feb. 1982. U.S. court of appeals upholds ruling that Hinckley's rights were violated. *Washington Post,* p. A9.

————. 6 Mar. 1982. Law on St. Elizabeth's commitments overturned. *Washington Post,* p. A7.

————. 31 Mar. 1982. Foster gives testimony in Hinckley proceeding. *Washington Post,* p. A10.

————. 17 Apr. 1982. Hinckley reportedly claims he wasn't aiming at president. *Washington Post,* p. A12.

————. 20 Apr. 1982. Judge reverses himself says he won't sequester jury. *Washington Post,* p. A10.

————. 23 Apr. 1982. Hinckley won't say he wasn't trying to shoot Reagan. *Washington Post,* p. A30.

————. 25 Apr. 1982. Hinckley expected to be greatest legal drama since Watergate. *Washington Post,* p. A2.

————. 26 Apr. 1982. Defense headed by a bulldog. *Washington Post,* p. A2.

————. 26 Apr. 1982. No-nonsense judge plans active role in Hinckley trial. *Washington Post,* p. A2.

————. 26 Apr. 1982. Top prosecutor intense veteran trial lawyer. *Washington Post,* p. A2.

————. 27 Apr. 1982. Hinckley trial opens. *Washington Post,* p. A5.

Kirchheimer, O. 1961. *Political justice: The use of legal procedures for political ends.* Princeton, NJ: Princeton Univ. Press.

Knapp, M. 1972. *Nonverbal communication in human interaction.* New York: Holt, Rinehart, & Winston.

Knight, A., & Henry, N. 1 Apr. 1981. Love letter offers clue to shooting. *Washington Post,* p. B1.

Kunstler, W. 1970. Introduction. In J. Clavir & J. Spitzer (Eds.). *The conspiracy trial,* pp. xiii–xvi. New York: Bobbs-Merrill.

Kuvin, H. A. 1965. *Trial handbook.* Englewood Cliffs, NJ: Prentice Hall.

Lannuzzi, J. N. 1981. *Cross-examination: The mosaic art.* Englewood Cliffs, NJ: Prentice-Hall.

Lapham, L. 25 Apr. 1981. Of gods and gunmen. *Washington Post,* p. A15.

Lardner, G. 16 Apr. 1981. Hinckley also stalked Carter, officials think. *Washington Post,* p. A6.

Lawson, J. D. (Ed.). 1919. *American state trials.* St. Louis: F. H. Thomas Law Book Co.

Lawson, R. G. 1970. Experimental research on the organization of persuasive arguments: An application to courtroom communications. *Law and Social Order, 1970, 579.*

Lawyers' column on lawyers for alleged Reagan assailant. 13 Apr. 1981. *Washington Post,* pp. C2, C22.

Lescaze, L. 1 Apr. 1981. Reagan in good spirits making a fast recovery. *Washington Post,* p. A1.

Levin, M. B. 1971. *Political hysteria in America.* New York: Basic Books.

Lieberman, J. H. 1980. *Free speech, free press and the law.* New York: Lothrop, Lee & Shepard.

Lindbergh, C. A. 1977. *Autobiography of values.* New York: Harcourt Brace Jovanovich.

Lofton, J. 1966. *Justice and the press.* Boston: Beacon Press.

Loftus, E. F. 1980. Language and memories in the judicial system. In R. W. Shy & A. Shunkal (Eds.). *Language use and the use of language,* pp. 257–68. Washington, DC: Georgetown Univ. Press.

Luchins, A. S. 1957. Experimental attempts to minimize the impact of first impressions. In C. I. Hovland (Ed.). *The order of presentation in persuasion,* pp. 62–75. New Haven, CT: Yale Univ. Press.

Lum, D. 1969. *The great trial of the Chicago anarchists.* New York: Arno Press.

Lund, F. H. 1925. The psychology of belief: A study of its emotional and volitional determinants. *Journal of Abnormal Social Psychology, 20,* 174.

Lundquist, W. I. 1982. Advocacy in opening statements. *Litigation, 8, 23.*

McCombs, M. E., & Shaw, D. L. 1972. The agenda setting function of mass media. *Public Opinion Quarterly. 36,* 176–87.

McCullough, R., & Underwood, J. 1980. *Civil trial manual.* Philadelphia, PA: American Law Institute.

Macdonald, D. 1970. Introduction. In M. L. Levine, G. C. McNamsee, & D. Greenberg (Eds.). *The tales of Hoffman,* pp. xi–xxvi. New York: Bantam Books.

McElhaney, J. W. 1979. Analogies in final argument. *Litigation, 6, 37.*

———. 1981. *Trial notebook.* Chicago, IL: American Bar Association.

McGuire, W. J. 1969. The nature of attitudes and attitude change. In G. Lindzey and E. Aronson (Eds.). *The handbook of social psychology,* pp. 136–314. Reading, MA: Addison-Wesley Publishing Co.

Marcus, P. 1982. The media in the courtroom: Attending, reporting, televising criminal cases. *Indiana Law Review, 57,* 235–87.

Martineau, R. 1985. *Fundamentals of modern appellate advocacy.* Rochester, NY: Lawyers Co-Operative Publishing Co.

Mauet, T. A. 1980. *Fundamentals of trial techniques.* Boston, MA: Little, Brown & Co.

Miller, G. R., & Burgoon, M. 1973. *New techniques of persuasion*. NY: Harper & Row.

Mindes, M. W., & Acock, A. C. 1982. Trickster, hero, helper: A report on the lawyer image. *American Bar Foundation Research Journal, 15,* 177–233.

Montgomery, J. D. 1981. Establishing a theme of defense. *Trial Diplomacy Journal, 4 (2),* 14–17.

Montgomery, R. H. 1960. *Sacco-Vanzetti: The murder and the myth.* New York: Devin-Adair Co.

Morgan, T. 3 Apr. 1981. D.C. attractions. *Washington Post,* p. A5.

Morrill, A. E. 1971. *Trial diplomacy.* Chicago, IL: Court Practice Institute.

———. 1972. Opening statements. *Trial Diplomacy.* Chicago, IL: Court Practice Institute.

Mott, F. L. 1941. *A history of newspapers in the United States through 250 years: 1690–1940.* New York: Macmillan.

———. 1952. *The news in America.* Cambridge, MA: Harvard Univ. Press.

Murray, R. 1964. *Red scare: A study of national hysteria: 1919–1920.* New York: McGraw-Hill.

Musmanno, M. A. 1939. *After twelve years.* New York: Alfred A. Knopf.

Nebr. Press Assoc. v. Stuart, 427 U.S. 539 (1976).

Nejelski, P. 1977. Judging in democracy: The tension of popular participation. *Judicature, 61,* 166–77.

Nichols, M. H. 1963. *Rhetoric and criticism.* Baton Rouge, LA: Louisiana State Univ. Press.

O'Connor, T. 1961. The origin of the Sacco-Vanzetti case. *Vanderbilt Law Review, 14,* 987–1006.

Okie, S., & Cohn, V. 1 Apr. 1981. Brady improves dramatically. *Washington Post,* p. A1.

Oliphant, R. E. 1978. *Trial techniques with Irving Younger.* Minneapolis, MN: National Practice Institute for Continuing Legal Education.

Oliver, R. T. 1965. *History of public speaking in America.* Boston, MA: Allyn & Bacon.

Paletz, D. L., & Entman, R. M. 1981. *Media power politics.* New York: Macmillan, Free Press.

Parker, J. 1950. Improving appellate methods. *New York University Law Review, 25,* 1.

Patterson v. Colorado, 205 U.S. 454 (1907).

Perelman, C. 1963. *The idea of justice and the problem of argument.* John Petrie (Trans.). New York: Humanities Press.

———. 1967. *Justice.* New York: Random House.

———. 1980. *Justice, law, and argument.* John Petrie (Trans.). Boston: D. Reidel.

Political trials, U.S. style. 2 Mar. 1970. *Nation,* pp. 126–27.

Pollack, J. 1972. *Dr. Sam: An American tragedy.* Chicago, IL: Henry Regnery Co.

Pound, R. 1923. The theory of judicial decision. *Harvard Law Review, 36,* 940.

Prentice, R. 1983. Supreme Court rhetoric. *Arizona Law Review, 25,* 85.

Prosecution cites security in seizure of document from Hinckley's cell. 4 Feb. 1982. *Washington Post,* p. A24.

Prosecution files papers in Hinckley case. 15 Dec. 1981. *Washington Post,* p. A9.

Prosecutors ask full court to rule on Hinckley evidence. 23 Mar. 1982. *Washington Post,* p. A3.

Radosh, R., & Milton, J. 1983. *The Rosenberg file: A search for the truth.* New York: Holt, Rinehart & Winston.

Ranney, A. 1983. *Channels of power.* New York: Basic Books.

Raspberry, W. 2 Oct. 1981. The insanity defense. *Washington Post,* p. A29.

Reagan shooting suspect given brain scan. 24 Apr. 1981. *Washington Post,* p. A3.

Reid, T. R. 1 Apr. 1981. Secret Service checking limousine position. *Washington Post,* pp. A1, A16.

———. 3 Apr. 1981. Secret Service cites lack of information on Hinckley's record. *Washington Post,* p. A3.

———. 9 Apr. 1981. No connection in assassination arrests is found. *Washington Post,* p. A13.

Replying to Szasz. 13 May 1981. *Washington Post,* p. B1.

Report of the committee on the scope of rhetoric. 1971. In L. F. Bitzer & E. Black (Eds.). *The prospect of rhetoric,* pp. 208–19. Englewood Cliffs, NJ: Prentice-Hall.

Rieke, R. D. 1982. Argumentation in the legal process. In J. R. Cox & C. A. Willard (Eds.). *Advances in argumentation theory and research,* pp. 363–78. Carbondale: Southern Illinois Univ. Press.

———. 1986. The evolution of judicial justification: Perelman's concept of the rational and the reasonable. In J. L. Golden & J. J. Pilotta (Eds). *Practical reasoning in human affairs,* pp. 227–44. Boston: D. Reidel Publishing Co.

Robinson, E. 1 Apr. 1981. A drifter with a purpose. *Washington Post,* p. A1.

Ross, W. S. 1976. *The last hero: Charles A. Lindbergh.* New York: Harper & Row.

Russell, F. 1971. *Tragedy in Dedham.* New York: McGraw-Hill.

Sacco case up today. 22 Oct. 1921. *New York Times,* p. 6.

Sannito, T. 1981. Psychological courtroom strategies. *Trial Diplomacy Journal, 4,* 30–35.

Scaduto, A. 1976. *Scapegoat: The lonesome death of Bruno Richard Hauptmann.* New York: G. P. Putnam's Sons.

Scholes, R., & Kellogg, R. 1966. *The nature of narrative.* London: Oxford Univ. Press.

Schopenhauer, A. 1942. The art of controversy. In Saunders, T. B. (Ed.). *Complete Essays of Schopenhauer*, pp. 1–42. New York: John Wiley & Sons.

Sears, D. O., & Freedman, J. L. 1965. Effects of expected familiarity of arguments upon opinion change and selective exposure. *Journal of Personality and Social Psychology, 2,* 420–25.

Secret Service agent Timothy McCarthy sues Hinckley. 30 Mar. 1982. *Washington Post,* p. C3.

Shaffer, R., & Henry, N. 31 Mar. 1981. Suspected gunman: Aimless drifter. *Washington Post,* p. A9.

———. 2 Apr. 1981. Hinckley pursued actress for months, letter showed. *Washington Post,* p. A1.

Shaffer, R., and Kiernan, L. 4 Apr. 1981. Tapes support theory of Hinckley motive. *Washington Post,* pp. A1, A10.

———. 28 May 1981. Hinckley takes overdose. *Washington Post,* A1.

Shapiro, W. 5 Apr. 1981. Attempted assassination of Reagan. *Washington Post,* p. C1.

Sheppard v. Maxwell, 231 F. Supp. 37 (S.D. Ohio 1964).

Sheppard v. Maxwell, 346 F.2d 707 (6th Cir. 1965).

Sheppard v. Maxwell, 384 U.S. 333 (1966).

Sheppard v. Ohio, 352 U.S. 910 (1956).

Sherbert v. Verner, 374 U.S. 398 (1963).

Siedman, L. M. 1977. The trial and execution of Bruno Richard Hauptmann. *Georgetown Law Journal, 66,* 1–48.

Simmel, G. 1968. The dramatic actor and reality. In J. E. Combs & M. W. Mansfield (Eds.). *Drama in life: The uses of communication in society,* pp. 59–61. London: Oxford Univ. Press.

Sinclair, U. 1928. *Boston.* New York: Boni Press.

Singer, T. H. 1977. Testimony as demonstrative evidence. *Litigation, 3,* 19.

Smith, L. J. 1978. *Art of advocacy: Summation.* New York: Matthew Bender & Co.

Smithburn, J. E., & Seckinger, J. H. 1983. Visual evidence. *Litigation, 9,* 33.

Spangenberg, C. 1977. Basic values and the techniques of persuasion. *Litigation, 3,* 13.

———. 1982 . What I try to accomplish in an opening statement. In G. W. Holmes (Ed.). *Opening statements and closing arguments,* pp. 247–52. Ann Arbor, MI: Institute of Continuing Legal Education.

Starr, V. H. 1983. From the communication profession: Communication strategies and research needs on opening statements and closing arguments. In R. J. Matlon & R. J. Crawford (Eds.). *Communication strategies in the practice of lawyering,* pp. 424–48. Annandale, VA: Speech Communication Association of America.

Stein, J. A. 1985. *Closing argument.* Wilmette, IL: Callaghan & Co.

Stephenson, D. G. 1979. Fair trial–free press: Rights in continuing conflict. *Brooklyn Law Review, 46,* 39–66.

Strawn, D. U., & Munsterman, G. T. 1982. Helping juries handle complex cases. *Judicature, 65,* 444.

Stryker, L. P. 1954. *The art of advocacy.* New York: Simon & Schuster.

Styan, J. L. 1973. *Drama, stage, and audience.* New York: Cambridge Univ. Press.

Sumpter, J. L. 1978. A trial lawyer's greatest tool: The opening statement. *Trial Lawyer's Quarterly, 12,* 34.

Swann, W. B., Guiliano, T., & Wegner, D. M. 1982. Where questions can lead: The power of conjecture in social interaction. *Journal of Personality and Social Psychology, 42,* 1025–35.

Szasz, T. S. 6 May 1981. Reagan should let the jurors judge Hinckley. *Washington Post,* p. A19.

Tanford, J. A. 1983. *The trial process.* Charlottesville, VA: The Miche Company Law Publishers.

Toulmin, S. 1969. *The uses of argument.* London: Cambridge Univ. Press.

Toulmin, S., Rieke, R., & Janik, A. 1979. *An introduction to reasoning.* New York: Macmillan.

Transcript of Record. 1886. *State of Illinois v. August Spies, Albert R. Parsons, Adolph Fisher, George Engel, Louis Lingg, Samuel Fielden, Michael Schwab, and Oscar W. Neebe [The Chicago Anarchists].* Reprint, 1919. John D. Lawson (Ed.). *American state trials.* St. Louis: F. H. Thomas Law Book Co. Albuquerque: Univ. of New Mexico Collections. Page citations in text are to the 1919 reprint.

———. 1921. *State of Massachusetts v. Nicola Sacco and Bartolomeo Vanzetti.* Reprint, 1969. *Trial record: The Sacco-Vanzetti case.* New York: Paul A. Appel. Page citations in text are to the 1969 reprint.

———. 1935. *State of New Jersey v. Bruno Richard Hauptmann.* Reprint, undated. Chicago: Univ. of Chicago Archives. Page citations in text are to the undated reprint.

———. 1951. *United States of America v. Julius Rosenberg, Ethel Rosenberg, Anatoli Yakovlev, David Greenglass, and Morton Sobell.* Reprint, 1952. The National Committee to Secure Justice in the Rosenberg Case. Page citations in text are to the 1952 reprint.

———. 1969. *United States of America v. David T. Dellinger, Rennard C. Davis, Thomas E. Hayden, Abbott Hoffman, Jerry C. Rubin, Lee Weiner, John R. Froines, and Bobby G. Seale.* Reprinted & abridged, 1970. Judy Clavir & John Spitzer (Eds.). *The conspiracy trial.* New York: Bobbs-Merrill. Page citations in text are to the 1970 reprint.

Tuchman, G. 1978. *Making news: A study in the construction of reality.* New York: Macmillan, Free Press.

U.S. court allows more time for examination of John Hinckley. 27 June 1981. *Washington Post,* pp. A1, A4.

U.S. court delays trial of John Hinckley. 22 Dec. 1981. *Washington Post,* p. A6.

U.S. court sets date for trial of John Hinckley. 10 Oct. 1981. *Washington Post,* p. A2.

U.S. House holds hearings on assassination arrests. 9 Apr. 1981. *Washington Post,* pp. A2, A13.

U.S. prosecutors to appeal ruling in Hinckley case. 17 Dec. 1981. *Washington Post,* p. C10.

Wallace, K. R. 1971. The fundamentals of rhetoric. In L. F. Bitzer and E. Black (Eds.). *The prospect of rhetoric,* pp. 3–20. Englewood Cliffs, NJ: Prentice-Hall.

Waller, G. 1961. *Kidnap: The story of the Lindbergh case.* New York: Dial Press.

Warner, A. 28 Sept. 1921. Sacco and Vanzetti: A reasonable doubt. *Nation,* pp. 343–45.

Weaver, R. M. 1953. *The ethics of rhetoric.* Chicago: Henry Regnery.

Wechsler, H. 1950. Toward neutral principles of constitutional law. *Harvard Law Review, 73,* 1.

———. 1964. The nature of judicial reasoning. In S. Hook (Ed.). *Law and philosophy,* pp. 290–300. New York: New York Univ. Press.

Weil, M. 16 Nov. 1981. Hinckley attempts to hang himself in jail cell. *Washington Post,* p. A3.

Weinstein, J. B., & Zimmerman, D. L. 1977. Let the people observe their courts. *Judicature, 61 (4),* 156–65.

Wessel, M. R. 1976. *Rule of reason.* Reading, MA: Addison-Wesley Publishing Co.

Wexley, J. 1977. *The judgment of Julius and Ethel Rosenberg.* New York: Ballantine Books.

Whipple, S. B. 1937. *The trial of Bruno Richard Hauptmann.* New York: Doubleday & Co.

White House considers replacing Ruff as U.S. attorney. 22 Apr. 1981. *Washington Post,* p. A1.

Who killed the Lindbergh baby? 1985. Public Broadcasting System television.

Wiener, F. 1950. *Effective appellate advocacy.* New York: Prentice-Hall.

Wilkie, C. 1981. The scapegoating of Bruno Richard Hauptmann: The rhetorical process in prejudicial publicity. *Central States Speech Journal, 32,* 102.

Will, G. 4 Apr. 1982. Slowness in judicial procedure in bringing Hinckley to trial. *Washington Post,* p. C7.

Young, W., & Kaiser W. E. 1985. *Postmortem: New evidence in the case of Sacco-Vanzetti.* Amherst, MA: Univ. of Massachusetts Press.

Index

Janice Schuetz received her Ph.D. degree in Communication from the University of Colorado and is presently an associate professor in the Department of Speech Communication at the University of New Mexico. Her other books include *Rhetorical Perspective on Communication and Mass Media* (with Richard J. Jensen and Robert L. Schrag) and *Participating in the Communication Process* (with Jean M. Civikly). She has also published numerous articles in journals in her discipline.

Kathryn Holmes Snedaker received her J.D. degree from the University of New Mexico and is presently associated with the law firm Van Cott, Bagley, Cornwall & McCarthy of Salt Lake City. Her journal articles have appeared in the *American Journal of Trial Advocacy* and the *New Mexico Law Review*.